# THE CITIZEN
# MACHINE

The public accepts the material benefits o
They like to drive GM cars, they like to have cl
synthetic fibers but they have certain subconsc
about the big businesses which make these mate
And it's attacks like those we've outlined th
foster this attitude.

## OBJECTIVE OF OUR PROGRAM (CHART VIII)

It's from this problem - the prob
that we derive the objective of our pro
"To create a better public understandi
role of the Pont as a large business i

*Also by*
Anna McCarthy

AMBIENT TELEVISION
Visual Culture and Public Space (2001)

MEDIASPACE
Place, Scale, and Culture in a Media Age (2004)

# THE CITIZEN MACHINE

## GOVERNING BY TELEVISION
## IN 1950s AMERICA

Anna McCarthy

THE NEW PRESS

NEW YORK
LONDON

All photographs are by Stephanie Broad.

Published in the United States by
The New Press, New York, 2010
Distributed by Perseus Distribution

LIBRARY OF CONGRESS CATALOGING-IN-PUBLICATION DATA
McCarthy, Anna, 1967–
The citizen machine : governing by television in 1950s
America / Anna McCarthy.
    p.  cm.
Includes bibliographical references and index.
ISBN 978-1-59558-498-4 (hc.: alk. paper)   1. Television and
politics—United States.   2. Television broadcasting—Social aspects—
United States.   3. Television broadcasting—Philosophy.   4. Political
culture—United States.   5. Advocacy advertising—United States.
6. Television advertising—United States.   7. Television viewers—
United States—Attitudes.   I. Title.
PN1992.6.M3775 2010
302.23'45097309045—dc22
                2009039029

The New Press was established in 1990 as a not-for-profit alternative
to the large, commercial publishing houses currently dominating
the book publishing industry. The New Press operates in the
public interest rather than for private gain, and is committed
to publishing, in innovative ways, works of educational, cultural,
and community value that are often deemed insufficiently profitable.

www.thenewpress.com

Book design by Pollen, New York
Composition by Westchester Book Composition
This book was set in Walbaum and Trade Gothic

Printed in the United States of America

2 4 6 8 10 9 7 5 3 1

*For* Bill

O Mediums! O to teach! To convey the invisible faith!

Walt Whitman, "Apostroph"
(*Chants Democratic and Native American*, 1860)

e attempted the treatment <u>so ewhat</u> in the style of the
al, barring only the real excesses in sentimentality
ch the book is already too well known.

not known for, at least not to me, is the high
its observations on the effect of slavery not only on the
d not only on the brutish tyrant, but on the most
intelligent, and generous of the white masters.

master was an inept farmer who could not make things
sold Tom to clear his mortgage. He no more wanted
han he wanted to lose his only plough; additionally
e were distressed at parting this way with this
they were fond. <u>But</u>, Tom belonged to Mr. Shelby
essed to the wall Mr. Shelby could sell Tom. And
master, Simon Legree, could kill Tom. And did.

# Contents

# Acknowledgments

In writing this book, I benefited immeasurably from the research support of a number of institutions. The Scholar-in-Residence programs at the University of Pennsylvania's Annenberg School for Communication and the University of Cologne's Center for Media and Cultural Communication provided me with time to write and present this work as it evolved, as did a faculty fellowship at NYU's International Center for Advanced Study and the Stephen Charney Vladeck Fellowship from NYU's Robert F. Wagner Graduate School of Public Service. I wish to thank the following individuals associated with these gigs for their feedback at critical stages in the project: Barbie Zelizer, Katherine Sender, Elihu Katz, Ilka Becker, Michael Cuntz, Friedrich Balke, Allen Hunter, Marilyn Young, Robert Vitalis, Sergei Kapterev, Alyosha Goldstein, and Nicole Sackley.

I am grateful also for commentary and critique from audiences at the University of Amsterdam's Department of Film and Media Studies, the Film Studies Program at Yale University, the University of Toronto's Center for the Study of the United States, the University of Montreal's Useful Cinema Symposium, the Department of Film and Media Studies at the University of California at Irvine, the Department of Critical Studies in the University of Southern California's School of Cinema-Television, the Rockefeller Archives, the Center for the Humanities at Wesleyan University, the Tamiment Library at NYU, the Columbia University Seminar in American Studies, the Columbia University Seminar in Film and Interdisciplinary Interpretation, the Visual Culture Colloquium at Bryn Mawr College, and the Department of Film and Media Studies at Swarthmore College. I wish to thank the following individuals for their comments on these occasions: John MacKay, Alondra Nelson, Charles Musser, Nicholas Sammond, Michael Cobb, Elspeth Brown, Vanessa Schwartz, Amelie Hastie, Jennifer Horne, Edward Dimendberg, Victoria Johnson, William Buxton, Joseph Reed, Jeanine Basinger, Jill Morawski, Stewart Ewen, Molly Nolan, Michael Nash, Amanda Claybaugh, William Luhr, Drake Stutesman, Christina Zwarg, Patricia White, Jane Caplan, and Homay King.

Many other readers and interlocutors have helped me refine the ideas in this book, both in conversation and in their generous readings of drafts over the years. I am indebted to Gustavus Stadler, Susan Murray, Dana Polan, William L. Bird, Steven Classen, Thomas Bender, James Schwoch, Elaine Freedgood, Toby Miller, S. Paul Klein, Nick Tanis, Mark Naison, Ellen M. Violett, José Muñoz, Laura Kipnis, Aurora Wallace, and Tavia Nyong'o. The argument of this book is particularly enriched by the exemplary work of Laurie Ouellette and Lisa Duggan, and I owe them particular thanks for the sustaining models they have established in their own publications.

Thanks must also go to the archivists who helped me navigate uncountable square feet of primary materials in film and manuscript collections: Marge McNinch and Roger Horowitz at the Hagley Museum and Library, which funded the research in Chapter Two with a grant-in-aid; Leith Johnson and Joan Miller at the Wesleyan Cinema Archives; Jonathan Greene at the Ford Foundation Archives; Lynda

The third white boy.


The negro girl.

DeLoach at the George Meany Memorial Archives; Margaret Compton at the Peabody Awards Archives at the University of Georgia; as well as archivists at the State Historical Society of Wisconsin, the University of Illinois at Urbana-Champaign, the New York Public Library's Schomberg Center for Research in Black Culture, and the Seeley Mudd Manuscripts Library at Princeton. I am especially grateful to J. Fred MacDonald of MacDonald and Associates and Rick Prelinger of the Prelinger Library for their help in locating audiovisual materials.

I am grateful to a number of individuals and institutions for granting permission to reprint film stills in this book: The Hagley Museum and Business Library; KETC-TY, St. Louis; Edward O. Bland; The Center for the Study of the Great Ideas; J. Fred MacDonald; The George Meany Memorial Archives.

For research assistance I thank the following current and former graduate student employees at NYU: Torey Liepa, Ragan Rhyne, Adam Segal, Anastasia Saverino, Alexander Kupfer, Michelle Kelley, Jose Freire, and Cortland Rankin. Juan Monroy was invaluable in the final stages of manuscript preparation when I broke my arm, and Stephanie Broad was a godsend when it came to photographing the illustrations. On the editorial end, I must particularly thank André Schiffrin—for his faith in the project, for his patience, and for his insights—and Marc Favreau, who wielded the scalpel of redaction with consummate skill.

Every page of this book bears witness to the love and support of Bill Vourvoulias, and, in dedicating it to him, so do I.

# THE CITIZEN
# MACHINE

BOY 3:   (lip sync)

Well, my school is in a pretty
fancy neighborhood and we had
some kids who broke in one night
and wrecked the place.


GIRL 2:   (lip sync)

Well, I think it's the individual
that counts, and how are you
going to know anything about
people if you never get to meet
them?

The FBI cannot in any major & complex field place all its bets on one man.

Further, let's don't be beguiled with the omnipotent influence of omnibus & all inclusive that good & names.

*Introduction*

# TELEVISION AND POLITICAL CULTURE
# AFTER WORLD WAR II

"TO GOVERN," Napoleon wrote in his will, "is to spread morality, education, and happiness."[1] A century and a half later, some powerful individuals in the United States decided that television was a perfect instrument for realizing such a vision. Inspired less by Napoleon than by the perceived threats of Soviet communism, class war, and racial violence, these members of what was then known as the Establishment were drawn together by a shared conviction that television broadcasting, although a debased and thoroughly commercial institution, could be a useful venue for governing. Not governing through the repression of people's wills, not governing as dominance from above by an all-powerful state, but rather governing as a process of cultivation that presumes individual liberty and seeks to preserve it through the ever-evolving medium of citizenship—a model of liberal rule described by Michel Foucault as "an administration of things that would think above all else of men's freedom, of what they want to do, of what they have an interest in doing, of what they think about doing."[2] As is the case today, talk of freedom circulated promiscuously throughout 1950s public culture, and state agencies, philanthropic enterprises. Even private corporations drew on it to develop an array of strategies for spreading education, morality, and happiness among the citizenry, their ostensible motivation the pressing need to safeguard the free world's economic and political systems against the spectral apocalypses of class, race, and nuclear war. Sponsoring television programs was among these strategies.[3]

The TV shows produced and proposed in the service of such lofty goals were often quite crude. Some, it should be noted, seem laughable from the perspective of the present: an animated cartoon about free enterprise, a brownface drama about land reform in India, a sketch comedy about civil liberties. Their sponsors, technocrats to the core and propagandists by inclination, nevertheless were convinced that they could help maintain social stability and national cohesion by exploiting the airwaves "for citizenship, for personality development, for general increase in enlightenment and taste," as one Ford Foundation staff member put it.[4] Yet, at the same time, many were men (as they mostly were) who saw television as the cultural equivalent of a sewage pipe.[5] Journalist Walter Lippmann, the media guru of the Establishment, disliked television so intensely that when his cook begged him to buy a set he insisted that it remain in the kitchen, with her.[6] How exactly, then, did TV come to be seen by some social and political elites as an appropriate vehicle for governing the habits, morals, and mental development of the populace? Why, for instance, would a man such as Robert Maynard Hutchins—the legendarily irascible public intellectual who once described television as a "fungus"— think that TV programs could help educate Americans about civil liberties and civil rights?

The answers to these questions can shed new light on the place of TV in the political landscape of the postwar United States. They also, as I suggest in this book, provide telling insights on the culture of governance that took shape in this period, and which lives on today in increasingly privatized—if contested—models of liberal rule and political subjectivity. Conceptualizations of democratic governance as a process best managed through the transfer of state responsibilities to the private sphere date back a long way, but the postwar years were their moment of ascendancy.[7] The multipronged corporate assault on New Deal social planning is solidly rooted in legislative campaigns against organized labor that were undertaken throughout the 1950s, even as the Keynesian welfare state appeared to flourish. At the same time, the monetarist theory formulated by Friedrich Hayek and other economists sowed the intellectual seeds of the neoliberal program, rationalizing as a science the upward distribution and concentration of wealth and social resources that would emerge as a coordinating historical force over the next four decades.[8] Throughout this period, concepts of self-regulation, voluntarism, and entrepreneurial initiative would come to define the rights and responsibilities of both individual and corporate citizenship, serving as ideological touchstones in evolving definitions of democratic government.[9]

Television broadcasting came into existence at the moment when this neoliberal paradigm first began to cohere, so it is worth paying close attention to the moments when the powerful and privileged, bent on reinventing government and redefining citizenship, turned to the medium as a tool for reaching those people they thought of as the masses. TV seemed easily adaptable within the system of soft power embodied in public relations and advertising, as well as in less top-down arenas such as documentary film production, civic forums, and adult education (especially in the areas of economics, history, and expressive culture). Often closely linked to each other, these domains for constructing civic identities and defining interests, aligning individuals with each other and with broader forms of political authority, could only be enhanced by television's highly regarded capacity to disperse ideas and automate perception and cognition, enabling, on a massive scale and at a suitably removed distance, the shaping of conduct and attitudes.[10]

This book is about television's place within the ambitions of rule associated with six distinct, if overlapping, sectors of the governing classes (as opposed to The Government): business, philanthropy, social reformers, labor leadership, public intellectuals, and the media profession itself. At a time when democratic nation building rested on the disavowal of the state as a source of direct political power, all were forms of authority capable of embodying some aspect of the idea of liberal rule that sits at the heart of modern conceptions of the citizenry. The shadow of state socialism demanded a sharp contrast between totalitarian rule and freedom-loving Western democracy. The state might administer the lives of the citizenry within the clearly defined confines of Keynesian welfarism—establishing social security, forming networks of knowledge and expertise to manage macroeconomic processes such as growth and inflation, establishing policies for housing and employment consistent with a liberal democratic idea of social citizenship, and so forth—but seeing to people's minds and attitudes was another matter. Such a project would have distinctly totalitarian overtones if undertaken by state and federal authorities, and into this breach, bringing their own agendas with them, stepped the men of DuPont, the AFL-CIO, the Advertising Council, the Ford Foundation, the Fund for the Republic, and other organizations interested in shaping, in Mortimer Adler's words, "the ideas that should be in every citizen's mind."[11]

But although Cold War exigencies were central to this project, its most revealing contradictions emerged when the citizenship struggles of black Americans entered the picture, especially after the Supreme Court's 1954 *Brown v. Board of Education* decision made desegregation a matter of national moral leadership. A broad array of racial rationalizations found expression in the visual and organizational culture of governing by television. Sponsors advocating corporate "rights," for example, pursued legitimacy by referencing civil rights, while broadcasters' policies of balance and fairness hampered the programming strategies adopted by liberal campaigns for racial justice. In part, such practices of racial containment reflected the economic and infrastructural relations between local television stations and networks, as advocates of integration within the liberal establishment mainstream discovered when they sought airtime for their programs in the South.[12] But these contradictory voicings of the relationship between race, rights, and citizenship in efforts to govern by television were also in part a result of the contradictions shaping white racial liberalism in the period. After viewing a 1965 Advertising Council TV spot about the importance of community self-management in achieving "better race relations," a group of social workers, labor leaders, and businessmen took the opportunity to complain about black people's attitudes toward those reformers who were trying to help them. As Helen Hall, a prominent social worker, protested, "It [is] not possible these days to have a Negro group visit any establishment without having them count the number of Negroes on the staff, and look to see whether they [are] being treated with the same degree of courtesy and importance as the whites."[13] In such moments, the combination of *ressentiment* and civic responsibility traces television's ambivalent place in postwar racial governance, and reveals the ambivalences of those who sought to use the medium as an instrument for improving democratic life.

These moments of racialized conflict in the process of television sponsorship contribute to our sense of the period's history, pointing toward connections between the liberal reformist discourse of reasonableness and the seemingly nonpolitical reasonableness that, as Lisa Duggan notes, secures today's neoliberal arguments for the upward distribution of wealth and political power.[14] In this respect, such moments also highlight the importance of contestation and cultural mediation in the study of modern government's claims to cultivate human capital. Specifically, they counter rationalist claims that particular programs of rule merely "administer the lives of others in light of conceptions of what is good, healthy, normal, virtuous, efficient, or profitable."[15] This concern with administration and its limits constitutes the field of power Michel Foucault called *governmentality*: "the ways in which one conducts the conduct of men."[16] To study governmentality is to scrutinize the *material* of rule: the techniques and theories, as well as the practices, that coalesce in Western democracy's constantly evolving process of conceptualizing political sovereignty. But recounting governmental reason should not automatically affirm its efficacy, nor discount its close connections to private interest. The analysis of governmentality, one group of political scientists notes, requires attention to the conflicts and contradictions involved in the "messy implementation" of particular governmental rationalities, approaching them not as abstract formulations, nor as equations for calculating the extent and depth of rule, but as contestatory scenes, rife with competing interpretations of human nature and culture.[17] Television occasioned many such scenes within the governing classes, even as it offered itself as the perfect instrument of liberal democratic rule, and emerging challenges to the "racial order of things" were central to the conflict.[18]

If television failed to resolve the racial contradictions implicit in the ideas about government it was asked to embody, in another sense it provided a vehicle for smoothing out some conflicting agendas among sectors of elite authority. A certain curiosity about television was perhaps the most concrete commonality between some of the sponsors considered in the following chapters. Business, labor, philanthropy, academia, and the media were, and are, incommensurate categories; business and philanthropic leaders have historically enjoyed far higher levels of access to the offices of the state than labor leaders, for example, and intellectuals, unlike labor and business, could not claim to represent particular constituencies within the interest group schema of the postwar polity. Moreover, their relations with each other were, to varying degrees, antagonistic. This may be why, with the exception of the obviously intertwined histories of labor and management, historians have tended to address the public work of these groups somewhat separately, the capitalists in one corner coordinating their assault on the New Deal, the intellectuals in another scratching out the texts of their edifying humanist lecture programs. But treating them in isolation obscures the ways their public activities resonate with each other, codifying and solidifying a common language of governance in which *freedom*, surely the period's most frequently used abstract noun, was a point of co-articulation for a host of otherwise discrepant agendas.[19] Television, or rather the intriguing possibility that television sponsorship could be a practice of governance, was a medium in which to develop that language. It brought members of these incommensurate sectors together figuratively, by creating a place in visual culture for the sponsor-citizen, a hybrid institutional entity embodying the period's technocratic fantasy of benign, voluntarist self-rule, and literally, in advisory boards, roundtable discussions, and other elite social configurations of the postwar pluralist ethos.

This may sound like the beginnings of a conspiracy, but it would be foolish to reduce the elite incorporation of television sponsorship into postwar arts of government to a cabalist tale of nefarious intrigue and cunning propaganda. For one thing, the cast of characters involved had distinct, sometimes clashing goals, none of which included the fantasy of effortlessly and totally persuading a compliant populace to act directly against their own interests (although corporate union-busting campaigns came close). Moreover, there is little evidence to suggest that television could achieve the Orwellian goals of total propaganda. If anything, the opposite is true—it is hard to believe, given the often soporific nature of programs produced with the goals of governance in mind, that such endeavors had much direct effect. In this respect, governing by television was just like any other effort to rationalize attitudes and behaviors among the governed. As Peter Miller and Nikolas Rose observe, "Government is a congenitally failing operation. . . . Things, persons, or events always appear to escape . . . the programmatic logic that seeks to govern them." But if the world in which we live is not "a governed world so much as a world traversed by the 'will to govern,' fueled by the constant registration of 'failure,' the discrepancy between ambition and outcome, and the constant injunction to do better next time," this does not mean that the will to govern is impotent or ineffectual, particularly when it comes to the distribution of resources and access to power.[20] When corporations, private agencies, philanthropic institutes, and other television sponsors expressed this will to govern, shouldering the burden of educating the population about the responsibilities of freedom in capitalist democracy, they often discovered a profound discrepancy between the effects they hoped to achieve and the responses of their viewers. Still, in the process of defining and adapting television as a technology of liberal rule, certain ways of thinking about the population emerged while others were marginalized, and these ways of thinking were as influential in determining the political horizons of everyday life as the medium itself, if not more so.

In other words, perhaps we are looking for "media effects" in the wrong place. If television helped implant the neoliberal program in U.S. political culture, it was not via its influence upon the so-called masses, but rather in its capacity to galvanize elites. From its inception, television assembled and connected members of distinct sectors of the governing classes who were seduced by, or at least curious about, its potential as an instrument for inculcating the values of liberal capitalist democracy. The existence of TV's mass audience provided these powerful people with opportunities to talk about and give form to the amorphous collectivity of the nation. These conversations helped ratify the existing power structure, rationalizing particular ways of ameliorating injustices and inequality over others. Instead of focusing on the proverbial living room, it makes more sense to look to the conference rooms and banquet halls of the Waldorf-Astoria or the Hotel Pierre for traces of postwar television's political effects and, in a sense, one of its most receptive audiences. In providing a venue in which elites could come together and exchange ideas about the citizenry, television sponsorship fostered interpersonal and institutional connections that were vital to the maintenance of political power and class interests.

Television also seemed to embody the technocratic ideals of liberal rule associated with these interests. Combining mass outreach with the potential for deep individual engagement, TV was a structural and conceptual model for benign, remote governance, dispersing power and authority outward, away from the bureaucratic, hierarchical, and potentially invasive offices of the state.[21] Although those who incorporated it into their agendas for governance also used print, radio, and nontheatrical film to communicate with the citizenry, TV stood for certain ideals of access, legitimacy, and popular identification, and it therefore occupied a privileged place within ambitions of rule. Its dominant configuration—commercial network programming—was admittedly a problem, especially as mass-culture critique began to gain prominence among intellectuals. But liberal democratic governance thrives on reform.[22] If television threatened tenets of citizenship in encouraging passivity, conformity, and the elevation of emotion over reason, this only strengthened the resolve of those who sought to activate the medium's potential for spreading rational civic practice among the populace. The "cozy functionalist fantasy" equating the television audience and the nation meant that the rehabilitation of television was the rehabilitation of society.[23] The process of maturing and rebalancing the ideas people encountered on TV was a way of maturing and rebalancing the interests that constituted the polity and, indeed, individual citizens themselves. Elite conversations about governing television and its audience, in short, were inseparable from broader national discussions about the relationship between culture, the economy, and the state.

These discussions ranged widely, delving deep into the central structures of liberal capitalist democracy: how to respond to and overcome looming challenges to the postwar social order, its distribution of wealth and power under threat from several fronts (the specter of communism, certainly, but more concretely, organized labor, black radicalism, and the residual energies of the Popular Front); how to link the abstract tenets of democracy—liberty, equality, and individual sovereignty—to programs and formulas of rule that might encourage some forms of conduct and marginalize others; how to ask and answer questions about the relationships between everyday, ingrained behaviors and the ethical obligations of good citizenship in a liberal democratic state; how to communicate the rational processes that bound individual citizens to the abstraction of the economy. Such grandiose concerns, couched in the language of reform, lay at the heart of the didactic TV projects undertaken by diverse public and private agencies in the medium's early years. In the act of voicing them, those in power collaborated across political divisions to identify areas of common interest, rendering concrete, in the highly projective figure of the TV viewer, the abstract entity of the citizen.

It is impossible to grasp the full significance of television in the political culture of the postwar period without first coming to grips with the basic assumptions about citizenship that took hold among those who saw TV as a form of governance by other means. Postwar experiments in governing by television certainly drew inspiration from prior efforts in radio and nontheatrical film, but the kinds of expectations attached to TV were most directly grounded in the historical moment of the 1950s.[24] Citizenship and liberal governance had specific meanings at the time, and a number of agendas were set and conflicts waged in the process of their definition. The large-scale shifts in U.S. culture and society that took place after World War II engendered broad efforts to redefine the institution of citizenship at the dawn of a new age. It was this moment of reinvention, its character greatly determined by the rapidly assembled consensus machine of Cold War ideology, that most profoundly shaped how and what television would teach its audience about culture and economy in a democratic society. When members of the governing classes spoke about citizenship, they stressed concepts such as freedom, equality, moderation, and balance. The only way to understand the persistent conflicts involved in translating these terms into the language of the era's newest—and potentially most transformative—medium of mass communication is to know the meanings behind these words, and the forms of inclusion and exclusion they helped to negotiate.

## INVENTING THE COLD WAR CITIZEN

"The making of citizens is a permanent political project for democracy," observes political scientist Barbara Cruickshank. "It seems that everybody has a scheme . . . for turning political subjects into democratic citizens, for transforming the apathetic into the politically active, the indolent into the productive, and the dependent into the self-sufficient."[25] Citizenship, in other words, is not the stable foundation on which democracy rests, but rather a category of personhood based on some kind of lack, a label describing political subjects who are "ethically incomplete," requiring ongoing training and reform if they are truly to live up to the title *citizen*.[26] The postwar mass media acknowledged as much in the programs they made to serve the public. "Citizens are made, not born," announced the title of a radio drama produced for ABC's *World Security Workshop* in 1946.

The Cold War overwhelmingly dictated ideas about the rights, responsibilities, and values associated with citizenship that emerged at this time. As a discourse of belonging and responsibility, implicitly opposed to the political subjectivity of the "comrade" in Soviet states, citizen talk in the United States helped to position individuals and their everyday actions in relationship to large-scale abstractions, not only the liberal democratic state, but also culture and the economy, as well as the emerging, highly projective image of a global society.[27] Spawning new exemplary figures of American freedom—recent scholarship has discovered the roles played by Mom, the teenager, the abstract painter, and the jazz musician in this regard—citizenship in the Cold War provided a capacious language through which to understand and manage the political and geopolitical meanings of individual behaviors, vocations, and values.[28]

Cold War citizenship talk was also, of course, a consummately contradictory discourse. To speak of citizenship in this period was to speak constantly and promiscuously of freedom, although it was a moment in American history that (until the Bush administration's War on Terror) saw an unprecedented assault on the "five freedoms" guaranteed by the First Amendment to the U.S. Constitution: freedom of speech, press, religion, assembly, and petition. This was also the moment when it became commonplace to describe economic entities as citizens—the corporation, the consumer, and even organized labor—in a conceptual move that transformed the production, exchange, and accumulation of goods into a moral and patriotic act.[29] And it was a period in international relations when the United States loudly proclaimed the superiority of American citizenship against the repressions suffered by people living in communist states, even though racist campaigns of terror against black Southerners revealed to observers in the free world and beyond the hollowness of such tenets of U.S. democracy as the right to vote and be represented, and to enjoy free and equal treatment under the law.

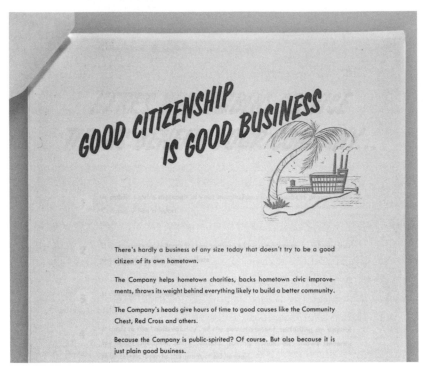

**GOOD CITIZENSHIP IS GOOD BUSINESS**

There's hardly a business of any size today that doesn't try to be a good citizen of its own hometown.

The Company helps hometown charities, backs hometown civic improvements, throws its weight behind everything likely to build a better community.

The Company's heads give hours of time to good causes like the Community Chest, Red Cross and others.

Because the Company is public-spirited? Of course. But also because it is just plain good business.

The Advertising Council worked hard to promote the idea of corporate citizenship in the 1950s, highlighting the public relations value of corporate good deeds.
*Image courtesy of Advertising Council Archives, University of Illinois.*

Citizenship's association with moral universals such as freedom, equality, rights, and responsibilities concealed these contradictions and allowed the category to serve diverse social, economic, and cultural agendas. The term was particularly useful in the corporate effort to identify the interests of business with those of the nation, an effort immortalized in the "what's good for General Motors" adage uttered by GM president Charles Wilson during congressional hearings on his appointment as Eisenhower's secretary of defense. Alongside invocations of corporate citizenship, business leaders' visions of the postwar polity often advanced the idea of workers as citizens of a corporation.

Management guru Peter Drucker, writing in the Catholic public affairs magazine *Commonweal*, proposed that the business enterprise was a new social order:

> For its employees, it is increasingly the community in which they spend the major part of their waking hours and from which they therefore expect the fulfillment of the social promises of their society . . . the status and function which make a person a citizen . . . and the equal opportunities of a democratic society. In other words, the workers look upon the enterprise as the place in which they realize both freedom and justice.

In Drucker's view, industrial corporations held the key to "the possibility of creating harmony, establishing again a moral community" among their employee-citizens and within the nation as a whole; in this possibility, he suggested, lay "the best chance for the survival of Western society as a free, strong, and prosperous society."[30]

Such paeans to corporate welfarism, implicitly advocating employer paternalism over union representation, supplied a Cold War context for classical liberalism's equation of free enterprise and democracy. This context also motivated popular education campaigns aimed at teaching free market principles, and creating favorable attitudes toward those principles, among the populace. Elizabeth Fones-Wolf has exhaustively detailed the place of these campaigns within an aggressive and wide-ranging assault on labor and economic justice movements, although in the public statements of many corporate visionaries, "economic education" was the business community's moral obligation, a way of serving those whose actions as consumers guaranteed the strength of the economy.[31] "American capitalism," one industrial psychologist noted, "has educated people in slogans about its products . . . but it has not educated the public to the moral significance of these slogans." Opinion polls, he continued, showed that "American industry has not been nearly so successful in selling *the principles of free enterprise* as it has been in selling its *products*."[32] Popular campaigns to improve economic education among the citizenry, designed to sway public opinion away from government regulation of commerce and industrial relations, both countered the redistributive ethos of FDR's New Deal and Truman's Fair Deal and advanced the cause of corporate citizenship. As the Advertising Council suggested in a 1954 filmstrip aimed at recruiting new members, business leaders should be careful not to forget "the essential nature of their citizenship as advertisers."[33]

Invocations of citizenship lent legitimacy not only to the corporate assault on the New Deal and organized labor but to many other antidemocratic causes besides. All kinds of acts, from price gouging to assassination to the suspension of constitutional rights, could be justified as efforts to protect the freedoms on which American democratic citizenship rested. For White Citizens Councils in the South, for example, the term lent a "respectable" public face to segregationism. To claim, as did one of the movement's founders, that integration was a "communistic disease" was to justify racist acts of intimidation as the duties of citizens acting on a sense of patriotic decency.[34] But anticommunist scaremongers, corporate shills, and hate-filled segregationists were not the only ones to draw on concepts of citizenship to gather support for their causes. The category was just as crucial for struggles against hatred and fanaticism in this period. The Southern Christian Leadership Council and other civil rights groups organized "citizenship schools" to assist black Southerners in the process of voter registration and qualification. Citizenship also figured prominently in the rhetoric of reform circulating at the socially liberal end of the Establishment. Organizations such as Robert Hutchins' Fund for the Republic, for example, aimed to revive the tenets of citizenship on which the American republic was founded. Because the vitality of those principles had been weakened by McCarthyism's seductive political hysteria and the culture of segregation, the Fund called upon Americans "to discuss, in a rational and orderly manner, the deep conflicts of liberty and justice that trouble us."[35] Citizenship, in short, was a category that circulated indiscriminately throughout Cold War era public speech, providing a capacious means of moral and political legitimization and a widely recognized vocabulary for framing particular political agendas as general issues at stake in democratic self-governance.

History played an important role in this legitimization process. Hutchins' effort to revive citizenship's republican roots was part of a broader postwar impulse to link the tenets of governance in the present to the ideals of the American past, an impulse manifested in festive spectacles of patriotism such as the rededication weeks and Freedom Train tours sponsored by the American Heritage Foundation. These instances of pageantry, along with the various centennials and sesquicentennials staged throughout the 1950s, asked Americans to reaffirm their commitment to the ideals fought for in prior struggles, discovering their civic selves through the reverent inspection of historical documents, as well as community-based speech and essay contests. In such moments, Richard Fried notes, "the past anchored a stormy present, and remembrances unnerved Americans for a stressful new global role."[36] Television programs were among such efforts to connect the heroic pursuit of freedom in past centuries to the domestic and geopolitical challenges of the day. *A Date with Liberty*, for example, based on a popular book by Supreme Court Justice William O. Douglas and sponsored by the Fund for the Republic, dramatized scenes from American history in order to remind viewers of the importance of hard-won democratic freedoms. "There's a law in our land bigger than any mob," avows abolitionist newspaper editor Elijah Lovejoy in one installment, right before he is murdered. "A free press is the precious right of a free people," intones a male voice-over, finishing Lovejoy's sentence—a rhetorical flourish that turned the antislavery struggles of the past and the anticommunist struggles of the present into points on the same continuum of freedom.[37]

It was the recent past, however, and not previous centuries, that most decisively shaped the expectations and agendas encoded in the Cold War conception of citizenship. In their efforts to shape national planning in the transition from war to peace, corporate leaders, politicians, philanthropists, and intellectuals spoke constantly of the unprecedented challenge of citizenship in a seemingly brand-new world. Recalling the heroic efforts of the war years, the hardships of the Great Depression, and the visions of social and economic justice associated with the New Deal, citizen talk characterized the present not only as

a time of rebuilding and making a fresh start, but also as a new stage in the development of a (progressively more virtuous) system of American governance. When Advertising Council president Theodore Repplier proposed in 1952 that "the free world badly needs a rearmament of ideas," he was speaking of the present as a world that had outgrown previous forms of social organization, most notably the socioeconomic conditions that led to the Depression and the more radical forms of redistribution associated with New Deal policies, as well as the leftist alliances that constituted the Popular Front of the 1930s.[38] Reconstruction in European nations meant recovery from war, but in the United States, for many members of the governing classes, it also meant recovery from the peacetime federal social mandates that preceded it.

Across diverse sectors of the Establishment, from liberal intellectuals to union-busting business groups, a rhetoric of the political and economic future emerged in response to such calls for democracy's rebirth. It was a rhetoric suffused with tropes of maturity and images of balance and moderation to counter the purported extremes of the past.[39] Although this rhetoric seemed motivated by an ethos of progressive enlightenment and deepening equality, its uses were not clear-cut, to say the least. Eisenhower, for example, used the idea of balance to justify his inertial stance on civil rights, refusing to meet with civil rights leaders because he said he would then have to meet with the Ku Klux Klan. As Thomas Borstelmann notes, this was "a calculus equating whites engaged in violence with polite, peaceful protesters seeking the fulfillment of their civil rights."[40] All too often, politicians and segregationists used the language of "extremists on both sides" to equate civil rights activists with white perpetrators of racial terror, a move that might be considered the "dog whistle politics" of the day. Such characterizations would lead Martin Luther King Jr., in his famous *Letter from Birmingham Jail*, to retort, "The question is not whether we will be extremists, but what kind of extremists we will be. Will we be extremists for hate or extremists for love? Will we be extremists for the preservation of injustice—or will we be extremists for the cause of justice?"[41]

In another sphere of postwar struggle, corporate activists used the concept of balance as a key strategy in their campaigns to pass the antilabor Taft-Hartley Act, suggesting that it might "equalize" the excesses of the 1935 Wagner Act.[42] However, the project of rebalancing democratic institutions around a seemingly centrist fulcrum was perhaps most crucial for American liberals, anxious to distance themselves from radicals and leftists in the postwar years. Arthur Schlesinger Jr.'s *The Vital Center* (1946), a manifesto for liberal anticommunism, was saturated with the language of parity and symmetry; similarly, J.K. Galbraith would argue a few years later for an approach to postwar economic planning that conceived of capitalism as a system of "countervailing powers."[43] Ideals of maturity and compromise also found expression in the period's cultural criticism, most notably in Lionel Trilling's influential 1950 essay collection *The Liberal Imagination*, which argued for the literary values associated with the psychological subtlety of a Henry James over the dogmatism of the social realist tradition in American literature.[44]

This new understanding of the polity, and the individual, as a set of forces in need of balance alienated some leftists. "If the master-image of balance is accepted," noted C. Wright Mills in a scathing critique, "many intellectuals, especially in their current patrioteering, are readily able to satisfy such political optimism as they wish to feel."[45] The conciliatory centrism that angered Mills was, as Mary Sperling MacAuliffe has detailed, a symptom of the disintegration of the United Front coalitions formed across class and ideological lines in the 1930s; it was also a hallmark of the emerging political and cultural formation often known as Cold War liberalism. The Cold War liberal was a figure embodied by Schlesinger, along with Trilling, journalist James Rorty, philosopher Sidney Hook, educator Mortimer Adler, and others. He supported "principled" anticommunism and expressed distaste for McCarthyism, a position justified, along with support for militarized containment overseas, as a return to the true liberal tradition—the latter summarized by Americans for Democratic Action founder James Loeb as "a complete dedication to the twin objectives of economic security and human freedom."[46]

But the political culture envisioned in Cold War liberalism was not only a revival of classical liberal philosophy; it was also a consolidation of class interest. In aligning themselves against mass culture and McCarthyist mass hysteria, postwar liberals found a way to sever any ties to populism and to the grassroots causes that might in the past have bound them to working-class politics. Instead of speaking of solidarity, postwar liberals *worried* about the so-called masses. "Is the common man too common?" fretted one book of essays on the perils of the mass.[47] The answer, it seemed, was yes; journalist Joseph Wood Krutch, in the title essay, concluded that "ultimate responsibility for the future lies with the thinkers and educators whose most important social task at the moment is to define democratic culture in some fashion which will both reserve a place for uncommon excellence and . . . emphasize the highest rather than the lowest common denominator."[48] In statements such as this, Cold War liberals diagnosed the potential contradictions emerging from the postwar economy's emphasis on mass consumption in terms of the inadequate moral education of the populace; the cure was the administration of culture by an elite class immune to the seductions of the mass.[49] Hence television programs such as *Omnibus*, sponsored by the Ford Foundation. As Robert Saudek, the director of the foundation's Television-Radio Workshop, explained, the mass dissemination of culture on television was a way to "raise the level of American taste."[50]

The liberal rejection of political and cultural populism required a shift in the languages of governance, as it placed "the people," a key term in the historical vocabulary of American citizenship, in opposition to the democratic process.[51] As MacAuliffe notes, "The 'people' with whom liberals had identified in the thirties . . . became in the fifties enemies of civil liberties and threats to the stability of the political system."[52] Liberal groups such as Americans for Democratic Action did use the term in their hesitant challenges to the blacklist, most notably in a New York public forum, "The People vs. McCarthy."[53] But generally, if the concept of "the people" entered into postwar citizenship talk, it was only to embody anticollectivist values. The Advertising Council's People's Capitalism project, for example, co-sponsored with the State Department, invoked "the people" as a tool for teaching the moral and ethical dimensions of capitalism at home and abroad. As one of its participants explained, American capitalism worked for the people "by enlarging the freedom of the individual and extending his potentialities." As a result, "the alertness and self-assertiveness of . . . citizens will contribute to the development and maintenance of free government in the world."[54] People's capitalism, from this perspective, was not a contradiction but the ultimate embodiment of democratic ideals.

This co-optation of the concept of the people was too much to stomach for some observers; labor author Art Preis wrote in the *International Socialist Review* that "the widely advertised 'people's capitalism' is a myth based upon massive falsifications about the conditions of the working people and their struggles for existence in this richest and most favored of capitalist countries."[55] Moreover, there is no doubt that *the people* remained a vital keyword in critiques of the system. A scathing 1957 letter from Richmond, Virginia, resident Thomas A. Dalton to the DuPont corporation, housed in the company archives, noted snottily that from watching the advertisements that aired during *DuPont Theater* "one would think that the 'Du Pont co.' was operated entirely on a philanthropic basis. . . . [S]top trying to kid the public but have some consideration for the people. Do something about the long winded, boresome, misleading commercial." (At the bottom of the page, someone from the advertising department has penciled "Not a stockholder.")[56] Yet the right-wing appropriation of "*the people*" and its collectivist meanings continued apace, reaching a notable milestone in 1965 with the formation of Up with People, the youth musical theater wing of the conservative Christian movement Moral Re-Armament. The group's redaction of the definite article reclaimed the word *people* in the fight against the antiwar movement, beatniks, and communism.[57] Still, at around the same time, radicals in the Freedom Summer movement were appropriating the term for their own uses; most notable were Jane Stembridge and Stokely Carmichael, who began a widely hailed Freedom School workshop with the provocation "The Peoples wants freedom."[58] As Daniel Rodgers notes, "This was the core rhetoric of the Cold War, translated into black vernacular, specified, sharpened into radically destabilized demands, appropriated by the most marginal of Americans."[59]

But such strident efforts to reclaim "the people" had been unfathomable ten years earlier, when liberals saw populism as an impediment to the realization of their centrist ideals. In place of the people, the new liberalism placed the *individual* at the center of the democratic process. The individual was a powerful moral touchstone in some of the most important documents of postwar state governance, from defense policy briefs such as NSC 68, the Truman administration's landmark argument for containment as an exercise of military as well as diplomatic power, to Supreme Court decisions such as *Brown v. Board of Education*. If the former document argued that "the fundamental purpose of the United States is to assure the integrity and vitality of our free society, which is founded upon the dignity and worth of the individual," the latter enforced this goal, defining the damage caused by segregation in terms of its effects on the individual child's mind.[60] However beneficial the decision was, this focus on the psyche allowed the court to avoid the question of structural and material inequalities between black and white schools, addressing the collective concerns of black Americans within a narrowly defined form of "therapeutic pluralism."[61]

If the individual belonged to a larger form of collectivity, it was not the masses or the people but rather the technocratically administered collective of the interest group, a pluralist political category that came to dominate U.S. public administration in the decades following World War II.[62] Invoked in implicit opposition to social movements (conceived as unruly factions confronting each other in disruptive power struggles), interest groups were artifacts of the technocratic imagination—"fairy tales," Mills suggested in 1958, "used as working justifications of power in America."[63] If movements and masses were embodied throngs engaged in active conflict, interest groups were abstract entities who would meet only indirectly, through the mediations of the policies and expert systems connected with, but not equivalent to, the state.

This concern with the preservation and development of the citizen as an individual (rather than as a member of a potentially insurgent collective such as the people) and as a bearer of interests (rather than, say, demands) was of course rooted in the ideological terrain of the Cold War, in which U.S.-based conceptions of identity and selfhood countered the soul-stifling conformity of Soviet collectivism.[64] Yet even as they asserted the importance of the individual self, Cold Warriors acknowledged the seductions of the mass. Addressing the Advertising Council's board of directors, CIA psychological warfare expert Nicholas de Rochemont compared methods of propaganda on both sides of the Iron Curtain. He explained, as the meeting's minutes reported, that "the communist countries employ mass agitation which appeals to the emotions of the masses, whereas the only form of propaganda used in the United States is an intellectual persuasion appealing individually to the mind." Still, he noted, private organizations, such as womens groups, might be successful in using "the communist form of persuasion" to appeal to their counterpart organizations overseas, adding that he was working with the council's president toward this end.[65] Individualism, it seems, was not a universal human quality to be upheld at all costs, but rather a (gendered) matter of interpretation and strategy.

As this might suggest, Cold War liberal discourse was not a simple celebration of individuality in all of its forms. Rather, the Cold War conception of the citizen as individual embodied a particular set of traits and qualities, linked to broader ideas about the nation and serving particular economic and political goals. Citizenship was a developmental journey, leading from the immoderate and intemperate excesses of childhood (or its political equivalent, irrational extremism) to the constitution of a rational, moderate, and self-managing self, informed enough to evaluate intelligently the choices it confronted in the marketplace, in the political arena, and in the realm of arts and culture.[66] As a well-balanced individual, the ideal citizen was a part standing for a whole, his or her self-control embodying a more general liberal pluralist conception of good governance.[67] The latter, after all, involved the achievement of a balance of interests, superseding the ideals of reform and redistribution associated with the New Deal.[68] But who could be trusted to bring about this balance of interests, judging the point at which equilibrium had been reached? Who was impartial enough to orchestrate the pluralist polity's ideal of a harmonious chorus of voices? The most suitable candidate was the disinterested expert, a kind of metacitizen identified with no particular interest but rather charged with adjudicating *between* interests in order that the people might govern themselves wisely.[69] Annexing and maintaining this disinterested position was the essence of Establishment realpolitik, which thrived upon the crucial impression that the governing classes were a bipartisan, rational-minded, and benevolent body of expert social managers, their image of impartiality rendered credible by the presence of self-proclaimed liberals in their ranks.[70] After all, in a polity defined by interest groups, power accrues within those positions that seem to *transcend* interest—or, alternatively, subsume all interests in the assertion of some kind of universal good.

It would be naive to conclude from the ubiquity of the centrist language of moderation and balance that social conflicts were in abeyance in the postwar period.[71] Rather, we must understand this language *as* a language of conflict. Reframing antagonisms as interests and attacks as forms of rebalancing, centrist rationality set the terms for mounting any kind of challenge to the period's economic and political common sense. Although it derived from the accomodationism of postwar liberalism, this language provided a general vocabulary in which all kinds of political positions claimed their legitimacy and marginalized others. It was an elite discourse insofar as the ideals it stressed—balance, freedom, and reason—were increasingly located within institutions and mechanisms set, as Mills noted in 1952, at a widening remove from the citizen-individuals it supposedly empowered.[72] And it was a sign that the philosophical tenets of classical liberalism, prioritizing individual freedom and personal sovereignty, understanding government as an art practiced through (but not by) the state, had achieved ascendancy over alternative models that might have seemed dimly possible in the 1930s. For Mills, who believed that "twentieth century

problems cannot be solved by eighteenth century phrases," these tenets were the source of liberalism's political impotence; to bring about
any meaningful social change, it had to be transformed from a discourse of government into an analytic of power.[73] But his invocations of
power relations were uttered from outside of the Cold War consensus.
Opposed to the consolidating class interest linking liberal technocrats and corporate opponents of the New Deal, Mills was a sociologist "studying up" by scrutinizing the culture of the power elite, and
his insights had no place in the Establishment liberal conversation.


## THE RISE OF THE SPONSOR-CITIZEN

For those among the Establishment committed to the postwar rehabilitation of citizenship, the important issue was finding techniques
of rule that would translate the new conception of the citizen into a
persuasive vernacular amenable to affirmative, enabling, and indi-
viduated strategies of moderate reform. Television was a commercial
and thus supposedly "independent" instrument of mass outreach. Regulated according to principles of balance and fairness and explicitly
charged with the task of serving the public, it was a highly promising
new venue. Not only was it a novel device that could both inform and
entertain (a bromide industry shills never tired of mouthing), it was
also a "free" organ of opinion, a realm of public culture seemingly un-
contaminated by the censorial or propagandistic influences of the state,
in contrast with the broadcast systems of other nations. On European
television, veteran Cold Warrior Lucius Clay noted, "you get this constant repeated propaganda without advertising and without break,"
whereas in the United States, "the advertising gives you a direct feeling of assurance that you haven't got propaganda in the program being thrown at you."[74] These kinds of arguments had been around
since the beginning of radio, but the Cold War lent them new legitimacy. Television's structural separation from the federal government,
coupled with its diverse modes of address, made the medium seem

like an ideal tool for nondirective persuasion; it could be used to educate (or reeducate) viewers' attitudes surrounding problems in a range of areas, from industrial relations to the Jim Crow South, while keeping them at a safe distance from the tentacles of the state.

Thus, rather than condemning people's capacity to consume mass culture, public campaigns for citizenship education on television cultivated it, directing consumption toward something other than entertainment. The implication, however, was that viewers were disinclined by nature to answer the call of citizenship on their own. As a TV consultant hired by the Fund for the Republic explained, sponsored civic programming could "[drop] an occasional idea into the kitchens of folks like my neighbor, who rarely, if ever, thinks about the Bill of Rights but who regularly watches her television machine."[75] Through such speculations about viewers, producers and sponsors developed ideas about how TV might bring its audience members into the domain of governance without subjecting them to direct state control—embodying, in other words, the ethos of liberal democracy as "government at a distance."[76] They approached TV as a mechanism of *security* rather than *discipline*, to borrow a distinction from Michel Foucault. If the techniques of the latter involved placing the act of watching TV under surveillance in order to control it, the former would foster TV viewing as a form of conduct that could, under the right conditions, allow the population to reflect upon the social realm and form opinions, regulating itself automatically without sacrificing freedom of choice.[77]

This understanding of viewership as the indirect exercise of self-governance, and of sponsorship as a means of enabling that process, reflected and extended suppositions contained within the framework of the U.S. broadcasting system as it developed in the early twentieth century.[78] Radio was envisioned by policy makers and business interests as part of a self-regulating corporate sector that was networked with the state and with private associations, forming a scientifically managed "organizational sector" that ensured the proper dispersal of responsibility and oversight in the governmental process.[79] Predicated upon an understanding of corporate leaders as moral guardians of the interests of the nation, this approach to governance, notes James Weinstein, emerged from the conflicts animating Progressive era civil society and indicated businessmen's success "in adapting to their own ends the ideals of middle class social reformers, social workers, and socialists."[80] Weinstein and others have labeled this vision of governance "corporate liberalism"; as Thomas Streeter details, the broadcasting policy that evolved in this period embodied the corporate liberal ideal. It placed the airwaves, a public trust, in the hands of commercial licensees whose task, with minimal state oversight, was to serve "public interest, convenience, and necessity."[81]

The prestige conferred upon corporate liberal broadcasters by the rhetoric of public trusteeship extended to sponsors as well. Fostering the free will of listeners, and positioning sponsors' quests for publicity as competitive mechanisms working on behalf of the listener, early radio policy forged an identification between sponsorship—even when motivated by private interest—and the public good. As debates over the intrusions of radio advertising stepped up, proponents of the commercial system worked hard to draw out the connotations of patronage associated with the idea of sponsorship, positioning sponsors as community institutions bringing culture and learning to mass audiences through "indirect advertising" designed to foster "goodwill." Even as pitch-heavy spot advertising took over and critics began to decry the excesses of the commercial system, indirect and so-called institutional (public relations) advertising remained counterexamples demonstrating the ways that sponsorship could provide a public service.[82] But the image of the sponsor as, in Erik Barnouw's words, a "modern potentate" continued to take hold, and in the New Deal era the public trusteeship conferred upon the private U.S. broadcasting system became an avenue for critique. New federal guidelines for public service programming distinguished between paid and unpaid broadcasts and required stations to set aside a number of hours per week for programming in the latter category—educational, cultural, and public affairs shows produced and/or sponsored by nonprofit groups, or by broadcasters themselves, as so-called sustaining programs. But although presented as reform, this separation of commerce and the public interest did not contradict the corporate liberal equation of private broadcasting and the public interest. If anything, it shored it up even further, demonstrating the self-correcting capacity of the system while remaining, as many critics have noticed, a largely unenforceable form of regulation.

This was not a new development for activists and reformers opposed to private broadcasting. From the first, the corporate liberal conception of public service was a bitterly contentious point for educators and nonprofit groups working to change the system. As Robert McChesney notes, broadcast reform began as a "radical criticism [that] identified ownership and support as the decisive elements in accounting for the nature of U.S. broadcasting and argued that any meaningful reform . . . would have to alter the existing patterns."[83] Serving the public interest, in this view, was structurally impossible within the extant profit-driven system. The arrival of television reawakened public service activism, and the presence of educational broadcasting advocates among the FCC commissioners led, for a short time at least, to a fear within the commercial TV industry that precious television frequencies would be allocated to nonprofit and educational stations. Among its responses was an avowed commitment to public service programming, seen as good public relations for the system as a whole. "Operation Frontal Lobes," an NBC-TV public service initiative, was a classic example. It was devised by the network's programming head, Sylvester "Pat" Weaver, who advocated "using commercial television networks and stations in adult education and not leaving education via television to educational stations and the educators" because the "showmanlike" sensibilities and mass audience associated with commercial TV made it a more effective tool for "the enlargement of the horizon of the viewer."[84] Others agreed; as James Webb Young of the Ford Foundation noted, educators "are not masters of the arts of holding non-captive audiences."[85]

Such arguments over commercial television's capacity to serve the public are still active today, in ongoing debates over broadcast reform and regulation. These debates are often understood in terms of the antithetical models of democratic governance established on each side—a disingenuous market populism on one hand and an ingenuous elite paternalism on the other, each claiming to be more truly democratic.[86] But such polarized interpretations obscure the points of commonality between each position. Despite their irreconcilable stances on the question of ownership and funding, the proponents and critics of U.S. broadcasting's private, commercial basis share a foundational assumption, namely, that the government of the airwaves is also the government of the people, or more precisely, that the airwaves must be governed in such a way that they can best help people govern themselves. It is an assumption that radical critiques of broadcast ownership must examine if they are to continue contributing strong and vital arguments to the ongoing leftist challenge to neoliberal political economy.

Tracing the history of governing by television is an opportunity to examine this assumption more closely. Rather than debunking one ideal of public service and replacing it with a truer one, we might be better off asking about the uses of the ideal for those organizations and individuals who see television as a form of government by other means. At stake, in other words, is not so much the issue of whether a particular television program actually does or does not perform a public service, but rather the matter of the strategies and rationales under which sponsors and broadcasters can claim to represent themselves as public servants at particular moments and, by extension, how their activities on the air come to be seen as enabling the rational exercise of freedom among the viewing population.[87] In the 1950s, to speak in the public service was to speak from a position *transcending* material and personal interests. Identification with this space of reasonable, seemingly neutral enunciation was perhaps most important for corporate public relations, which often disavowed the pursuit of profit in order to identify the interests of business with those of the public. (It is hardly surprising that the running banner at the bottom of the Advertising Council's letterhead for many years was "The Best Public Relations Advertising Is Public Service Advertising.") But this aspiration to speak in the public interest was certainly not confined to the corporate sector. It was a matter of intense struggle for any number of groups—organized labor, civil rights activists, and liberal philanthropists among them, as this book's case studies detail. To be able to speak to the public as its servant was to inhabit the authoritative position of the universal liberal subject, responsible and worthy enough to think and act on behalf of others. It was to link sponsorship to citizenship.

comparisons with the special character of both subject and
little meaning. As you know, our belief is that the
created by this approach are not readily identifiable
when they can be consciously absorbed, are subject to
irrelevant influences, pro or con, which in our opinion
statistical appraisal into question.

Even if we assume, however, that the "pl
represent a valid index of memorability or accepta
yet established a par. The field is new and untri
are no yardsticks that we know of to indicate whe
percentage is good, bad, or indifferent.

Certainly, it is true that acceptance
dealing with the large corporation's role in soc
susceptible to identification and attribution th
matter such as "Du Pont makes materials for fas
or even "Du Pont works with smaller companies."
hand, we feel that, no matter how desirable the
be, the goal of most long-term significance is
approval of big business on an emotional as we
plane. If this is true, then obviously it is
to reassure one person about unspoken fears o
than to convince a dozen people of conclusior
ment exists. It is much more difficult to w
big business idea and it takes a great deal
in public attitudes, but I am sure we all a
warrant a determined effort, even if the di
able.

I hope this review gives you the
our thinking as a guide to your conversati

al character of both project and technique, ...
...ble types of ... the ...
know. Our belief is that the ...
... are not readily identifiable and ...
...ously absorbed, are subject to all sorts of
...pro or con, which in our opinion calls any
...nto question.

...sume, however, that the "playback" does
... of memorability or acceptance, no one has
... The field is new and untried, and there
...we know of to indicate whether any given
...d, or indifferent.

...t is true that acceptance of any concept
...corporation's role in society is less
...ication and attribution than purely factual
...t makes materials for fashionable apparel"
...s with smaller companies." On the other
...o matter how desirable those objectives may
...long-term significance is understanding and
...ess on an emotional as well as an intellectual
...ue, then obviously it is of greater importance
...n about unspoken fears of bigness in business
...ozen people of conclusions on which no argu-
...much more difficult to win acceptance of the
...d it takes a great deal longer to make a dent
...but I am sure we all agree that the stakes
...effort, even if the difficulties are formid-

...s review gives you the picture you need of
...ide to your conversations with Gallup and

*Chapter One*

# SPONSORS AND CITIZENS

"THE WHOLE structure of modern business," wrote critic Philip Rieff in 1953, "is enveloped in an aura of political legitimation, and indeed, of identification with government. This is the function of institutional advertising."[1] With these blunt words Rieff summarized the growing relationships between governance and public relations in the postwar period. Over the course of the twentieth century, public relations had become increasingly integrated into attempts to regulate people's everyday lives, shepherding their conduct and, to paraphrase PR guru Edward L. Bernays' uncannily Chomskian 1947 essay title, engineering their consent.[2] For some, this was a utopian moment in the history of democracy. As one optimistic British observer proposed, the skillful techniques of the public relations profession could help bridge the gap "between 'we'—the millions of plain men and women—and 'they'—the thousands in business, government, the churches, organized labor, the universities, and elsewhere, who constitute the effective ruling class."[3] For many others, however, the profession was merely a propaganda factory populated by "snide, weasel-minded, smart, sharp, conscienceless lads who, if necessary . . . could make a chiseling steel firm which rooked the Government of millions seem to be the liberal lover of labor, blind widows, and infantile paralysis victims."[4] Institutional advertising, a public relations format in print and broadcast media born out of corporate responses to Progressive era reform in the 1920s, was notorious for promulgating exactly this kind of disingenuous spin.[5] More ominously, as Rieff's observations suggest, it was a formula through which corporations assumed the authority to address the public as fellow citizens, just as politicians or government officials might. Distancing the business enterprise from the taint of private profit, institutional advertising was a kind of indirect political speech that sought to locate corporate interests on a moral plane that transcended the market, rendering them equivalent to the public good.

Although the term *institutional advertising* has slipped out of common usage today, the public relations goals it served will no doubt seem wearyingly familiar to television viewers and magazine readers in the United States. If you have ever come across an advertisement from an oil company avowing its commitment to saving the planet rather than destroying it, you have been exposed to institutional advertising. Historically, the term referred to a kind of advertising that downplayed sales in favor of public relations—the adjective *institutional* reflecting the modern firm's increasing interest in defining itself as an establishment on a par with church, state, and family. As the genre evolved, it became increasingly concerned with *humanizing* the corporation, redefining its relationship with its public as that of "favorite, friend, neighbor, and even family member."[6] These anthropomorphic metaphors transported the activities of business from the sphere of economic accumulation into the familiar, comforting terrain of everyday life.[7]

To get a sense of what institutional advertising looked like in early television, consider an advertisement for the American Machine and Foundry Corporation that aired on the CBS network on January 25,

1953, which happens to be the same year Rieff published his remarks characterizing the format as an exercise of the corporate will to govern. The ad begins with a shot of pretzels in a bowl. A hand reaches in and picks one up. "Have you ever wondered how the pretzel gets twisted?" a male narrator asks in voice-over. This quirky invitation shifts the scene to a factory, where we see the hands of human pretzel twisters at work on an assembly line. As dough strips glide by, the hands grasp and twist them one by one. The job seems to require an awfully large number of employees. Quality control appears to be a problem too; one of them makes a mistake as we watch. Then, in close-up, a complicated machine appears, its cunning little pincers twisting dough into pretzels in a fraction of a second. The narrator invites us to compare the fiddly task of hand-twisting pretzels with the lightning contortions of the machine, incapable of making a mistake. The process is fascinating to witness, and it seems even more awesome when we learn about the scale of pretzel production it involves. "In just one eight-hour day a single battery of AMF machines can twist as many as one and a half million pretzels. Perfectly. Endlessly. Without ever stopping." A slow-motion shot shows us just how perfect the machine's movements are. "The thinking fingers you see here are typical of AMF invention in action. Typical of how the skilled specialists of AMF continuously put invention into action to make things best for industry and for you."

Although it focuses closely on the pretzel, a consumer product, this is obviously not an advertisement for something you can buy. It is, most immediately, a public relations exercise trumpeting the research and development program of the American Machine and Foundry Corporation. But more important, it is an advertisement for something that was highly controversial in conversations about the national economy in the postwar period: automation. In keeping with industry arguments at the time, the advertisement presents automation in terms of its benefits to the consumer—in this case, the idea of a cheap pretzel supply, guaranteed never to run out. The ad also personifies capital-intensive industry (a category to which the majority of institutional sponsors belonged) on a human scale, in the figure of the

skilled specialist whose expertise ensures the ongoing expansion of consumer markets. And we can hear the governmental rhetoric that so concerned Rieff in the advertisement's insistence that automation is the best thing both "for industry and for you." Such statements presume a paternal relationship between consumers and industry analogous to the relationship between the state and its subjects, or rather, as management guru Peter Drucker suggested in an apologia for welfare capitalism also published in 1953, between the community and its citizens—a relationship in which the corporation, a "new autonomous institution," emerges as "the local self-government of modern society, the logical successor to manor, village, and town."[8] In its earnest explanation of the shared interests linking consumer, corporation, and nation, rendered concrete in the story of how goods are made, the advertisement credits business with the values of transparency and accountability associated with good government, rewriting the calamitous postwar narrative of deskilling and job loss as a necessary progression toward a greater public good.

The big question, of course, is whether people actually bought the premises of advertisements like this, welcoming the humanized, benevolent corporation as an institution of American democracy. The effects of institutional advertising were notoriously hard to evaluate, and one company, DuPont, conducted extensive research on audiences for its television programs and ads in the 1950s, hoping to answer this very question.[9] I spent many hours pondering it myself as I paged through the records of the company's advertising department, archived in a bunkerlike building originally built to store nitrate of soda for a gunpowder mill on the banks of Delaware's Brandywine River. (The mill, along with the first du Pont family estate, now houses the Hagley Business Museum and Library.) Like the advertising managers whose memoranda and marginalia I pored over, I was curious about whether the institutional advertisements they painstakingly crafted had any discernible effect. Such questions are very seductive, tempting the researcher to search obsessively for telltale documents that will gratify suspicions about corporate brainwashing. But I concluded quickly

that to fully understand the place of these advertisements, and indeed television, in postwar projects of corporate governance, I needed to stop searching for evidence of their direct effects. Instead, I began asking how the very process of audience research in institutional advertising, constituting a realm of encounter between corporation and citizen, helped to rewrite relations between economy, culture, and state at a moment that, in retrospect, seems to have marked the beginning of the long erosion of New Deal liberalism as a governmental paradigm.

As several historians have shown, corporations staged their assault on the New Deal in the postwar period in a number of different media.[10] But what makes institutional advertising on television a particularly interesting venue for exploring these campaigns is the fact that rapidly evolving techniques of audience research provided corporations with a tangible framework for evaluating and adjusting the ways they spoke to the public as servants and fellow citizens. Moreover, as Roland Marchand has shown, the research process itself could serve as a means for advancing the corporate agenda, as it was easily presented to viewers as a democratic structure, a way of giving them their "say" in national debates over corporate power.[11] Institutional advertising presented itself as a form of civic education, and its audience research was, inevitably, also an occasion for people to define their relationships to public policies, to corporations, to evolving languages of citizenship and governance, and to mass culture in general. In this respect, audience research for institutional advertising had more in common with opinion polling than with product-based market research—it was a means, via the research encounter, for the corporation to refine its techniques for knowing, and governing, its public.

Because it positioned television audiences as both receptacles and originators of opinion, institutional advertising research facilitated particular kinds of interactions between corporations and citizens. Research professionals approached individuals as proxies of the polity at large; subjects in turn treated researchers as proxies of the governing classes, and as representatives of the apparatus of mass communication more generally.[12] They approached these encounters as conversations about how (and sometimes whether) a corporation might participate in democratic rule, and about television's limits as the instrument through which firms might communicate their civic intentions. If this type of interaction was an approximation of the mechanism of representative government, it was certainly not a conversation among equals. Rather, the audience research process surrounding institutional advertising transformed the medium's fusion of intimate and mass communication into a technique for exercising corporate power while appearing to work in the best interests of the population.[13] Finding out what people thought about television was easily represented as an effort to democratize and render transparent the mechanisms of media representation, even if the citizen whose interests it ultimately served was the corporate one.

However, as it turned out, the question of what to make of the patterns of speech and attention that emerged from audience research was always a bewildering one. To examine the ways that people negotiated the relationship between PR and governance when they entered the audience research process is to discover that institutional advertising's place within the ideological terrain of the postwar period extended well beyond the ongoing debates about national economic policy and monopoly power that DuPont sought to influence. The research process was a conversation about how corporations might legitimately represent themselves to the public, although at times it went much further. Discussing advertising and programming with representatives of the company, viewers not only took the occasion to express their attitudes toward the interrelations of corporations, consumers, and government in the postwar economy, but also invoked the growing critique of mass society and the embryonic national debate about desegregation, prejudice, and civil rights. Talking to DuPont audience researchers and ad managers was a way of voicing concrete concerns about pressing issues in government, from the shortcomings of public schools to Southern racial violence. Such dialogue was taking place in a range of venues in this period—in local community and service organizations, in labor halls, in churches—but the research encounter was a novel and privileged context insofar as it seemed to offer ordinary citizens a chance to speak into the ear of power.[14]

For its part, DuPont used institutional advertising to participate in these public dialogues, voicing the key liberal values of the day—dignity, individualism, equality, and the elimination of prejudice—in order to stress the importance of the "fair treatment" of the corporation.[15] What is most significant about DuPont's uneasy relationship with its viewers is its creation of a language of governance—a way of talking about civic responsibility—out of the process of watching, thinking about, and expressing an opinion of television. Indeed, the mundane practices of institutional advertising research are a good place to begin this book's exploration of television's place in postwar governance because they open out so readily to encompass broader conversations about liberal democratic rule.

Appropriately, given DuPont's identification with chemistry, viewers emerge within the knowledge framework of audience research not as agents in the democratic process but rather as reagents—participants in the measurement of a reaction, and indicators, in their behaviors and in the speech they produced, of the pace and extent of a process of change ultimately directed, or so DuPont advertising managers hoped, toward the population's willing acceptance of the corporation's interests as its own. This identification of interests was, as later chapters will make clear, common to all of the individuals and organizations that sought access to the process of democratic rule through television in this period. But few could afford to research their audience's reactions so extensively, and some of them, in truth, were too attached to their own imagined templates of the viewer-citizen to care much about what their audiences had to say, especially in situations where economic profit was not at stake.[16] DuPont, on the other hand, had the resources and the motivation; its ad managers, like policy makers, academics, and other members of the expert classes, worried constantly about how to shape the conduct and attitudes of the people on the other side of the screen, drawing upon various techniques of representation to imagine television's viewers: informants, pupils, customers, collaborators, experts. The resulting archive, amounting to thousands of pages of audience research, provides a unique opportunity to explore the horizons of political experience within which sponsors and citizens conceptualized each other, and the medium of television more generally.

## THE ALCHEMY OF GOODWILL

DuPont emerged as a pioneer in the field of institutional advertising in the 1920s, long before television came along. Its motivation was damage control. Members of the du Pont family were vocal supporters of the United States' entry into World War I, although only one of them, Victor du Pont, would see combat. When the war was over, the company had reaped huge profits from the sale of gunpowder, explosives, and poison gas to the United States and its allies, considerably expanding DuPont's manufacturing facilities; meanwhile, the family's gross income grew to exceed $1 billion.[17] When congressional investigations in 1921 probed the government contracts under which the company had built its munitions plants, a House committee found that one factory, Old Hickory in Tennessee, had cost the government $116 million but "produced no nitrates prior to the armistice, and contributed nothing toward winning the war."[18] In the 1930s, branded "merchants of death" and hounded by Senate investigations of the munitions trade, the company turned to public relations consultants to help overhaul its corporate image.

The solution they settled on was institutional sponsorship. In 1935, DuPont announced that it was producing a new radio program, *The Cavalcade of America.* A weekly biographical drama focusing on instances of individual heroism and service in U.S. history, the program featured advertisements that aimed not to sell DuPont products but rather to "foster the confidence, respect and goodwill of the company."[19] The program ran for almost two decades, its longevity indicating the extent of DuPont's commitment to broadcasting as a public relations venue. When network television became a reality after World War II, the company asked its advertising agency, Batten, Barton, Durstine, and Osborne (BBDO), to explore sponsorship options in the new medium. After considering, and rejecting, such genres as comedy-variety (tasteless and undignified), quiz shows (contestant ad libs could be risky), and news and public affairs (too controversial), BBDO recommended that the company consider the possibility of doing a series on the lives of ordinary Americans—a Cape Cod fisherman, an Iowa farmer, and so forth. In the end, however, it concluded that "straight drama," while costly, was the best.[20] Accordingly, DuPont launched a half-hour filmed version of *Cavalcade of America* on the NBC television network in 1952 (the show moved to ABC the following year).

*Cavalcade of America* belonged to a television format closely associated with institutional advertising: anthology drama. Anthology programs were the kind of shows that included the name of a giant monopoly corporation in their titles, such as *Westinghouse Studio One* and *General Electric Theater*. They presented a varied selection of short plays each week and were considered among advertising agencies to be a "prestige" programming form.[21] The format is most often remembered today as the symbol of everything that was good about the "golden age" of television. But it was also an everyday context in which Americans might routinely encounter the corporation in its guise as a public servant or citizen. Because of its association with aesthetic quality, anthology drama was an ideal venue for cultivating a modern, progressive corporate image. "We wanted . . . to reflect tremendous prestige on Ford Motor Company for having the originality and the courage to present something new, different and spectacular for the American public," gushed an account executive at the Kenyon and Eckhardt advertising agency, referring to the lavishly expensive anthology series *Producers' Showcase*.[22] Such programs fostered the impression that their sponsors were patrons of the arts, the seemingly philanthropic relationship between corporation and viewer underscored by codified announcer phrases such as "brought to you by." Appearing as a civic entity donating cultural goods to viewers and asking only for their goodwill in return, the anthology drama sponsor was a powerful figure of corporate benevolence, positioned at the forefront of artistic innovation and contributing to the cultural life of the nation.

Like other institutional sponsors, DuPont used the anthology format as a vehicle for commercials that would speak to the population about the affairs of the nation, especially those concerning the economy—repairing any ideological damage caused by the New Deal, antitrust suits, labor radicalism, and other forces deemed antithetical to the free enterprise system. These issues were infused with acrimony in public debate, but the tone of DuPont's institutional advertising remained unfailingly positive and statesmanlike, relying on the prestige of the anthology drama format to create, in the words of William L. Bird, "a cultural climate conducive to the autonomous expansion of enterprise."[23] As it would turn out, the one incontrovertible truth about advertising to emerge from the feedback DuPont received from audiences over the years was, paradoxically, the fact that the less of it there was, the more people liked it. Indeed, it was clear that the restricted commercial address associated with anthology drama was one of the format's most tangible assets as a vehicle for public relations. "As a rule we lower the volume in disgust to avoid listening to advertising," Mrs. T.J. Vaala of Orange, New Jersey, wrote in a letter to DuPont praising *Cavalcade*, "but since you don't try to force it down our throats in the middle of your program and because of its dignified, informative nature, we listen to your advertising willingly. If only others would learn a lesson from you, television would move forward."[24] DuPont ad managers decided not to add a middle commercial in *Cavalcade* when they discovered how much their audience appreciated this aspect of the show, even though this limited the amount of time they had to make a case for DuPont's corporate citizenship.

Indeed, as they set about making their case, the men of the DuPont advertising department—Robb DeGraff, George Nielson, and other public relations professionals—recognized that the position of the institutional sponsor was always a fragile one. Overly direct propagandizing could backfire and draw unwelcome scrutiny, as it did in 1957, when Albert Gore Sr.'s senate subcommittee investigating lobbying in the 1956 election found "numerous instances of institutional advertising, either clearly political in nature or with definite political implications."[25] DuPont, battling antitrust suits over the course of the decade, could not afford to alienate the public with direct propaganda; it thus defined the goal of its institutional advertising in modest terms, as the friendly fostering of "goodwill." A frequently used PR keyword, *goodwill* referred to a climate or atmosphere rather than an overt directive. In order to sustain it, institutional sponsorship needed to be dissociated from persuasion, manipulation, and other paths for accessing the citizen's mind that could be perceived as illiberal or illegitimate, and which might raise the specter of domination. "A viewer once wrote us," De Graff told a BBDO production coordinator, to say "that he liked 'Cavalcade' because 'it leaves a nice taste in your mouth.'" This, De Graff explained, was what DuPont was looking for in its sponsorship of television—"a feeling we can leave with the viewer that he has invested a half hour of his time wisely, [a feeling] that he is better for having seen it and that DuPont has done a real service by bringing it to him."[26] Fearful of crossing the thin line between cheap hucksterism and political manipulation, ad managers constantly worked to perfect the recipe for creating this feeling in *Cavalcade* and its institutional commercials.

Ratings were never particularly high, however, and at the end of the 1954–55 season, DuPont decided to investigate its audience's responses further, hoping to find a way to make the program more popular. *Cavalcade* had reached a milestone: although only twenty of the eighty or so episodes thus far broadcast had been written for TV (the remainder were based on scripts from the radio version), this was the first season in which episodes written for TV outnumbered those adapted from radio.[27] As the program left radio behind, it was time to take stock of its direction and reception. In June 1955, the company's executive committee asked the advertising department to "study the possibility of developing additional techniques . . . for determining the effectiveness of 'Cavalcade' television programs."[28] In response the department proposed a massive, multifaceted research program, contracting with several firms, at a cost exceeding $100,000.[29] The methods employed by these firms were quite divergent, ranging from the quantitative data gathering of Nielsen to the idiosyncratic techniques of John Dollard, a Yale psychology professor who applied diluted forms of Freudian textual analysis to program and advertisement scripts, following up with in-depth audience interviews.[30]

This audience research formed a large part of the complex network of expertise in which DuPont's advertising department was embedded, and ad managers incorporated it into the lengthy process of information management that went along with the production of programs and advertisements. When a script for a commercial arrived from BBDO, it went to scientists and manufacturing executives who reviewed it to ensure that it accurately depicted products and their production. They suggested any necessary changes, sometimes requiring reshoots. Members of the legal department then checked it for truth in advertising and patent protection, and advertising department managers, while collating and coordinating these changes, themselves worked on issues of structure, narrational tone, and visual style. They did the same with program scripts, which were reviewed by professional historians to make sure that DuPont took no excessive liberties with the past. When episodes had been shot, combined with commercials, and scheduled for broadcast, Dollard reviewed shooting scripts for both programs and ads to assess their internal psychological meanings and predict audience response. Then, after they aired, Dollard (and sometimes researchers for other firms) interviewed viewers in selected markets, either by telephone or in person. Each firm submitted a report interpreting the resulting responses. These lengthy analyses, their binding and their authority reinforced with embossed leather covers, circulated from one advertising department manager to another for comment. Researchers also provided raw responses, in the form of unedited transcripts or playback recordings, in case these reports raised further questions.

Although we have no record of their conversations about these reports and transcripts, the annotations that ad managers left behind on their pages give us a partial sense of the kinds of dialogue that emerged around the research process. Along with memoranda and other internal communications, these marginalia provide a window into the organizational culture from which the voice of DuPont's corporate citizenship emerged. It was a culture governed by an uncompromising attention to detail and a high degree of skepticism in relation to both the conventions of television advertising and the claims of audience research. Even Dollard, who enjoyed a long and profitable career as the advertising department's psychological consultant from 1954 until 1960, was not immune to criticism. "A guy has to be a PhD to be aware of this?" wrote George Nielson in the margins of one of Dollard's more obvious research predictions.[31] When it came to programming and advertising styles, DuPont ad managers had strict, narrowly conceived ideas about tone and mode of address. They reacted with horror at BBDO's early efforts to inject a sense of audience participation into *Cavalcade* via such gimmicks as a fan club and contests awarding a free trip to Hollywood; one man, reading the agency's proposal, registered his disgust with graphic marginalia depicting a queasy-looking face and a pile of manure with a pitchfork sticking out of it.[32]

However, feedback from the 1955 research initiative made it clear that some changes were necessary in the *Cavalcade* format. In response to viewer preferences, the series began to incorporate more contemporary biographical portraits and to intersperse episodes about actual individuals with ones focusing on fictional characters whose stories embodied the American values with which the company strived to identify itself. The research also led to a name change: in the fall of 1955 *Cavalcade* was renamed *DuPont Cavalcade Theater*, and a year later it was titled simply *DuPont Theater*. In 1957, however, ratings were still low, and ABC refused to renew DuPont's Tuesday evening time slot for another season.[33] At that point, the company abandoned the half-hour telefilm format altogether, moving to CBS, where it sponsored the ninety-minute *DuPont Show of the Month*. Usually airing as a live broadcast, the show presented adaptations of literary classics, often using stars from Hollywood and Broadway, and ran until 1961.

But although the program format changed over the course of the decade, the commercial spots surrounding DuPont's television programming remained fairly constant, at least until the shift to *DuPont Show of the Month*. They were, after all, the most important moments in the broadcast; as ad manager George Nielson explained, the purpose of each episode's uplifting dramatic narrative was to put people in the right mood "to consider and accept the ideas we wish to put before them . . . it sets the stage, as it were, for our commercials."[34] Advertisements stuck closely to the institutional format as the program evolved, telling stories of DuPont's amazing chemical discoveries, its excellent industrial safety record, and its philanthropic contributions to education. They never failed to incorporate the catchphrase "Better things, for better living, through chemistry." Redolent with connotations of wise government, the slogan combined ideals of virtue and wealth to conjure the image of a prosperous population living the good life and a company committed to research furthering the well-being of all.

As this slogan suggests, DuPont's institutional advertising tended to place a heavy premium on the scientific research that made these better things associated with the American consumer economy possible. Associating itself with science lent cultural legitimacy to the firm as it continued to battle its association in the public mind with munitions profiteering. Moreover, stressing its identity as a research firm was a strategic ploy in light of DuPont's constant battle against charges of monopoly. The company's aggressive absorption of smaller firms over the course of the twentieth century had led it afoul of antitrust laws more than once.[35] Research was a form of intangible mental labor that added hidden value to products, justifying the profit levels of monopoly capital. It lay at the core of DuPont's claims to public service and provided a rationale for the economy of scale on which the firm operated. Given this association with science, it is not surprising that the first television broadcast of *Cavalcade*, in October 1952, was a profile of the inventions and writings of Benjamin Franklin.[36]

But stories of scientific research did not necessarily make for good television. Chemical formulae and bubbling test tubes were unexciting visual fare, and DuPont advertising managers were perennially concerned that viewers, particularly female ones, would be bored by the arcane facts of scientific discovery. This concern extended to the nonscientific stories that aired on *Cavalcade* too, causing anxiety among DuPont ad managers from the very beginning. In 1951, the company previewed two pilot shows on a local Los Angeles station, each of them focusing on the achievements of an eighteenth-century man: inventor Eli Whitney in one case, newspaperman John Peter Zenger in the other. Unprompted feedback from industry professionals predicted that women would not watch the program. "Both stories should have had more love or family interest," explained Harold Blackburn of BBDO, relaying these opinions to DuPont ad manager F. Lyman Dewey, who ruefully noted the depth of the problem in a marginal note on Blackburn's letter: "We knew it, but history couldn't help us."[37] History apparently remained unhelpful for the next three years, as only fifteen or so *Cavalcade* episodes in that period focused on the lives of women. Of these, eight concerned courageous women in wartime, diplomacy, and the pioneer West. The other six were about the wives of famous Americans. Only one episode highlighted the achievements of women as professionals, telling the story of Elizabeth Blackwell, the first female doctor in the United States. Its title was "Petticoat Doctor."

## THE GIRL IN THE MYLAR SWING

If historical drama proved an inflexible instrument with which to secure female interest, advertising was a chance for DuPont to make up for history's masculine emphasis. Ad men thought they knew a great deal about the desires and interests of women—at least as far as product-based commercials were concerned.[38] A commercial focusing on the properties of Mylar, widely considered exemplary in the ad department, tried to solicit both male and female viewers while telling an "institutional story" about the contributions of DuPont chemical research to the American consumer products industries. The advertisement opened with a dramatic shot of a baseball player throwing a fastball directly at the camera, its lens protected from the force of impact by a transparent Mylar screen. In case this vignette might seem to appeal primarily to men, a subsequent scene presumably awakened female interest by

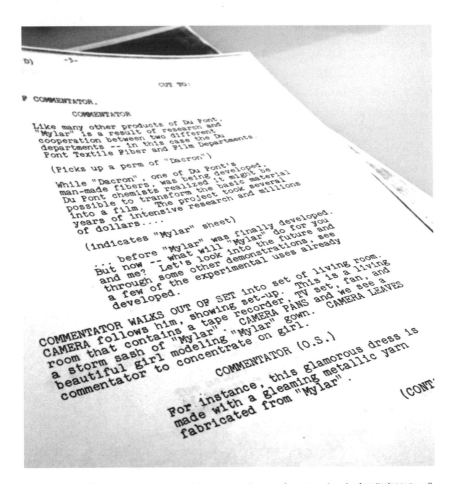

**Many DuPont advertisements promoted the company's commitment to developing "miraculous" substances like Mylar, which was presented as proof that large profitmaking enterprises were helping to improve all areas of human life, from architecture to fashion.**
*Image courtesy of the Hagley Museum and Library.*

showcasing "a beautiful girl" in a gown made entirely of Mylar, sitting on a Mylar swing—a choice of images that no doubt would maintain men's attention too.[39] The dual-gendered address carried over into the commercial's mise-en-scène, a home-of-the-future set that appeared in several DuPont commercials. The open-plan set was a hybrid space, part suburban home and part laboratory. Women, presumably, might admire the modern living room with abstract art on the walls, minimalist furniture, and floor-to-ceiling windows shrouded with vertical blinds; men, on the other hand, could find interest in the laboratory occupying the space where the kitchen should be, its glass counter providing a surface on which to demonstrate the futuristic powers of products produced from DuPont innovation. It was a setting in which "better things" and "chemistry" quite literally merged.

Although they seemed to solve the problem of attracting female viewers, commercials such as this one raised a larger set of questions about audience responses for DuPont ad managers. The Mylar ad and many others like it were based on the idea that viewers were capable of taking away from the commercial not only images of products but also particular ideas about the company and economic policy. But there

DuPont ads were frequently shot on a set that combined elements of theater, home, and laboratory—a highly artificial setting that communicated a sense of connection between chemical research, everyday life, and show-business glamour.

was no guarantee that this was the case, particularly in the sexist imagination of the DuPont ad department, where women viewers were concerned. Reflecting on this problem in a 1958 speech that appears to have been written for an audience of noninstitutional sponsors, advertising manager George Neilson explained,

> A product may sometimes be so compelling of viewer
> attention that an institutional point slips by unnoticed. Since
> your concern is entirely with the product story, it might
> appear that you have no such problem. But if you were doing
> a commercial on wash 'n wear, for instance, and the dress
> you were using as an example was too outstanding and too
> much detail was given to it, all the points about wash 'n wear
> might not register well.[40]

As this invocation of the housewife entranced by a dress suggests, the question of gender and audience interest was also, always, a question about *excessive* interest. DuPont ad managers hoped that audience research would clarify viewers' capacity to derive the moral meaning of laissez-faire capitalism from displays of the material properties of DuPont products and point them toward new techniques for making clear the connection between ideas and things.

They had reasons to be optimistic about this goal. Telegenic products such as Mylar were, in a number of ways, ideal vehicles for getting viewers to see parallels between the physical properties of man-made substances and the magical physics of the free market. The durability, convenience, and safety attributed to Mylar and other miracle materials such as nylon, Orlon, and Teflon were metaphors for the durability, convenience, and safety of the "miracle of America"—a term in wide circulation in the postwar years, referring not only to the nation's miraculous levels of economic growth and productivity but also to the rewards of faith in the capitalist system.[41] If the home-lab setting of the commercial helped personify DuPont as a benevolent, scientifically oriented technocrat, products such as Mylar, which "took several years of intensive research and millions of dollars" to develop, linked this image of corporate citizenship to the broader well-being of the population. As the commercial explained, Mylar had any number of potential applications. It might be used in products such as storm windows and magnetic tape, or even provide weightless insulation to enhance the portability of "the television set of the future."[42] In its pure potentiality, Mylar was indeed the substance of the future. Its uses envisioned but not yet realized, it signaled all the untapped po-

tential of the postwar economy, wherein the application of knowledge in new and expanding spheres—product development, automation, market research—would ensure a better life.

But while audience research showed that viewers, or at least male ones, appreciated such commercials for their "valuable scientific information," it also suggested that they did not tend to associate that information with the corporation. Asked what he recalled about the Mylar commercial, a forty-two-year-old man told researcher John Dollard, "It was about stuff that was so strong it held up this girl on a swing. . . . I liked that gal on the swing very much. I remember that part, but that's all."[43] Even when viewers did recall the name of the sponsor, there was no guarantee that the ideological message had reached its target. Asked why he liked the Mylar commercial, a man interviewed by John Dollard explained, "It was short and to the point. It was much better than most commercials—educational. Most commercials are so silly I wouldn't buy the product if I wanted to. DuPont makes the point good."[44] This viewer's response foregrounded the style rather than the substance of the advertisement; if he recognized a larger purpose, he failed to distinguish it from the sales-motivated purpose of product advertising.[45]

Viewers' repeated inability to grasp the idea that the primary message of DuPont advertising was the social benefit of free enterprise pinpointed a key distinction between institutional advertising and product-based advertising. Each was interested in stimulating the unconscious, triggering the emotions and arousing processes of identification in order to convince the viewer. But if the goal of regular commercials was to implant a will to purchase in the mind of the consumer, DuPont advertising sought access to a different, less well-charted part of the viewer's unconscious: the mysterious psychic processes shaping people's relationships to the economy and the state. As Charles Hackett, the company's public relations director, explained, "The negative attitude toward large scale business enterprise is vague and inarticulate with an emotional rather than a rational foundation"; the goal of institutional advertising was to allay the "unspoken fears of bigness in business" that lurked in the minds of viewers.[46] The question, however, was how best to pursue this goal. Hiring John Dollard to

- 11 -

The public accepts the material benefits of big business. They like to drive GM cars, they like to have clothing made of synthetic fibers but they have certain subconscious emotional fears about the big businesses which make these material benefits possible. And it's attacks like those we've outlined that tend to nurture and foster this attitude.

OBJECTIVE OF OUR PROGRAM (CHART VIII)

It's from this problem - the problem of "big business" - that we derive the objective of our program, which simply sta... "To create a better public understanding and appreciation of... role of Du Pont as a large business in our society." We f... If people know us better, understand what we do, how we ...

By the middle of the 1950s, DuPont advertising managers increasingly saw anticorporate public sentiment not as a political position but as an irrational, emotional reaction that could be cured with the right kind of advertising.
*Image courtesy of the Hagley Museum and Library.*

probe the Freudian dimensions of DuPont's advertising imagery was one solution, but it did not address the more general matter of what stylistic and rhetorical approaches to adopt.

## ECONOMY AND PSYCHE

One obvious obstacle the advertising department faced in devising ads that addressed viewers' emotional response to business was the fact that the recognizable conventions of the hard sell were off-limits, lest they demean the corporate citizen or—equally unwelcome—invite the label "propaganda." But at the same time, the ideological message could not be so subtle as to be unrecognizable altogether. This conundrum was the source of immense frustration. As DuPont's audience research continually demonstrated, unconscious feelings about the economy were much harder to measure than viewers' ability to recall a brand name or recount details about a product and its uses.[47] All too frequently audience researchers, striving to detect evidence of institutional advertising's effects on attitudes, encountered subjects who were overly familiar with the expectations of conventional market research. These viewers labored to provide concrete evidence that sales figures were rising, without realizing that the study in which they were participating was designed to measure their thoughts about, not their behavior in, the marketplace. In conformance with the period's gender norms, women, in particular, tended to focus on products. "I always ask the dealers for these products when I am shopping," a chirpy San Antonio *Cavalcade* viewer told researchers from the Advertest corporation in 1955, unwittingly hindering the study's goals in her effort to comply with the dictates of product-based advertising research.[48]

Other viewers who responded similarly did seem to recognize the company's ideological objective, pointing to their use of DuPont products as an affirmation of the company's economic and political stance. "They said it was a pretty good company and I agree with that," one man told Gallup and Robinson researchers. "I told the party I was watching it with to go out and buy some DuPont products tomorrow. . . . Actually, I said to go buy some DuPont, and she said 'you mean socks,' and I said that I didn't care."[49] Affirming the identity of consumer and citizen simultaneously, responses like these really should have made DuPont's advertising managers happy, as they indicated basic acceptance of the market ideology of "better living." But as often as not, viewers who focused on products in their commercials failed to notice what one ad manager described as "the ideological points that we believe are 'Cavalcade's' chief burden."[50]

Because of this problem, ad managers turned to commercials that dispensed with the product altogether and exposed viewers more directly to the forms of corporate propagandizing known at that time as "economic education."[51] Between 1952 and 1958, DuPont produced twenty-three commercials that explicitly engaged the viewer as a citizen in need of training on the rudiments of macroeconomics. The ads spoke in the language of liberal governance, addressing crucial issues in postwar debates about economy and society. The bulk were produced after 1956, a period in which DuPont was involved in two antitrust suits, winning one of them (concerned with cellophane manufacturing) and losing the other, which targeted the company's controlling interest in the General Motors Corporation. Twelve addressed attitudes toward big business—its relationship to small businesses, its contribution to high productivity, its capacity to meet growing levels of demand, and so forth—although members of the advertising department tried to avoid the actual term *big business*, dismayed by its unsavory, thuggish connotations in popular culture.

These commercials were part of a broader campaign of economic education that employees of DuPont and other large firms received at work, via mandatory lectures and films programmed by management

our own Chestnut Run Laboratories devoted to customer service.
3. There are arguments that big business is bad for the people in it, that they are treated poorly, inconsiderately, exploited. Yet we know as employees that we've been getting more and more benefits over the years, and most of these have come about without the prod of legislation. 4. We touched upon restrictive taxation earlier. 5. There is also a current attack against the "fantastic profits" of big corporations.

The not-so-obvious attacks or influences are directed toward the moral and the intellectual aspects of big business. They are primarily prevalent in the arts, particularly in fiction. For instance, in television we've had such plays as "Patterns"...whe the big businessman is symbolized as being ruthless and greedy only interested in profits and with little moral or social re sibility. There have been such novels as "Cash McCall," "Ex Suite"...in plays we've had "Point of No Return," "Death of man"...in the movies, we've had "Born Yesterday" and "Gian appeals all are based on what we call the "Goliath appeal is, where bigness (Goliath) is bad, and smallness (David
course, ever since our childhood we
fairy tales s

In the face of antitrust suits against DuPont, one advertising manager wrote a memorandum analyzing negative portrayals of "big business" and "bigness" in popular culture.
*Image courtesy of the Hagley Museum and Library.*

during work hours.[52] GE, for example, required that its employees attend a course about laissez-faire economics. Another course entitled "In These Hands," developed jointly by Inland Steel and Borg Warner for distribution through the conservative American Economic Foundation, reached one and a half million workers in heavy industry between 1950 and 1953.[53] Historically seen as union-busting management propaganda, these workplace information programs had been outlawed with the comprehensive protections set in place by the Wagner Act of 1935, which established collective bargaining rights, federal oversight, and other key elements of twentieth-century industrial relations. But the 1947 Taft-Hartley Act, promoted by the National Association of Manufacturers and other powerful antiunion lobbies (heavily funded by firms such as DuPont), made workplace propaganda programs legal once again, as long as they refrained from coercive or threatening speech.[54]

Although Taft-Hartley applied only to the imagery and rhetoric of management communications aimed directly at employees, it signaled a shift in the general tone of corporate public relations. It purported to establish limits for corporate speech, but the bill's assertion of speech codes rooted in ideals of civility actually helped management refine its techniques of antiunion communication by affirming in legislative language the idea of the benevolent corporation concerned merely with educating employees for their own good. Viewed in this context, DuPont's interest in using the direct and didactic techniques of economic education in its television commercials is not surprising. The new medium's arrival on the heels of Taft-Hartley was an opportunity to integrate the kindly, authoritative voice of the corporation into living room conversations, backed by visual evidence and bolstered by the intimate rhetoric of TV.[55]

Indeed, the company's advertising department experimented with adapting for television its own multimedia employee economic education program, called HOBSO (How Our Business System Operates), and in 1951 it considered getting Disney involved in the project.[56] But HOBSO, which was distributed by the National Association of Manufacturers for widespread use not only in the workplace but also in schools and other educational venues, was a very crude instrument.[57] As one reviewer described it,

> The HOBSO equipment consists of a flannel-covered board on which the teacher places colored, descriptive symbols to construct four charts entitled: "Our American Business System," "Accomplishments of Our System," "The Importance of Competition," and "Individual Freedoms under Our System." The symbols are backed with flocking, a material that adheres to the flannel, thus permitting the step-by-step building of each chart.[58]

Flannel symbols are not exactly television material, and HOBSO's dry economic pedagogy was hardly going to appeal to the emotions. After reviewing BBDO ideas for a commercial based on HOBSO entitled "Miracle of the 20th Century," George Neilson forwarded the agency's scripts to his boss with the handwritten assessment, "We're not so hard up for subjects that we should tackle these themes until we have a better vehicle for our points."[59] To avoid the pitfalls of product stories and HOBSO-style didacticism, the ad department turned to animation. The advertisement based on HOBSO ended up using sections of an animated film called *It's Everybody's Business*. It was produced by John Sutherland, who made a number of films about the free enterprise system for Harding College's film education program, underwritten by an extensive grant from the Alfred P. Sloan Foundation.[60] DuPont's previous research had indicated that audiences found it hard to derive abstract concepts from the tangible properties of products when animation was involved, but it seemed a promising technique for softening the edge of free market didacticism in ads focusing on economic education. Things got confusing only when animation was combined with products, as their juxtaposition brought to mind the sales pitches of conventional commercials.[61]

As this turn to animation might suggest, DuPont institutional advertisements tended to infantilize the viewer. One cycle in particular, a series of ads produced for *DuPont Show of the Month* in 1957, relied on folksy comparisons and associative arguments that stretched the boundaries of credulity as they labored to rationalize corporate monopoly. "Changing Times," for example, featured a little girl in a gingham dress and braids buying gumballs from a machine with her father, followed by shots of a teenage girl trying on a poodle-skirted dress, Dad looking on fondly. A smiley-voiced male narrator explained the connection: "When Mary was a little girl her allowance wasn't very big. But of course she didn't need much then. At seventeen, Mary gets a lot more money from Dad. As she grew, her needs increased too. Well, that's how some of the things in our country developed and grew—as the *need* for them developed." The commercial went on to explain that the desire to meet America's growing needs gave rise to "large industries" (one of several euphemistic ways of saying "big business"), leaning on the comparison between human development and the rise of economies of scale to make monopoly corporations seem natural. "It's all part of a healthy, familiar process of growth, development, and progress," the upbeat narrator explained at the end.[62]

Against the rational if highly ideological economic lessons offered by HOBSO, the goal of this cycle of advertisements was to access the viewer's unconscious. "The public accepts the material benefits of big business," noted one ad manager in a speech explaining *DuPont Show of the Month* ad strategies to DuPont department heads, "but they have certain subconscious emotional fears about the big businesses which make these material benefits possible."[63] This focus on the unconscious explains the repetition of certain generic scenes in the cycle in question. These scenes recycled the semiofficial iconography of postwar national life in a dreamlike, hypnotic sequence of associations: A white family watches television. Workers enter a factory. Mom bustles about in her well-appointed kitchen. A car pulls into a suburban driveway and a ponytailed girl rushes outside to greet her father behind the wheel. Dreamlike tropes such as gigantism figured throughout the series too. "It's a Great Big Country" compared large manufacturing interests with icons of "the grand scale of American ideals," from the Hoover Dam to Paul Bunyan, while "The Grand Design" asked viewers to accept a strained analogy as a logical proposition: its voice-over,

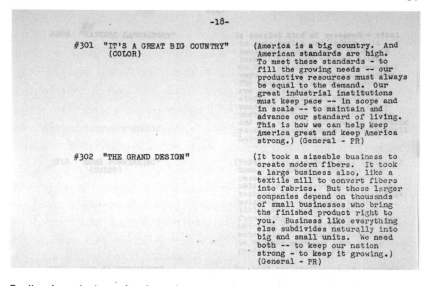

-18-

| #301 | "IT'S A GREAT BIG COUNTRY" (COLOR) | (America is a big country. And American standards are high. To meet these standards - to fill the growing needs -- our productive resources must always be equal to the demand. Our great industrial institutions must keep pace -- in scope and in scale -- to maintain and advance our standard of living. This is how we can help keep America great and keep America strong.) (General - PR) |
| #302 | "THE GRAND DESIGN" | (It took a sizeable business to create modern fibers. It took a large business also, like a textile mill to convert fibers into fabrics. But these larger companies depend on thousands of small businesses who bring the finished product right to you. Business like everything else subdivides naturally into big and small units. We need both -- to keep our nation strong - to keep it growing.) (General - PR) |

To allay viewers' subconscious fears about monopoly corporations, DuPont made a special series of advertisements in 1957. As these summaries illustrate, they were designed to make the concentration of capital in large firms seem like a natural and inevitable social good. *Image courtesy of the Hagley Museum and Library.*

juxtaposed with shots of big and small things in the natural world and in human industry, reasoned that just as there are large and small things in nature, so there must be large and small firms in business. Large and small depend upon each other, it claimed, and "we need both—to keep our nation strong—to keep it growing."[64]

One of the long-standing goals of DuPont institutional advertising was to reach people in "all walks of life," and this 1957 series of advertisements strived to identify the goals of the company with the interests of the population as a whole, regardless of class, occupation, or region. A commercial entitled "The Public Interest" made this point explicitly. The ad showed people signing in at a stockholders meeting, while the narrator revealed their occupations: machinist, schoolteacher (there's always a schoolteacher in these ads), farmer, housewife. "Real people like these . . . make up the American business system," he trilled. "And it's people too who *own* American business." The ownership of stock, he continued, was a way of exercising civic responsibility for those "thousands of average citizens who, through their investments, have a stake in the progress of American business." He went on to explain that people "play different roles in life. At one and the same time we are stockholders, consumers, employees, and citizens. In each role, they, and the companies of which they are a part, are representative of the American public." With the air of someone drawing an inescapable conclusion from the reasoned presentation of facts, the narrator summed up the point of the commercial at its conclusion: "It's easy to see why the interest of the business organization and the interest of the public coincide. Each is an essential part of the other."

The identity established between corporation and citizen took institutional advertising's goal of humanizing business to an extreme, depicting the firm as, like the American republic itself, a democracy composed of ordinary people. The comparison between corporate power and democratic structure continued in ads such as "All Size Is Relative." Reminiscent of contemporary political rhetorics championing small business owners, the ad explained that although the scale of the U.S. consumer economy made large corporations necessary, their only purpose was to assist small businesses in meeting the demands of the American public. Instead of leading toward monopoly, the expansion of large-scale manufacturing interests would establish the conditions under which small firms could thrive, facilitating self-determination on all levels of economic life much as a well-managed federal administration might enable state government to flourish. These were highly controversial, if not counterfactual, assertions. In a statement that somehow manages to read like a script for the soothing intimations of a hypnotist, Charles M. Hackett, the company's public relations director, explained the basic concept: "These messages were designed [to] suggest that large business enterprises are as acceptable a part of life today as large educational enterprises or large organizations of whatever purpose, and are simply part of a normal and familiar pattern."[65] Determining whether viewers responded positively to such suggestive and tenuous analogies was not easy, however. Indeed, it is clear from their responses that viewers were not particularly inclined to draw upon the resources of the unconscious when they shared their feelings about these commercials.[66] Rather than embarking upon pleasant free associations, they approached the ads as a chance to comment on corporate power. Like the ad managers who consulted the tea leaves of their responses, viewers also understood the television audience as a representation of the nation, and in voicing their ideas about DuPont's most overt efforts to speak as a corporate citizen, they stepped into the role of citizen themselves. Their responses traced a pattern of thinking about television's place in governance, one in which delineating appropriate rhetorical and stylistic limits for corporate speech seemed fused with the process of democratic participation. Looking closely at these viewer responses, we can tease out the assumptions they brought to bear upon the process of opinion gathering, and which shaped the roles they adopted within it.

## THE VOICE OF THE VIEWER

In 1958, BBDO conducted tests of audience responses to the commercials targeting unconscious fears of big business DuPont had produced the previous year. Two of the advertisements, "It's a Great Big Country" and "The Grand Design," drew particularly negative audience responses. When asked, "Is there anything in the film you disagreed with and found hard to believe?" one respondent protested that "It's a Big Country" tried to represent DuPont as "just another social welfare agency." Another disputed the commercial's suggestion that "DuPont helps small business," acidly remarking that "'gobbles them up' would be closer to the truth." "The Grand Design" prompted similarly strong reactions. Quite likely echoing sentiments from *The Hidden Persuaders*, Vance Packard's recently published bestseller on the manipulations of advertising, one person recognized the commercial's attempt to probe the unconscious, complaining that "DuPont ... must justify its size with an appeal to the emotional and unthinking." The associative mode of address was clearly a matter of concern, as the study asked subjects in a separate question whether anything about the ad felt condescending. This provoked some hostile responses too; one viewer retorted, "DuPont was saying they were doing me a big favor by staying in business and producing things for me. They may be right but it rubs me the wrong way." Another felt "propagandized" by the ads.[67]

For some viewers, audience research was a chance to register a critique of economic power; for DuPont, it was a reminder that institutional advertising could awaken such critiques rather than address them. Indeed, BBDO's report detailed in bar graphs that none of the viewers at the test screening thought of DuPont as big business before they viewed the commercials, but some did afterward.[68] This was obviously a matter of strong concern among DuPont ad managers. Chuck Crowley highlighted this section of the report as he read it, noting particularly the possibility that the commercials reminded people that DuPont was getting "bad publicity." The effect apparently extended beyond the laboratory conditions of the test screening. When "The Grand Design" aired on *DuPont Show of the Month* in the fall of 1957, one man told Gallup and Robinson researchers, "It would take them a long time to convince me that they were more interested in my organization than in making ammunition."[69]

The reference to ammunition would seem to indicate awareness of DuPont's antitrust history and of its role in the 1936 Senate hearings on war profiteering, an awareness perhaps spurred by press coverage of the recent Supreme Court decision ordering DuPont to dispose of all of its General Motors stock. Another Gallup and Robinson respondent, apparently more sympathetic to DuPont's position in the antitrust proceedings, may also have been thinking about this context when he explained, "*Off the record*, they were showing that Du Pont really isn't a monopoly and how they were a company that wanted progress for themselves and other companies as well. The idea was that Du Pont is the mainstay of small businesses in America (emphasis added)."[70] The small phrase "off the record" is worth remarking upon. It positioned the speaker as a public subject and imbued his words with an ambiguous, quasi-official status, as if the creation of a legally binding transcript were involved. Referring to language that is at once attributable and deniable, the phrase aligned the process of audience research with the broader mechanisms of political journalism, indicating the respondent's assumptions that the kind of speech produced in the research encounter was part of a larger governmental process.

Viewers such as this seemed to understand their interactions with researchers as a form of consultation in which their job was to give feedback to the company on its techniques of persuasion. Such assumptions were not limited to highly ideological advertisements. "The man last night sounded a little too 'rote,' he'd learned it too well," one Syracuse viewer told researchers from the Advertest company in 1954, referring to an ad in which DuPont company spokesman Larry Livingston rattled off an excited spiel about the use of Teflon in TV manufacturing.[71] Another Syracuse viewer registered approval of Livingston's in-depth scientific explanation: "I think they will put over DuPont's point. All selling is on an educational basis." An Omaha viewer in the same study questioned the appeal of this educational approach: "I like them, but they lack glamor." Addressing the technique rather than the message, these kinds of comments repositioned viewers not as destinations in the transmission of particular ideas or indicators of advertising's effects but rather as collaborators in the process of defining how sponsored images might most appropriately serve as forms of corporate speech and as mass cultural vehicles for governance. Needless to say, DuPont ad managers did not see things this way. "Asking him to be an advertising expert?" Crowley wrote grumpily on the draft of a Gallup and Robinson audience questionnaire asking viewers to evaluate whether a commercial made "a strong case."[72]

The interesting thing about these moments when viewers assumed the role of advertising expert is the degree to which their assessments of the commercials projected broader ideas about the capacity of the population to govern itself. As is often the case when people speak of governance and television together, these "expert" viewers tended to imagine another set of viewers, less capable than they, when they spoke about the effects of DuPont advertising. Responding to "It's a Great Big Country" and the claim that DuPont works with small businesses, one viewer told Gallup and Robinson researchers, "I think it is important for those who don't already know this that there is more than one industry involved in this particular thing." A viewer in the same survey made a similar point: "I think that most people are aware of those materials but they don't know DuPont makes them and was responsible for them, but the commercial would put this in their minds more firmly."[73] In suggesting that advertising might be a form of civic or economic education, viewers tacitly affirmed the idea of governing by television. But when they envisioned the medium as a necessary supplement to existing governmental realms, such as the educational system, in which individuals learn the foundations of citizenship, they always saw it as a corrective to the shortcomings of other people, rather than themselves.

In fact, among positive viewer responses to *Cavalcade* commercials, avowals of their educational value greatly outnumber any other kind. DuPont's viewer mail and audience research files were full of testimonies praising its commercials as "intelligent," "dignified," and "full of information," often contrasting them with other forms of television. Viewers who complained about other, more irritating commercials connected their complaints to broader frustrations with television as a medium, drawing upon the emerging mass culture critique of the period as a form of public speech about citizens and media in which they might claim expertise. Mrs. R. Ellis Roberts wrote to DuPont to describe her experience after watching *Cavalcade* one evening: "There was a dignified and interesting commercial from Du Pont, the usual almost unendurable silliness of a Nestle's commercial, a commercial about candied California fruit, and perhaps others. . . . I wonder if sponsors realize how boredom and annoyance at the frequency of the interruptions for commercials makes an intelligent viewer determine never to purchase *that* commodity, at any rate?"[74] An Omaha viewer interviewed by Advertest researchers reported, "I don't like far-fetched commercials. I like a commercial that assumes I have intelligence enough to understand what they are talking about," and a Syracuse viewer in the same study made a similar point: "I think so many commercials treat you like children. DuPont's are on a higher level. I like them."[75] In voicing their approval of DuPont through critiques of dominant advertising styles, viewers claimed authority to judge the acceptable limits of corporate speech on television. Calling for educational, rather than infantilizing, rhetorical styles that might elevate the sensibility of the population as a whole, they corroborated the corporate image of DuPont as a benevolent scientific entity, treating the company, and the medium of television, as institutions endowed with educational, quasi-governmental, responsibilities.

When viewers praised DuPont's advertising strategies in these terms, their remarks frequently extended beyond the advertisements in which the company spoke to them directly to include the program itself. These responses awakened the connotations of public patronage that were originally associated with the idea of sponsorship in early commercial radio broadcasting and that were vestigially present in the sponsorial styles associated with anthology drama. Eschewing direct sales, radio sponsors in the mid-1920s had begun to adopt the guise of philanthropists with the altruistic goal of uplift, bringing art, culture, and education to a mass audience.[76] Recognizing this genre of commercial speech, a number of *Cavalcade* viewers expressed their gratitude to DuPont for the edifying tales and talented performers it brought to them. As with DuPont advertisements, they frequently characterized *Cavalcade*'s social benefits in terms of the program's effect on other people. "This type of entertainment is beneficial to the mental stature of the millions of viewers watching it," wrote Carl DeBiasi of Waterford, Connecticut, in a letter congratulating DuPont on the quality of a *Cavalcade* episode. "It is a step above the comic book, slap stick type of entertainment that is being transmitted daily. You must have given the nation an intelligence pill."[77] These *Cavalcade* viewers attributed to DuPont the prosocial goal of "improving" television. As this was the explicit motivation for *Omnibus*, the experimental arts and culture program sponsored by the Ford Foundation, such projections of corporate intent effectively equated institutional sponsorship with philanthropic largesse.

The story lines that aired on *Cavalcade*, stressing liberal democratic tenets such as freedom and individualism, served as an indirect form of corporate speech. Many viewers interpreted program content as evidence of DuPont's corporate citizenship, appearing to perceive its motivation in presenting these stories as public service rather than public relations. One broadcast that prompted an outpouring of interpretations in this vein was the 1955 episode of *DuPont Cavalcade Theater* entitled "Toward Tomorrow." The program told the childhood story of Ralph Bunche, the black American diplomat and winner of the Nobel Peace Prize. It aired on October 4, 1955, a month after a white jury acquitted the defendants in the savage murder of black teenager Emmett Till by white residents of the town of Money, Mississippi. Thirty viewers wrote letters to DuPont praising the company for sponsoring the broadcast—an unusually high number of responses—and several of them referenced the trial.[78] Indeed, to the extent that they interpreted the program as public relations, these viewers saw it as PR for the civil rights movement, not DuPont. In their unprompted feedback, and in the reactions solicited in the audience research Dollard conducted in New Haven, Connecticut, we can see viewers defining the act of television sponsorship as a form of political speech that might help clarify questions preoccupying postwar governance, and possibly advance solutions to the contradictions emerging within it.

## INCORPORATING CIVIL RIGHTS

The broadcast of "Toward Tomorrow" marked a turning point in DuPont's television sponsorship. The episode was one of the first to air under the new series title *DuPont Cavalcade Theater*, a change that reflected the company's decision to lose its white-wigged costume drama image, expanding the series to include chronicles of contemporary American lives. This shift to the present diversified the roster of heroic individuals whose stories were featured in the show. Between 1955 and 1957, the program incorporated inspiring tales of the achievements of Chinese, Mexican, and Japanese Americans, and addressed controversial subjects such as criminal insanity and alcoholism. It should be noted, however, that this seeming liberalization went only so far. Shortly after "Toward Tomorrow" aired, Four Star Pictures, the production company that filmed the program, submitted some story outlines to the DuPont ad department. Among them was a proposal for an episode about black businessman Charles C. Spaulding, a leader in the life insurance industry. Robb DeGraff nixed the idea, writing on the draft, "Made $ on so-called contrib[ution] Hold Negro for year."[79] Although both radio and TV versions of *Cavalcade* abounded with stories of inventors and entrepreneurs who profited from their contributions to American life—including several versions of the biography of Irénée du Pont, the company's founder—the program's celebration of capitalist ingenuity stopped short at the color line. Having aired the story of Ralph Bunche, DuPont had apparently filled its racial quota.

Or perhaps DeGraff recognized that some viewers would appreciate DuPont's broadcast of "Toward Tomorrow" more if they perceived it as an exception—a possibility that makes sense when one ponders the implications of its title, which bears more than a passing similarity to the contemporaneous "gradualist" rhetoric of patience on the question of integration. One of Dollard's New Haven respondents, identified as a white maintenance mechanic with an eighth-grade education, suggested as much when he remarked on the novelty of encountering a show about a black American on network television. "First time I've seen one," he confessed, adding, "It wouldn't be as good if there were more colored stories."[80] Perhaps anticipating such responses, the depiction of Bunche's early life in "Toward Tomorrow" placed great emphasis on mythological and deracinated American universals such as the rewards of hard work and determination. The episode also stressed the importance of family in shaping individual destinies; it was as much a chronicle of the self-sacrificing efforts of Lucy Johnson, the grandmother who raised Bunche and convinced him to pursue his educational goals, as it was the story of the great man's beginnings. Dollard's research confirmed that for some viewers, this emphasis on triumph over adversity and the strength of family bonds transcended racial divisions, serving as "a dramatic affirmation of the American Dream."[81]

Bookended by two commercials—one promoting DuPont fellowships in higher education (a predictable tie-in given the episode's focus on Bunche's struggle to achieve an education), the other detailing DuPont's role in the development of odorless paint—"Toward Tomorrow" traced Bunche's early life through melodramatic set pieces: an affecting maternal deathbed scene, an encounter with a tough-but-fair

This newspaper advertisement for DuPont's biography of Ralph Bunche downplayed his race, focusing instead on American universals: hard work, self-sacrifice, and the pursuit of education.

basketball coach, the distractions of a good-for-nothing teenage friend. Johnson's constant demand that Bunche make something of himself dominated the story line, along with her own selfless efforts on his behalf. Defying doctor's orders, she works tirelessly to pay for Ralph's hospital costs as he recovers from surgery. She keeps a scrapbook recording all of his achievements, and when Ralph finally gets a graduate scholarship to study political science at Harvard, she looks to heaven and sighs, "It's been a long time. A long, long time." Although she doubles over with heart trouble immediately after this utterance, Johnson insists that Ralph take the scholarship and "do the things we could never do." He is about to graduate from Harvard when he learns that she has died; he skips her funeral and attends his graduation instead, knowing that she would have wanted it that way. This is deep melodrama, and some scenes—namely, Bunche's interactions with his stern basketball coach and a sequence that cuts between Johnson working late as a dressmaker and Bunche studying at Harvard—are deeply affecting. It is easy to see why viewers might have responded emotionally to the program. (Dollard, in his typically glib fashion, catalogued these responses in terms of "lumps" and "tears.")[82] Indeed, while DuPont may have balked at the idea of doing another story about a black American, viewers who wrote to express their appreciation of the broadcast made a point of requesting more programs like it.

But what made the program especially appealing, it seems, was its ability to combine melodrama and social pedagogy, elevating television to a cultural status akin to that of abolitionist literature of the previous century. Many viewers voiced this sentiment via the commonplace complaint that most TV programs underestimated audiences' intelligence and taste. Evelyn Snyder of Portland, Oregon, pleaded, "Couldn't you producers give the public credit for some taste and feeling and produce something like this a bit more often?"[83] Patricia Herzog of Santa Ana, California, made a similar point when she congratulated DuPont on the show: "The treatment on TV of Negroes, showing them as mature, intelligent humans, is very rare and your program should be a model for other shows. Although I am not Negro, I feel that a substantial lift is given to the betterment of race relations by the screen portrayal of Negroes as people rather than stereotypes."[84] A viewer from nearby Long Beach who signed her letter "Donna Lane (white)" took the point even further, suggesting that providing more airtime for black Americans would constitute a kind of argument with the white Mississippians who perpetrated and abetted the Till murder. Referring to "that 'unmentionable' town in Mississippi," she requested that television "give us more all colored folks performances. It would be a good rebuttal for the crime they (those folks from that town in Miss) commit against us the white race."[85]

In these instances of viewer feedback, the screening of a television program about a black man's journey out of poverty served a broader, exemplary purpose within the institution of television and, more generally, within an imagined version of national political culture in which social change occurred through the setting of good examples—a vision that extended from the diplomatic sphere, in which the containment of communism flowed from the free world's ostentatious practice of freedom, to the activist creed of nonviolent resistence in the civil rights movement. The sense of exemplarity these viewers attached to Bunche as a model of Negro citizenship extended to DuPont, which they characterized as a courageous and responsible model of the sponsor-citizen. Bruce Wheeler Sr. of South Gate, California, wrote, "We are not only grateful for your excellent choice of story, but very cognizant too, of your position in having to face reality in presenting a racial controversial feature over [an] open television network. But, that is America! And exactly as it should be."[86] Sponsorship appears in this statement as an act of bravery akin to defying the color line, creating a momentary equivalence between Bunche's struggles to overcome prejudice and DuPont's corporate image. Mary Louise Grey, a social worker from Los Angeles, praised the show as a contribution toward global governance: "It's *good* to see that television can be both entertainment and helpful toward better appreciation and understanding among peoples of our rapidly shrinking world. This, I feel, is part of the industry's social responsibility, and I am personally very appreciative to the DuPont corporation."[87] Mrs. I. Tourian of West New York, New

Jersey, echoed this point, suggesting that the show be shown overseas by the United States Information Agency (USIA) to "arouse admiration both for Ralph Bunche and this country."[88]

This was a prescient suggestion, as the USIA did in fact purchase a print of "Toward Tomorrow." Stripped of its advertising, the film circulated widely overseas, enjoying a long afterlife in cultural diplomacy. That the program should end up representing U.S. racial progress on the international stage is no surprise. As Melinda Schwenk points out, its narrative conformed closely to the vision of black Americanism the USIA sought to foster in its film programming, affirming Algeresque individualism over collective values and "claim[ing] for democracy the ideal of individual success through personal improvement."[89] Viewers who wrote to DuPont after the ABC broadcast readily identified these elements. "I was feeling low, reflecting on the Till case and wondering if people will ever learn the worth of the individual," wrote Alicia Palma of Paris, Illinois. "I hope that thousands saw your program and got the point, thanks to DuPont."[90]

Dollard's interviewees echoed sentiments similar to these spontaneous expressions of gratitude to DuPont, using the research encounter to air their own, generally liberal, views of race relations in the United States. Dollard had anticipated these affirmative responses in his close reading of the program's "unconscious content," predicting that because "most Americans have a feeling of guilt about the prejudicial treatment of the Negro . . . they would be glad for a chance to express approval of Negroes and deplore social injustice." However, he failed to note the subtle ambivalences underlying white viewers' responses. "Lots of times colored people are pushed aside," one woman noted. "I think that up to marriage itself, they should be treated as equals and people should mix and do things together." Another, referring to Bunche, said, "It's too bad that there aren't more like him," a comment that could be interpreted as either an assertion of black Americans' inferiority, with Bunche figured as an exception, or an acknowledgment of the effects of inequality on their mobility in the class and educational system. The latter seems more likely, as this viewer, alone among white respondents, recognized that Bunche's success did not necessarily signal racial progress: "Rank in the UN and all, he's still a Jim Crow. And all the prejudices that seemed to be lifted on the surface are still in effect underneath."

Black viewers (there were 29 in Dollard's 238-viewer sample) focused closely on the issue of Bunche's success, measuring it against their own experiences of race in the United States. One middle-class black respondent, a public relations consultant, identified strongly with Bunche's determination to succeed: "It wasn't just the story of Ralph Bunche; it was the story of any Negro. . . . [T]here are an awful lot of Negroes doing just as much as he who aren't well known. It indicated that he had an unusual struggle, but most Negroes have the same struggle." Another black viewer, identified in the report as a housecleaner with an eighth-grade education, offered a sharply different perspective: "There aren't many of us like him. A few, like the man who discovered how to use the peanut for a lot of worthwhile things. No, there aren't enough who'll give us the push we need. . . . [I]t brings to mind what you could have done, or what I could have done, when the opportunity was there." This viewer spoke approvingly of DuPont: "I figured that if the DuPont Cavalcade of America was doing it, it would be done well." The middle-class black viewer, on the other hand, quoted again in another section of Dollard's report, responded indignantly when he discovered that DuPont was the sponsor. "If I'd known that I wouldn't have watched!" he exclaimed, his anger palpable in the words transcribed on the page. "If you ask me, DuPont would do a much better job in their race relations if they had just one Negro on their payroll. . . . Is DuPont trying to lure Negro trade?" Invoking the State Department's use of prominent black Americans to exemplify progressive U.S. race relations overseas, he speculated bitterly that the film was just "propaganda for foreign consumption."[91] Dollard was surprised by this response, recording it in a separate section under the heading "Interesting Findings Not Predicted About the Commercial." And indeed, of all the viewers to share their responses to the program, this man was the only one to register incredulity at the aura of socially liberal corporate citizenship DuPont affected in its sponsorship of "Toward Tomorrow."[92]

There were no significant findings on the commercial which have not been discussed in some part of this report. We found a couple of interview excerpts that seemed of interest, however, even though they reflect only individual negative responses.

Illustrative Excerpts from Interviews:

Man, 50 or over, graduate of a four-year college, public relations, colored.

Interviewer: "Do you know the sponsor of this program?"

Viewer: "No."

Interviewer: "It was Du Pont."

Viewer: "If I'd known that I wouldn't have watched! I just don't like Du Pont. If you ask me, Du Pont would do a much better job in their race relations if they had just one Negro on their payroll. Du Pont is just as bad as Ruppert Beer. Neither of them hire Negroes except to sweep the floor. And Ruppert Beer knows that no Negro in the United States will buy their beer. Is Du Pont trying to lure Negro trade? It makes one suspicious as to whether they're after the Negro market or whether this film is propaganda for foreign consumption. Du Pont is a Southern outfit and have never had, outside of servants, any Negro employees. I'd like them to name just one above unskilled workers. They have no Negro chemists or professional people. I just don't like that Du Pont Company!"

Woman, 30-49 years old, 7th grade, wife of a road-worker.

"It's very nice to get rid of the paint smell, but when I paint I like some paint smell, because I think paint fumigates and the paint smell gets the cockroaches and bedbugs out of the house. And odorless paint wouldn't fumigate, too. Perhaps they'll think up something that'll do that too. Then I'd use their new kind of paint."

But although this viewer's insistent, angry voice is anomalous, it is worth paying attention to it as it raises the question of what, exactly, the episode's message of racial uplift had to do with DuPont's motivations. What value was there in identifying its corporate image with the period's most visible public image of black achievement? One answer lies in the company's psychologized understanding of citizens' relationship to big business. In championing Bunche, DuPont likely sought a way of complementing its campaigns to stamp out "prejudice" against business by attacking the supposedly widespread belief that "bigness is badness."[93] Throughout the 1950s, DuPont defined resistance to free enterprise ideology as a pathological and phobic response akin to racial bias. Like the liberal race relations talk of the period, postwar discussions of antibusiness "bias" tended to characterize the problem in terms of unconscious fears; the purpose of sponsorship, DuPont ad managers felt, was to instill "understanding and approval of big business on an emotional as well as an intellectual plane"—an objective that resulted in the dreamlike commercials they produced in 1957.[94] The parallel between opposition to corporate power and racial prejudice originated with Taft-Hartley. Advocates of the bill claimed that New Deal policies had unleashed "prejudice" against business; its final language, promising to create "equality between employer and employee," was a decisive victory in management's ongoing battle to rewrite class struggle in the increasingly race-focused language of liberal democracy.[95]

DuPont advertising personnel echoed Taft-Hartley's spurious call for corporate rights throughout the 1950s. In a 1952 trade journal article, Donald Carpenter, general manager of the DuPont film division, heralded the election of Eisenhower as the end of "20 years of hostility toward business" and the arrival of "a more normal period of fair treatment to be accorded to all citizens of our country." Carpenter wrote approvingly of "fair treatment regardless of race or creed, of course." But he continued with a plea for "fair treatment regardless of the individual's means of livelihood or his membership or lack of membership in some special group," employing the antiunion right-to-work rhetoric used by management in struggles over Taft-Hartley and in

IDEAS FOR DU PONT "SHOW OF THE MONTH'

The writer has been appointed as a member of the (
to develop ideas which may be used as the basis for
general company television program. Since the "veh
commercials use to convey their messages are Du Por
activities, and Du Pont science, it is apparent the
sources of ideas. You can be of help to the commit
your own Du Pont background and experience and sub
you may have. In order to assist your thinking, I
salient features about the company television prog

Background

In each of our ten 90-minute television programs,
more than 25 million viewers to three 3-minute me
The primary reason we have this type of program t
segment of the American public is to overcome a p
company and other large businesses face today: a
"bigness" in business. The apparent implication
"power" and "control" which go with the idea of '
latent fears which only a small percentage of th
Du Pont and other large businesses will prosper
operate in a favorable environment, it behooves
emotional and subconscious fears which many Amer
business", whether they stem from ignorance, in
"stereotyped images" which are contradictory to
large businesses in today's American economic s

Throughout the 1950s, DuPont ad managers maintained that negative attitudes toward corporate power were a form of prejudice, one as irrational and stereotype-driven as racism. *Image courtesy of the Hagley Museum and Library.*

subsequent legislative activism in individual states. Warming to the metaphor of prejudice, Carpenter came out with a statement that sounded like a call for corporate civil rights: "Give us equality of opportunity and let us show you what we can do for this glorious country of ours. Let us practice the free enterprise system again and let it demonstrate again what miracles it can perform for all Americans."[96] Drawing on a similar liberal language, an account executive at BBDO told George Nielson in 1954 that "the fight for the right to conduct business on a big scale is not over," adding, as if DuPont were an orphan of the storm rather than a massive corporation, that "nobody is going to do it for big business."[97] Complaints about antibusiness prejudice appeared frequently in ad department communiqués, often accompanied by pleas for institutional advertising that would correct "negative 'stereotyped images.'"[98] Much as liberal reformers in this period might speak of the need for blacks and whites to interact and get to know each other, dispelling myths and preconceptions that might impede racial progress, DuPont ad managers proposed wistfully that "if people know us better, understand what we do, how we fit into the economic and social picture of our country, they will understand us and be more favorable to us."[99]

This commitment to a public relations approach modeled along the same lines as racial outreach explains the decision to hire Dollard, whose Freudian methods of close textual analysis were hardly in the mainstream of audience research. But in fact, Dollard was not primarily known as an audience researcher.[100] He was, rather, widely hailed as an expert in race relations. His 1937 study, *Caste and Class in a Southern Town*, which remains his most famous work, was a classic in midcentury social psychology.[101] This expertise makes Dollard's failure to anticipate negative responses to "Toward Tomorrow" among black viewers particularly striking; despite his training as a psychologist of race, his analysis of the script confined itself to Freudian themes, such as the narcissistic tendencies of Bunche's grandmother, and the possibility that their relationship constituted "an incest bound object choice."[102] We might interpret Dollard's neglect of racial issues as evidence of poor research technique, but it is more appropriately understood as a reflection of his skill in assessing what DuPont ad managers expected of his studies. The forms of prejudice that interested them were unconnected to race, and the call for racial progress implied in "Toward Tomorrow" was primarily a way of rendering the corporate rhetoric of fairness and equality after Taft-Hartley more palatable. People might not have agreed with DuPont's radical positions on government regulation or collective bargaining, but they could perhaps accept the more centrist conception of equality as a matter of fairness implied in the propositions advanced by DuPont's commercials about big business: "commercial institutions are neither less worthy or less necessary to society than any other institutions" or "big business occupies the same relationship to society as a whole as other elements comprising it."[103] Such claims exploited the tenets of postwar interest group pluralism, inserting the monopoly corporation in the spectrum of figures deemed worthy of political recognition and whose rights and interests deserved protection.

In the same vein, words such as *dignity* made frequent appearances in DuPont audience responses. The word had a special meaning in postwar political culture, and it was often invoked in implicit opposition to political stances deemed extremist. As John Nickel points out in his analysis of the disabled black man in racial message films, "Dignity . . . was a catchword in the postwar and civil rights eras, lavished on those who took persecution on the chin and did not deign to fight back."[104] It was also essential to the "politics of respectability" through which Bunche and other prominent black Americans advanced the claims of the desegregation movement.[105] As Bunche wrote in 1949, "The privileges and rights of the American citizen . . . guarantee to every citizen of this great nation all of the essential attributes of a free and dignified existence."[106] Indeed, the word *dignity* seems indelibly associated with Bunche in the postwar period, appearing countless times in writings and speeches both by him and about him. The mayor of New York City praised him for "saving the dignity and structure" of the United Nations in 1949; in 1954 Bunche praised former Ford Foundation head Paul Hoffman for "his intense belief in the dignity and rights of man"; and in 1960 he spoke of Africa's "aspirations for independence, human rights, and dignity."[107]

As it turns out, the angry black viewer interviewed by Dollard was right in his suspicion that company hiring policies did not reflect the image of social responsibility and racial outreach that other viewers of "Toward Tomorrow" attributed to DuPont. Indeed, it would be fair to say that the opposite was true. In the 1950s, DuPont invested increasing amounts of capital in the construction of factories in the South. Wages in the eleven southern states were up to 20 percent lower than in the North, and ten were right-to-work states that hobbled labor organizing with statutes prohibiting closed shops. Racial injustice played a large role in maintaining this situation. Organizations such as the Southern States Industrial Council, which counted DuPont among its top contributors, lobbied not only against unionization but also against desegregation, denouncing it as a violation of states' rights.[108] Racial tensions in the Southern workforce were an asset to DuPont, as the combination of Jim Crow and right-to-work laws undermined

efforts during Operation Dixie, the CIO's large-scale Southern organizing effort, to unionize plants where nylon and other DuPont products were produced.[109] This does not mean, of course, that DuPont
factory towns were Klan havens, although they were certainly fraught
with racial animus; textile industry historian Timothy Minchin notes
that Operation Dixie representatives "found workers at DuPont both-
ered by 'the Negro issue.'"[110] In the end, there seems to be no question
that while DuPont may have benefited from its association with the
cause of racial equality in national television, on the local level it prof-
ited greatly from Jim Crow.

Given this context, it is difficult to avoid the conclusion that "Toward Tomorrow" was an effort to preempt public criticisms of DuPont's
investment in groups such as the Southern States Industrial Council.
And indeed, the company's promotional plans for the episode support
such an interpretation. In the week preceding the airdate, BBDO arranged screenings for New York City civil service and housing commissioners, representatives of the black press, the Urban League, NAACP
leaders, and other "prominent Negroes."[111] The NAACP supported the
effort with mailings to twelve hundred branch offices throughout the
country. After the broadcast, Norman B. Johnson of the NAACP wrote
to John Procope of BBDO's Specialty Marketing Department (read:
Negro marketing department) to arrange further screenings, proposing that "with the national impact of the Mississippi (Till) case, it is
our studied opinion that the continued and continual showing of 'Toward Tomorrow' will be invaluable in emphasizing the basic American
concepts of equality and fair play."[112] Such evaluations rendered DuPont
and the NAACP as partners in a shared goal of striving for a truly democratic society. The program's availability for screening at meetings reinforced the idea of DuPont as a social service agency, its dramatized
public representation of the ideal of equality substituting for actual
economic and racial justice within its own organization.

DuPont's appropriation of Bunche's story suggests that institutional
sponsorship in commercial television was a valuable testing ground
for corporations seeking legitimacy through association with progressive causes. Similarly, today's jargon of "corporate social responsibility"

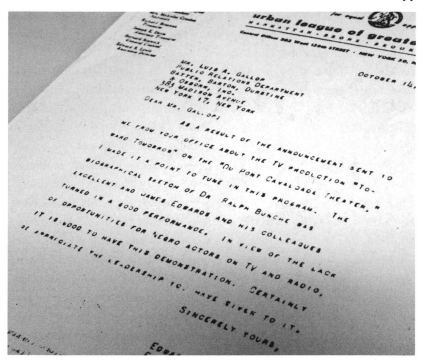

Organizations such as the NAACP and the Urban League provided free publicity for DuPont's broadcast of Bunche's life story, seeing it as a contribution to the cause of civil rights. *Image courtesy of the Hagley Museum and Library.*

(CSR) goes hand in hand with the push for privatization and decentralization, with charitable investments and projects providing multinational firms with a rich public relations resource through which to voice their claims to corporate citizenship, especially when partnered with nongovernmental organizations (NGOs). The resulting vision of governance, Toby Miller observes, is a "shared fantasy structure of social movements and corporations," an ersatz civil society dominated by a "CSR/NGO fetish." Of course, he notes, this fetish, made more teasing and powerful by the capricious funding tactics of corporations, "is no substitute for compensation derived from justice, whereby wrongs are adjudicated and compensated responsibly, with the parties on an equal footing."[113] The NAACP's partnership with DuPont and grateful viewer responses to "Toward Tomorrow" indicate, however, that this substitution happens all too easily, and that it has been going on for quite some time.

The public relations benefits of such demonstrations of social responsibility through institutional sponsorship extended to television itself. Institutional advertising's pseudophilanthropic mode of address added credence to the broadcast industry's long-standing claim that the U.S. system, based in the private exploitation of the publicly owned airwaves, could serve the public effectively. Indeed, viewed from such a perspective, commercial television appears as its own kind of public-private partnership. DuPont audience research certainly shows viewers actively engaging with the medium in these terms. Although they tended to question the campaigns through which DuPont addressed the absurd idea of a widespread "prejudice" against big business, they were more than willing to embrace the idea that its television sponsorship could contribute, in a pedagogical and entertaining way, to the cause of progressive governance in other areas of postwar American life. In later chapters, as we examine the various forms of sponsorship through which both the powerful and power seekers laid claim to this prized position of the sponsor-citizen, other agendas and other audiences come into view. But all were connected, in their disavowal of sponsorship as merely a technique for selling products to consumers, to the tenets for governing by television that originated in institutional advertising.

## "TOWARD TOMORROW" AND THE CULTURE OF DISCUSSION

A final question remains: what was the relationship between "Toward Tomorrow" and other forms of racial outreach staged on the television screen in the 1950s?[114] When I watched the program in the Peabody Awards archives at the University of Georgia, I was struck by the way many of the dialogue scenes were photographed. Perhaps because of budgetary constraints, there are surprisingly few group

shots. Instead, actors deliver their lines in close-ups that isolate them from their settings, giving their speech (especially that of Ruby Good-win, who played Bunche's grandmother) a sermonlike quality. This odd framing pattern signals that a message is being delivered—an idea made literal at the end of the program, when James Edwards, the actor who played Bunche, appears out of character and reads a telegram from the great man himself. Bunche's message distills the themes of the show, highlighting his grandmother's "simple dignity and nobility of spirit" and emphasizing the psychological dimensions of racial prejudice: "People are bad only as they are taught bad lessons from the environment around them."

This focus on the influence of environment and the sermonizing mode of dialogue linked the show to liberal social activism in this period, particularly the coalition of service and social work organizations known as the intergroup relations movement. Viewers certainly seemed to understand the program in these terms, their letters praising it as "a significant contribution in the field of human relations" and predicting that it would "advance the cause of brotherhood and understanding."[115] Terms such as *human relations* and *brotherhood* were keywords in the language of postwar racial fellowship, and the numerous publicity screenings DuPont held for civil rights organizations in preparation for the broadcast certainly positioned "Toward Tomorrow" in this context. But these 16 mm screenings differed from the broadcast version of "Toward Tomorrow" in one fundamental way: the commercials had been cut, leaving no trace of DuPont's corporate presence. I am left wondering exactly what NAACP audiences would have made of the paint commercial, officially entitled "Easy to Use—and Odorless Too," had it been left in. Paint signifies color, so odorless paint might convey the inoffensiveness of "colored" Americans' struggles for equality. But perhaps, reading more elementally, "odorless paint" simply says "whitewash"—the whitening universals of liberal humanism, a troublesome language of sameness under the skin—and focuses attention on the thin veneer of racial outreach that DuPont applied, temporarily, to advance its public relations goals. As the next chapter explains, the humanist values of racial transcendence the company borrowed to

legitimize itself were themselves part of a wider project of governing by television, one that had nothing to do with the defense of free enterprise but which, like DuPont's institutional advertising research, was greatly concerned with what audiences had to say. But rather than capturing their speech in the market research process, the agencies and civic groups of the intergroup relations movement hoped to liberate it through guided discussions, striving—not always successfully—to re-create the democratic process on the scale of the small group.

Men in police car look up.

Detective looks up.

Newsman reaches for his camera.

Kids going up the steps of the
school.

We cut to police car moving.
We are inside the car. The kids
going into the school.

C.U. policeman talking into car
radio.

POLICEMAN:
Car 57. There's nothing doing
here. We'll cruise on over
to McKinley...

We see car pull away from
school as the kids go up the
steps into the building.

No violence the first day...no
stories for the newspapers...
Now the real problems began.

We dissolve to last of kids
coming in the door to the classroom and we follow them as they
take their seats.

An integrated class...

...with the worst kind of
segregation...self segregation.

The teacher looks over his class.

We see blocks of negroes
together and blocks of whites
together.

What do you do? Mix them up?
Seat them alphabetically?..
Lean too far forward, or too
far backward?

C.U. teacher.

We see the class waiting for the
teacher to begin.

TEACHER:    (lip sync)

This is Civics 1. W
to be studying gove
local, state and n
we're going to lo

_ker sits on the edge of his

in police car look up.

etive looks up.

...man reaches for his camera.

...s going up the steps of the
...ool.

cut to police car moving. The kids
are inside the car.
...ing into the school.

...U. policeman talking into car
...dio.

POLICEMAN:

Car 57. There's nothing doing
here. We'll cruise on over
to McKinley...

We see car pull away from
school as the kids go up the
steps into the building.

No violence the first day...no
stories for the newspapers...
Now the real problems began.

We dissolve to last of kids
coming in the door to the classroom and we follow them as they
take their seats.

An integrated class...

...with the worst kind of
segregation...self segregation.

The teacher looks over his class.

We see blocks of negroes
together and blocks of whites
together.

What do you do? Mix them up?
Seat them alphabetically?...
Lean too far forward, or too
far backward?

C.U. teacher.

We see the class waiting for the
teacher to begin.

...her sits on the edge of his

TEACHER:      (lip sync)

This is Civics 1. We're
to be studying governmen
local, state and nation
We're going to look at
...ich we govern...

*Chapter Two*
# THE POLITICS OF WOODEN ACTING

DR. JEAN GRAMS, an intergroup relations consultant, was pale with nerves. She knitted her brow in concentration as she spoke her first halting lines, squinting under the lights of the KETC-TV studio. It was February 1955, and the subject under discussion in this live broadcast—the desegregation of St. Louis schools—was a highly sensitive one. Full integration of elementary schools was on schedule for the fall semester, a little over a year after the Supreme Court's landmark *Brown v. Board of Education* decision. This local television broadcast was one of many public discussion forums designed to bring together white people and Negroes (the terminology of the time) and facilitate the process. Some of these community dialogues were teacher workshops and parent meetings organized by the school board. Others were administered by groups such as the Urban League, the Parent-Teacher Association (PTA), and the organization Dr. Grams was here to represent, the National Conference of Christians and Jews. Everyone was anxious to see integration happen smoothly.

The program was part of a popular public affairs series called *Soap Box*, its host a lanky, crew-cut thirty-year-old named Ranlet "Ran" Lincoln. The St. Louis PTA was sponsoring this particular episode and, as Lincoln explained to viewers, tonight's broadcast was somewhat unusual. Four PTA members were going to role-play community concerns about integrated classrooms, acting out "typical ideas, feelings, and attitudes in a more concentrated form than we would find in real life." Neither Dr. Grams nor the other role-play participants were accustomed to theatricals. But although they stumbled on their words, glancing uncomfortably at cue cards, the sincerity of their performances underscored the PTA's commitment to television as a vehicle for democratic communication. Its members were active in the Educational Television Commission, the civic body that administered station KETC-TV (known locally as the "panel channel"). And the group had raised $100,000 through door-to-door fund-raising to help build the studio in which *Soap Box*'s guests were sitting, a converted women's gymnasium housing two cameras, a control room, and the 16 mm kinescope machine on which this episode was being recorded.[1]

Their enactment that evening centered on the preconceptions teachers and parents might bring to a particular hypothetical situation: a Negro fifth-grade teacher has awarded a low conduct mark to Johnny Jones, a white boy. To address the problem, Dr. Grams asked the role-playing parents and teachers to talk with each other about solutions. Throwing himself into the part, the man playing Johnny's blustery father confronted the teacher. "Mrs. Clark" (a white teacher who had previously taught his son) had never contacted him about any problems, he said, insinuating that the fault lay with the Negro teacher and not his son. The teacher, "Miss Smith," listened patiently, then responded in a way that focused on their commonalities, offering the ecumenical observation that "we both are fearful" and suggesting that she and he meet on an individual basis to discuss the problem.

The discussion stretched on, touching on the pros and cons of large and small meetings, letters and phone calls, home visits, open houses, voluntarism, and other ways that teachers and parents might interact with each other. Dr. Grams tried not to glance at the camera as she offered her summation. "At a time of integration too, perhaps, if Mr. Jones *meets* Mrs. Adams [a Negro parent], he perhaps would understand about the new situation too." She repeated her words out of nervousness, but the message was clear: face-to-face interaction was the only way to achieve "understanding" in this "stressful" period. At the end of the program, Lincoln stepped in and suggested to the viewer that watching the preceding role play was one way of starting such conversations. "You've been participating in the last of three teachers meetings on education," he announced, making it clear that watching *Soap Box* was neither rote entertainment nor the passive reception of a civics lesson, but rather a form of active democratic involvement.

Combining role play, group discussion, and expert advice, *Soap Box* embodied some key midcentury ideas about how people might govern themselves through television. Some of these ideas were carryovers from New Deal–era civic culture. In the 1930s and 1940s, the Federal Forum Project fostered participation in local and national government through town meetings; these were complemented by radio discussion programs such as *America's Town Meeting of the Air*, which sought to engage

*Soap Box,* which aired on St. Louis station KETC in 1955, featured parents and teachers role-playing scenarios that might arise with school integration. The real star of the show was the bespectacled Negro teacher "Miss Smith," who radiated calm, patience, and rationality even when confronted by an ornery white father.

citizens in their homes in conversation about pressing civic matters.[2] Television programs such as *Soap Box*, produced by and for the citizens of St. Louis, exemplified the enduring power of broadcasting as a means of realizing these earlier ideals of civic discussion. But their approach to discussion as a means for exemplifying conduct drew on new ways of thinking about civic life in the postwar period. The use of role play to teach viewers about productive social interactions across the color line might seem to suggest that unscripted discussion posed too great a threat of conflict, and that citizens adjusting to integration would learn better from awkwardly pantomimed "character types" than from actual people. But this interest in hypothetical conversations between social types was not simply a reflection of racial anxiety. It was actually one of several techniques through which postwar social scientists, philanthropists, and opinion researchers, as well as grassroots reformers and activists, worked to identify and encourage the workings of American democracy in the face-to-face interactions of people in groups. They categorized discussion participants in any number of ways, worrying over them like pieces in a chess puzzle. Sometimes they treated them as positions in a process of knowledge and information management: the expert, the layperson, the opinion

leader. Sometimes they divided them according to their roles in the economic system: the worker, the labor leader, the manager, the consumer. Sometimes they parsed the discussion group's demographics in terms of age and race: Negro youth, white youth, Negro teacher, white parent—the cast of characters in *Soap Box*. At other times, they imagined discussants as cultural aspirants, hoping to improve themselves through conversation about great books and great ideas.

Television occupied a small but privileged place in these postwar visions of discussion as a tool for the making of citizens. It could present arguments, promote grassroots reform, and meet people's needs for personal development on a mass scale, and it provided a battery of expressive forms—reenactment or role play, documentary film, the authoritative speech of experts—from which reformers might draw techniques for civic education. The specific reform context surrounding *Soap Box*'s mobilization of television for civic role play was an area of liberal interracial outreach known as intergroup relations. The intergroup relations movement sprang from a meeting of minds and commitments rooted in social science, social advocacy, and adult education. It drew much of its urgency from the events of the war years, when the unspeakable atrocity of the Holocaust and the segregation of the

armed forces made problems of race prejudice and anti-Semitism a matter of vital importance for reformers and activists, both in the Establishment and in those sectors of liberal activism able to withstand the anticommunist backlash of the immediate postwar years. Although it was a grassroots movement, intergroup relations took shape outside of the populist, and often more radical, networks for class and racial solidarity associated with the Popular Front of the 1930s and 1940s, and it was largely untouched by the anticommunist scaremongering of the immediate postwar period. Located at the nexus of psychology, sociological research, social work, civic practice, and school and adult education, the intergroup relations movement aimed at the abolition of prejudice and inequality through concerted forms of interpersonal contact rather than political agitation.[3] Stuart Svonkin points out that while the movement's methods and approach might seem dated today, "a number of these ideas—that the mass media can and should be used to influence individuals' attitudes and behavior, and that clashes between groups of people who happen to be identified with different ethnic or racial backgrounds are best understood in terms of 'race relations' or cultural identity—could as easily be derived from recent headlines."[4] If my account in the following criticizes some of the suppositions on which the intergroup relations effort rested, the issue is not so much its failings or shortcomings as a liberation movement but rather the relationship of its racial logic of common humanity to the broader political culture of the period and evolving tenets of black radicalism, which would eventually change the substance of interracial dialogue within that culture.

*Soap Box* exhibits many of the suppositions associated with the intergroup relations movement, which is not surprising: the 1955 desegregation of the St. Louis school system was widely upheld as a model example of successful integration, and many observers and participants credited the numerous public forums sponsored by intergroup relations organizations.[5] The program used the radical sociometric technique of role play, and enlisted the talents, or at least commitments, of ordinary citizens. In so doing it channeled newly minted assumptions about the ways that direct experience, interaction, and play could lead to therapeutic group governance. Dr. Grams' performance, emphasizing her involvement as a sympathetic participant rather than a neutral moderator or disinterested expert, reflected current social scientific thinking on how this process might proceed. Focusing not on abstract concepts but on concrete situations, her interjections moved the dialogue toward active problem solving, in order that the group might collectively identify possible courses of action.[6] Indeed, the survival of this particular episode of *Soap Box* into the present day indicates the sense of timeliness and innovation attached to it at the time; the kinescope was submitted, along with three other episodes, to the annual Peabody Awards, which today houses in its University of Georgia archives many examples of mainstream liberal ambitions in television from this period.

But this sense of prestige is somewhat paradoxical, given that programs such as *Soap Box* were marginal and infrequent in postwar television.[7] Their emphasis on localism and community involvement exemplified the ideals of the Blue Book, the FCC document that laid out public service guidelines for broadcasting in terms highly reminiscent of New Deal–era civic culture, and which enshrined liberal ideals of broadcasting as a public service infrastructure. But commercial monopoly of the airwaves meant that such programs were inevitably relegated to the struggling educational television system, which formed the building blocks of the public television network created by an act of Congress in 1969, or else programmed in the "cultural ghetto" time slots—Saturday and Sunday mornings—when commercial stations aired unsponsored public service programs.[8] These were for the most part syndicated films supplied free of charge by national service organizations, ecumenical religious groups, business lobbies and labor unions, educational institutions, and local chapters of organizations that might range politically from the National Council of Christians and Jews to the White Citizens Councils created after the 1954 *Brown* decision. (Black civil rights organizations did not, as far as I can tell, find a voice in the democratic conversation that public service and educational programming was supposed to provide, although at the end of the decade, as we shall see, some enterprising independent producers made an effort to exploit the format of discussion and the wooden performance styles of role play as an entrée into the discourse.) Still, despite their marginal status, postwar public service and educational programs are an important window into the workings of liberal civic culture. In their highly didactic and artificial efforts to model appropriate forms of civic conduct—especially, as this chapter details, those following from the radical shifts in everyday life associated with school desegregation and the burgeoning civil rights movement—these programs provide unique access to the uneasy encounters between liberal idealism and racial reality that shaped the practice of civic governance in this period.

The discussion program was one of the formats most commonly identified with television's role in civic governance, and philanthropic organizations, most notably the Ford Foundation's Fund for Adult Education, gave grants to a number of local stations to foster its development.[9] Testifying before FCC hearings on network programming in 1959, educational broadcasting advocate Morris Novik told the commission that viewers expected more than chirpy public service announcements, or PSAs. "Slogans don't replace discussion programs in depth. They can sell soaps, breakfast foods, headache remedies, but they cannot adequately inform the public." The kinds of programs Novik had in mind were conversations among members of the community, debating such issues as "selecting the site of a new public school, pay raises for policemen or firemen, slum clearance and the construction of new public housing."[10] But most often, discussion programs on TV were either network-produced or nationally syndicated, featuring experts, journalists, and other authorities debating each other, in some cases prompted by the occasional question from the audience. These national shows, such as *American Forum of the Air* (NBC) or *Face the Nation* (CBS), constituted an arid, talky world defined by the democratic furniture of roundtable and panel and populated entirely with besuited white men in hornrims.[11] These programs were not intended to bring citizens together in deliberation but rather sought to stage a sense of proxy contact between everyday citizens and experts charged with the administration of their conduct, a model of civic practice articulated by Walter

Lippmann in 1922 when he argued that deliberative discussion must always moderate "partisan voices" with the reasoned and knowledgeable opinions of experts.[12] As Novik's testimony might suggest, local programs such as *Soap Box* were more valuable to TV reformers because they were embedded in local community governance and were oriented toward advocacy. They worked at the grassroots level to effect changes in conduct and attitudes within particular localities—and, potentially, to build a more democratic polity from the ground up.

The Ford Foundation's Fund for Adult Education supported the production of civic discussion programs on a number of local stations, including WOI-TV in Des Moines, Iowa, the birthplace of the New Deal–era Federal Forum project.
*Image courtesy of the Ford Foundation Archives.*

## TV AND LOCAL CIVIC CULTURE

To understand this conceptualization of television's role in community governance and liberal activism, it is important to understand the local audiovisual culture in which civic programming circulated. It is difficult to count the number of local television programs with civic missions on a par with *Soap Box*. The Peabody Awards archives contain hundreds of panel discussions and community meeting programs, but it is hard to know what fraction of a station's broadcasting ecology they represent. A more contextual reason why such grassroots broadcasts are hard to quantify is the fact that they were distributed on the local level across a hybrid exhibition network comprising both broadcasting and 16 mm film exhibition. *Soap Box*, for example, was a live broadcast, but the program likely was available also as a 16 mm kinescope recording for screening on film in the community after it aired, as part of the wide-ranging public education campaign mounted by the St. Louis PTA and other civic groups around the time of integration. This was the case with another KETC-TV discussion program, *Free Assembly*, in which ordinary citizens gathered at the courthouse to air their opinions on civil issues. The program was initially presented as a live remote, but its producers planned to shoot subsequent episodes on 16 mm film, allowing them to "edit out the dull and weedy and . . . make a half-hour package for other uses," including distribution to civic groups for use in their own discussions.[13] Such efforts to extend the reach of a television program through 16 mm distribution were common in local educational broadcasting. Indeed, when we talk about educational television in this pre-PBS era we are often, necessarily, talking about nontheatrical film at the same time.

Civic groups were relegated to the margins when it came to the sponsorship of network public service programs, but on the local level they were key intermediaries between national distributors of public affairs media and individual stations. For example, the 16 mm distribution agreement for *A City Decides*, a 1956 documentary about the integration of St. Louis High Schools, included local television rights for civic groups that purchased a print. As the film's distributor, Leo

Dratfield, explained to its sponsor, the Fund for the Republic, these groups "could attempt to place the film with their local stations, possibly with a speaker or forum."[14] The two media complemented each other for the purposes of the community groups and reform agencies that used them. TV brought larger audiences, but nontheatrical film venues—churches, classrooms, military bases, service organizations, union halls, company cafeterias—were more likely than TV to stimulate viewer discussions of the ideas the films contained. Still, the very fact of a television broadcast was an opportunity for publicity and, often, for recruiting and networking. In February 1957, when *A City Decides* aired on NBC stations in public service time, as part of the annual Brotherhood Week sponsored by the National Council of Christians and Jews, the Fund for the Republic coordinated a mass mailing by groups such as the Southern Regional Council and the United Church Women to alert members to the broadcast and to encourage them to notify others in their community.[15] On such occasions, television helped civic organizations draft new members and introduce them to the civic modes expected of them at the same time.

The films that aired in local civic culture, on TV and on the collapsible screens of 16 mm screening venues, used many different visual formats—documentary, filmed lectures, and dramatized narratives, among others. But the act of *watching* the act of *having* a discussion was a particularly valuable technique in these contexts. It was a form of directive training, showing audience members appropriate and inappropriate forms of civic conduct and providing them with the opportunity to practice with each other. A series of "films without endings," distributed in the early 1950s both for 16 mm nontheatrical screening and as a template for a half-hour television program, incorporated the play of onscreen and offscreen discussion for this very purpose.[16] Produced by Columbia University's Center for Mass Communication and entitled *The Challenge*, the series included titles such as "Human Rights," "Rumor," "Can We Immunize Against Prejudice?," and "Freedom to Read." The viewing context was tightly controlled. Each film began with a role-played scenario that dramatized the issues alluded to in its title and which featured a discussion between individuals with opposing points of view. In 16 mm screenings, the projector was shut off after this preliminary segment so that viewers could discuss the issues; when conversation concluded, the group watched a one-to-two-minute closing segment that summarized the various points of view to which viewers had been exposed. In television broadcasts, according to one advocate promoting the series to a group of labor media representatives, the audience discussion session would be replaced with "a live panel made up of a prominent labor [leader] and other community personalities."[17] Through watching and then engaging in discussion, the film's producers (and civic reformers) reasoned, individuals would discover their sovereignty and freedom as citizens of a liberal democracy.

This idealism was rooted in New Deal civic republicanism, but it acquired a sense of urgency and momentum in the context of the Cold War. For some members of the governing classes, the discussion group embodied American commitments to free speech (as opposed to the repressions of Soviet culture) and contributed to the ongoing leveling of the American class system. As one political scientist, seemingly blind to the chilling effects of the emerging anticommunist bloc, proposed in 1947, group discussion was a social setting in which "John Citizen . . . swaps stories and matches arguments with the banker, the farmer, the carpenter and the village socialist."[18] For those involved in educational research and policy, the discussion group was a means for combating despotic tendencies in adult and youth classrooms. "Skepticism concerning the use of group discussion . . . is closely aligned with the problem of authoritarianism in teaching," wrote two expert advocates of the technique, identifying discussion with the antitotalitarian sentiments shaping postwar political psychology.[19] Discussion groups figured prominently in new sociological methods such as action research, pioneered by social psychologist Kurt Lewin, which combined research and activism in areas of social reform, probing group dynamics as the key to counteracting tyranny in human behavior. Describing his method as "democratic social engineering," Lewin saw in the delicate conversational spiderwebs of discussion group interaction a way for both researchers and participants to gain "better insight into the legitimate and non-legitimate aspects of power."[20] Lewin and his associates were interested in activating discussion's reformist promise for race relations, but it was in reality a highly flexible technology of governance, freely adapted to suit a range of political agendas. Because it appeared to produce "a modification of extreme points of view," group discussion supported the goals of postwar pluralism. It also provided evidence for research in education and mass communications that interpersonal contact was at least as important as structural, socioeconomic change in shaping opinions and attitudes.[21] And because of its associations with free speech (and, by dubious extension, free enterprise), it was a useful tool in union-busting corporate "economic education" programs in the workplace, although critics were quick to argue that the idea of free discussion in such contexts was a joke.[22]

Television programs devoted to discussion acted out contradictory Cold War ideals of democratic freedom—they were independent from the (potentially authoritarian) influence of the state, yet closely monitored via the mediating figure of the discussion leader. A public affairs program called *On Camera*, airing on CBS affiliate station KRNT in Des Moines, embodied this dualism in its regular call-in segment, called "Private Line," which combined on-screen and offscreen discussion with expert opinion. The January 15, 1957, episode addressed the topic of civil liberties in Iowa, a topic that encompassed the question of civil rights for nonwhite citizens. It opened with an image of a state map emblazoned with markers. As announcer Richard Hopkins explained, each one indicated the location of a discussion group organized through the city's Department of Adult Education for the occasion of the broadcast. The groups had been instructed to meet for ninety minutes prior to airtime, and they would be calling in with questions over the course of the broadcast. As the half-hour program unfolded, Hopkins and his guest, Kenneth Everhardt of the Iowa chapter of the American Civil Liberties Union, fielded questions from viewer groups around the region about topics ranging from freedom of religion in schools to racial discrimination in public accommodations, aided by Mrs. Betty Elvender, who answered the phone.[23]

Des Moines was the birthplace of the Federal Forum movement in the 1930s, and *On Camera* was a continuation of the local governance tradition the movement established.[24] But the program retooled this emphasis on the local for the postwar era, incorporating not only the technological capacities of television and telephony but also one of the period's reformist preoccupations: how to exploit the dynamic interaction of group members with each other and with experts for the good of the polity as a whole. The program was not just a call-in show, connecting isolated individuals to the experts directly, but rather a kind of event in which the broadcast and the phone conversation were just one segment of a longer process in which group discussion was central. This emphasis on context also referenced a point of consensus between postwar social scientific research and social work: the idea that the individual is the product of a group environment and that changing the individual required more than TV's mass dissemination of expertise via an intimate mode of address; it had to be combined with the discussion group's interpersonal contact.[25] Real changes, one observer noted, could only come about if screenings included "personal contact and personal participation."[26]

Still, handbooks and manuals also acknowledged the many ways that personal interaction through discussion might serve to entrench, rather than overcome, particular attitudes and roles. Recounting an awkward encounter between a Protestant minister and a rabbi watching television together at an intergroup relations conference, the authors of the 1955 *Manual of Intergroup Relations* noted that "persons inexperienced in intergroup relations frequently alienate minority persons with whom they wish to be friendly by inadvertently using the language of prejudice."[27] The task of the well-trained discussion leader, clearly, was to turn such moments into vehicles for further understanding. Combining group screening and discussion allowed intergroup relations experts to engineer the social environment, as a microcosm of representative democracy. It also encouraged emotional identification on the part of the spectator. "Through movies, panel discussions, and bull sessions we soon learned what it felt like to be a Negro in this country," recalled one intergroup relations trainee, who felt that this awareness never would have been awakened were participants simply required to "sit through all the lectures ever given on theoretical race relations."[28]

## HOW CITIZENS ACT

The use of role play to model the act of having a discussion, especially an interracial one of the sort dramatized in *Soap Box*, might seem like a curious technique given the wooden acting styles it inevitably involved. But role play was seen as a particularly potent tool for overcoming the attitudes that gave rise to such awkward and alienating social interactions. Although it involved the adoption of false personae, it seemed at the time to provide a means for discovering social truths that conformed closely to broader ideas about representative democracy. U.S. political culture was moving away from the New Deal model of civic life as a dynamic of forces and fronts and toward the technocratic conception of the polity as an aggregation of interest groups governed through processes of balancing and centering.[29] Role play, coupled with group discussion, was a way of demonstrating the postwar idea of democratic deliberation as a process of voicing and balancing interests. As sociologist Claude C. Bowman explained in the left-liberal journal *Social Forces*, "Situations involving thousands or millions of persons can be reduced to a relatively few type-roles."[30] Distilling the diversity of the nation into a microcosmic collection of types required a commitment to impartiality on the part of the role player. Psychologist Jacob Moreno, who first conceived of role play as a therapeutic technique in the 1920s, explained that "in sociodramatic procedure, the subject is not a person, but a group." The situation demanded that the participant "detach himself as far as possible from everything in his own collective life which might bias him toward one or another of the cultures portrayed."[31] Role play, in short, was not only a laboratory for exploring the threshold between individual psychology and interest group politics and for demonstrating the connection between the two, it was also a means for balancing antagonism by encouraging identification with the other.

Although films that used nonprofessional actors to role-play discussion are easily criticized for their bad acting, it is important to consider that part of their educational value lay in the manifestly antinaturalistic performances they contained. Wooden acting provided viewers with a tangible reminder of the valued sociological distinction between individuals and their social roles.[32] Method acting, the lauded technique in which the actor's internal self-discovery creates characters marked by an aura of authenticity, exemplified Cold War ideas of the well-developed individual. But wooden acting carried negative Cold War connotations too. In popular Hollywood films of the fifties it could signify brainwashing or alien influence—think of the affectless monotone spoken by the possessed townsfolk in *Invasion of the Body Snatchers*—and in that sense it might also be considered a kind of Cold War ideological shorthand, signifying the depersonalizing effects of totalitarianism against the depth and individualism associated with Method acting. In discussion group films, wooden acting also telegraphed Cold War ideology, but in a very different way. Role play asked actors to think of themselves as mere mouthpieces, and required a disconnect between the performer and the social position he or she ventriloquized. This performance mode conformed to a technocratic ideal of personhood closely associated with Cold War–era models of the rational citizen, a subject capable of transcending personal interests in the service of self-governance.[33] *Soap Box* and other such film and television programs used role playing in this way, striving to objectify different personality types and political interests. And as they used nonprofessional actors, they also tried to show how ordinary people could detach from their personal biases and identify with the situation of another in the course of conversation. Wooden acting was thus, in a sense, a civics lesson.

Another important aspect of role play's appeal in this Cold War context was the emphasis it placed on play. Although it might seem to contradict the ideal of rationality on which rested republican models of civic participation, play was a key term in the period's conceptualization of the cultivation of citizens. Intertwined with the cherished antiauthoritarian value of freedom, the language of role play shaped Cold War epistemologies across a range of fields, from military science to social psychology to corporate decision making.[34] The popularity of role play reflected the increasing centrality of personal identity in popular and specialized discourses of human development at the time; game-based methods for incorporating the viewpoint of the other nurtured the healthy growth of both the individual ego system and the group dynamic through what one proponent called "emotional reeducation."[35] If the pathology of the authoritarian personality stemmed in part from an overly rigid, controlling childhood environment, role play and discussion corrected authoritarian tendencies by demonstrating to participants the democratic values of creativity, choice, and freedom.

Role play's advocates envisioned television as a tool for the mass dissemination of these values, but their utopian vision was hard to reconcile with the conventions of mainstream broadcasting. Moreno hoped that televised role play could serve "as a check and balance to cultural tensions and hostilities" that would bring about "collective catharsis" on a large scale by "reaching millions of local groups and neighborhoods in which inter-cultural conflicts and tensions are dormant or in the initial phases of open warfare."[36] But with its wooden acting and its ordinary-looking people, role play was obviously not network material, nor was the direct advocacy it was generally asked to perform. These aspects of sociodrama were most palatable in the documentary form, which in this period allowed for extensive reenactment—often by the documentary's subjects or by amateur actors drawn from the community—in its search for greater moral clarity and social exemplarity.

A classic example of a documentary that exploited the stiff, declamatory style of role-play in the service of civic pedagogy is *A City Decides*. Released in 1956 and aired in public service time by NBC affiliates the following year, the film reenacted events at Beaumont

High School in St. Louis during the first months of integration, and examined how teachers handled conflicts between black and white youth. The film was nominated for an Academy Award in the documentary short subject category, and it was distributed widely to civic and educational groups for screening and discussion. It was produced and written by Charles Guggenheim, the first station manager of KETC-TV, in collaboration with other station staff members, and it included in its cast at least one of *Soap Box*'s PTA-member performers (the blustery racist father, here playing a blustery racist teacher). Group discussion, with all its complex social triangulations, figures prominently throughout the film. In one notable scene, the camera visits a crowded meeting hall where parents are gathered to pose questions about integration to a panel of teachers, school administrators, educational psychologists, and intergroup relations specialists. The parents' blushing performances indicate that they are not actors but participants recruited from the community, modeling examples both good and bad; the officials on the panel, on the other hand, appear to be playing themselves.[37] As the parents recite their half-memorized lines, the main character, a teacher, interprets in voice-over the real meanings of their questions for the viewer. "I'd like to know what our school plans on doing about things like social dancing," a white man asks, clutching his infant son out of nervousness. The voice-over whispers the subtext underlying his words: "He's worried about intermarriage." The scene made an impression on the Educational Committee of the National Council of Negro Women, whose members commented that "there was great skill in having parents state their opinions and then having the commentator interpret the implications."[38] What the committee appreciated, it seems, was the candor with which the film addressed the illiberal motives that might drive white participants' seemingly civil speech in the context of the discussion group.

The importance of this acknowledgement seems to have been lost on one of the film's only academic reviewers, New York Public Library film librarian William J. Sloan.[39] In a 1965 review of integration films released over the previous ten years, Sloane pointed out in the *Journal of the Society of Cinematologists* that although the film was noteworthy

in revealing "the fears of Negro parents in having their children attend school with white children," it was "aimed primarily at preparing
the white community for integration." Writing at a point when the
cinema verité style was ascendant, Sloan judged this goal as a limit on
the film's progressive political value. But this assessment failed to take
into account the centrality of the discussion process, both on-screen
and off, in the political meanings ascribed to such films; the scene sin-
gled out by the National Council of Negro Women made examples of
the white parents by exposing their euphemistic racism, and this provided validation, and potentially preparation, for black viewers facing
white people as constitutional equals in a civic context.[40]

Still, there is no question that *A City Decides* strived to set a fairly
narrow agenda for conversations about integration, placing heavy emphasis on the responsibilities of the individual. Its role-played reenact-
ments of the discussions that took place during the integration of the
St. Louis school system focused attention on the interpersonal scale in
which democracy succeeds or falters, emphasizing, like *Soap Box*, the
need for people to get to know each other. This focus excluded questions
about the roles of social institutions and structural inequalities in the
process of racial oppression. Conforming closely to the tenets of sacred
individualism on which the so-called free world defined its opposition
to other political systems, most pressingly communism, it sidestepped
questions of white privilege by asserting the universal commonalities
of the population it spotlighted, ultimately positioned as all-too-human
teenagers rather than whites or Negroes.

## THE BURDEN OF THE EXAMPLE

The strain of liberal humanism that connected the earnest reenact-
ments of *A City Decides* and *Soap Box* placed a particular burden on
black participants in intergroup relations role play, as it often typecast
them in a very particular role: leading by example. Describing an intergroup relations meeting in which participants discussed a role-playing

skit about Miss X, "a minority group nurse," Cleo Harter of Indiana's District Nurse Intergroup Relations Committee approvingly recounted the summation offered by Negro committee member Daisy Thomas, who emerges in Harter's telling as the moral conscience of the meeting. Interestingly, at least in Harter's paraphrasing, Thomas appeared to speak at first from the position of a white person: "I believe Miss X can be quite happy in our city . . . if she will not be too sensitive and will know that most of us are trying—and if those with whom she works will understand that when Miss X makes mistakes it is because she is human and not because she is Negro." Audience response affirmed Thomas' role as the universal liberal subject and truth teller in the group: "Thoughtful silence, and finally applause, indicated that most of the audience agreed with her summing up. A member commented later, 'Until that moment, I would have been reluctant to discuss a racial problem with a Negro; now I know I can.'"[41] Performing this cathartic role in the service of the district nurse meeting's group conscience, Daisy Thomas' repeated reference to the humanity of Miss X and her co-workers underscores the humanity of all of the workshop's participants. On-screen participants in interracial discussion in *A City Decides* performed a similarly authoritative and authentic modeling of humanity and civic depth. After listening to the concerns of some white teenagers, a poised young black woman speaks up at an intergroup youth meeting: "I think it's the individual that counts. How are you going to get to know a person unless you meet them?" she asserts, echoing the movement's ethos of interpersonal contact and setting an example for the rest of the group.

What was it like to be put in that position, as the moral conscience of the social microcosm and an exemplary figure of humanity as a whole? J. Saunders Redding, a historian and the first black professor hired by an Ivy League school, raged against such expectations in his anguished 1951 memoir *On Being Negro in America*. He condemned "the specialization of the sense and talent and learning . . . that is expected of Negroes by other members of their race and by whites," calling it "tragic and vicious and divisive." He was particularly upset by Richard Wright's 1941 classic, *Twelve Million Black Voices*, writing

| | |
|---|---|
| The first white boy. | BOY 1: (lip sync)<br><br>Well, I don't mean to say any-<br>thing about anybody, but we hear<br>stories about what happens in<br>negro neighborhoods -- delinquency<br>-- and things like that. |
| The third white boy. | BOY 3: (lip sync)<br><br>Well, my school is in a pretty<br>fancy neighborhood and we had<br>some kids who broke in one night<br>and wrecked the place. |
| The negro girl. | GIRL 2: (lip sync)<br><br>Well, I think it's the individual<br>that counts, and how are you<br>going to know anything about<br>people if you never get to meet<br>them? |
| The white girl. | GIRL 1: (lip sync)<br><br>I think we all get along fine. |
| A group shot of the kids talking<br>around the table. | TEACHER:<br><br>When the Supreme Court looked at |

*A City Decides* was full of staged discussion scenes; Negro role players often articulated the moral conscience of the group, understood in this scene as a commitment to interpersonal communication and respect for the individual.
*Image courtesy of Princeton University Library.*

of "the effrontery of one who a few years ago undertook to speak for me and twelve million others."[42] Like the unnamed famous singer Redding described as "weary of the obligation" to sing spirituals at every concert "'as if they were theme music,' wholly identifying her," Redding and other black intellectuals at the time recognized all too well the burden that white liberalism forced upon them.[43] As Ross Posnock notes, Redding's memoir was "one of the frankest confessions of disgust with exemplarity and the 'obligations imposed by race.'"[44] To be seen only as a figurehead or a mouthpiece was to experience a profoundly one-dimensional life, flattened by the pressure not only to look perfect in white eyes but also to help white interlocutors hone their own self-awareness for personal enrichment and the greater social good.

At the end of the decade, when Redding traveled to India as a cultural ambassador for the United States, he encountered these burdensome expectations in all their geopolitical complexity, bristling when

Indian Marxists treated him not as an American but as a representative of the black American struggle.[45] As this might suggest, leading by example was a process with multiple layers of meaning in the postwar period. It was central to foreign policy, specifically the strategy of containment, which placed great stress on the importance of international example setting. Although it developed into a template for militarized intervention overseas, George F. Kennan, the policy's original architect, initially conceived containment as a diplomatic practice in which the United States would exemplify statehood for the rest of the world, setting standards in domestic and international governance that would sway nonaligned nations to reject communism. "The United States . . . must demonstrate by its own confidence and patience, but particularly the integrity and dignity of its example, that the true glory of Russian national effort can find its expression only in peaceful and friendly association with other peoples and not in attempts to subjugate and dominate those people," Kennan wrote in 1947.[46]

For many observers overseas, however, the entrenched state of Southern segregation meant that the example set by the United States was a negative one. U.S. race relations pointedly undermined containment's pieties, providing highly visible examples of subjugation and domination within the borders of the United States. To counteract this problem, Cold War institutions of cultural diplomacy such as the USIA used film and other media to promote, in the words of Penny Von Eschen, "the achievements of individual Black Americans as examples of American democracy at work," exploiting the international visibility of figures such as Ralph Bunche, Louis Armstrong, and many others.[47] Along with hundreds of U.S. cultural workers sent abroad by the State Department to exemplify the artistic and intellectual freedoms supported by capitalist democracy, black artists, athletes, and writers found themselves embodying a paradoxical kind of exemplary exceptionalism intended to counter overseas impressions of the United States as a racist society.

Within the borders of the United States, the film and television projects of the intergroup relations movement embodied a pervasive trope in the visual culture of progressive racial reform in the United

States: the "exemplary Negro." A figure familiar to us today from the spate of Hollywood films in which, as K. Anthony Appiah notes, black characters embody a deeper "ethical principle," the exemplary Negro has occupied a privileged place in the liberal humanist imagination since the voluminous popular culture of the abolitionist movement.[48] Not simply a "model minority" accepted and approved of by whites—think of the Negro persona associated with Sidney Poitier in this period, indelibly stamped with the adjective *dignified*—the exemplary negro is also a figure of therapeutic reparation whose oratorical self-presence facilitates white liberal self-realization, setting an example of authenticity and "civic depth."[49] Kindly Miss Smith, the Negro teacher who handled the racist imprecations of a difficult white parent with patience and wisdom in *Soap Box*, was playing not only the role of the teacher but also the voice of reason and conciliation, displaying the exact qualities that Kennan ascribed to the United States and which made it an exemplary model of democratic statehood—patience, dignity, and integrity.

## THE EXAMPLES TALK BACK

Critiques of the burden of example setting gathered force within the broader U.S. discourse on race and racialization throughout the 1950s, but they remained largely absent from on-screen discussions of intergroup relations. There was, however, one notable exception: a controversial 1959 essay film called *The Cry of Jazz*. Although it aired on U.S. TV only once, excerpted on Boston station WHDH-TV in 1959, its producers—four young black men from Chicago who formed a production company called KHTB—saw the film as a commentary on the liberal pieties that frequently characterized movies made for discussion in civic and cultural education contexts.[50] The film is about the conflicts that explode during an interracial discussion at a meeting of the Parkwood Jazz Club. The wooden acting of the young, semiprofessional cast is highly reminiscent of an educational film's staged role play, but the dialogue exudes a level of antagonism rarely, if ever, encountered in the genre. Whites protest the idea that only Negroes could have created jazz, accusing blacks of "always singing the blues." Blacks tell whites that they have no souls, that they are not and never can be human. Alex, a black jazz arranger who serves as the de facto narrator, lectures the young white audience in the film with acid condescension, demolishing their suppositions about rock-and-roll, the liberal idea of sameness under the skin, and the authenticity of white jazz. These didactic discussions are interspersed with performance footage of Sun Ra and other musicians, and scenes in which the camera roams lyrically through the vernacular landscape of black Chicago life, visiting jazz clubs, barbershops, churches, and pool halls, as well as apartments where living conditions bear witness to the degradations of poverty. Alex's voice-over annotates these images with a complex and esoteric theory, at once musicological and cultural, that locates both jazz and Negro experience in the tension between structure and play, the escapist reward of the eternal present, and the legacy of suffering.

*The Cry of Jazz* took the conventional roles of the intergroup relations film and rearranged them to expose the implicit hierarchies on

*The Cry of Jazz* upended the conventions for showing interracial discussion in educational film and television. Staged as a meeting of the Parkwood Jazz Club, the film's scenes of open racial animosity are orchestrated by the supercilious character of Alex, who lectures the group about jazz and Negro suffering while politely informing white members that they have no souls.

which they rested. The character of Alex embodies both the role of the expert within the film and the figure of the Negro truth teller, and transforms both of them entirely. Instead of serving as the liberal exemplar of common humanity, he takes the position of the provocateur, doggedly asserting that American Negroes' experience of suffering and oppression renders them fundamentally different from white Americans. It is a schism that the film never resolves. Bemoaning exemplarity, "the terrible burden the Negro has in trying to teach American whites how to become human," Alex proposes that "America's soul is an empty void," asking, "Where else does its future image as a world power reside but in the dark soul of the Negro?" This concluding question, posed over a slow zoom into the face of a carved African statuette, references the Cold War politics of expediency in which the need to solve America's international image problem motivated the push to solve its segregation problem, the image serving as a reminder of the rising tide of decolonization and the demands of the nonaligned movement. But the instrumentalist logic of expediency has been inverted by this point in the film. Invoked at the conclusion of Alex's invective, this mainstream argument for integration seems to serve primarily as a legitimizing vehicle for black expressions of rage, demonstrating

the falsehood of the assimilationist liberal creed of sameness under the skin.

The film was immediately controversial. Numerous educational groups, jazz appreciation clubs, and film societies rented the film, but many who saw it worried that it was divisive.[51] The *Christian Science Monitor*'s Robert Colby Nelson echoed the pervasive mainstream concern when he asked nervously, "Will this bring enlightenment or just more upset thinking about racial affairs?"[52] One educator suggested that the film could have a positive impact if "an exceedingly experienced and competent person (discussion leader) is present to ameliorate different and conflicting viewpoints"—a suggestion that denied any pedagogical authority to Alex, who leads the discussion in the film.[53] And although many critics and audience members appreciated the jazz interludes in the film, they were horrified at the wooden acting in the discussion scenes. Jazz writer Leonard Feather described them as "clumsy (especially the girls)" and "offensive."[54]

But if the discussion group scenes were maddening, they were undeniably part of the educational film format, and in keeping them in the film, the KHTB team ingeniously managed to both attract and antagonize a cluster of target audiences in the 16mm film distribu-

tion market. Indeed, the Parkwood Jazz Club's Northern, middle-class, college-age whites (Parkwood is clearly Hyde Park, the mixed South Side neighborhood surrounding the University of Chicago) are a mockery of the very demographic that would account for the bulk of the film's viewers—it was apparent to the KHTB team early on that screenings at educational institutions would outnumber all others by far.[55] They gave the group's white actors ridiculously pat lines of dialogue that reduce them to mouthpieces of liberal orthodoxy: "America needs the Negro to teach us how to be American, right?" asks sympathetic, moderate Faye, later proposing that "jazz and the Negro could win friends for this country more readily than other things we're doing in the Cold War." The unpleasant Natalie is the most cartoonish figure of the lot: "What's this, a Mau Mau meeting?" she shouts. "This is nothing but black chauvinism!" "It's black Americanism," Alex spits back. Such antagonistic depictions of the film's viewing demographic, along with the musical interludes and the roving scenes of Chicago life, distinguished *The Cry of Jazz* from standard intergroup relations films. But perversely, the discussion scenes actually helped the film achieve the intergroup relations goal of setting an example, albeit on an entirely different level. Judging from the accounts of participants and eyewitnesses, the group discussions that took place around screenings of the film uncannily mirrored those modeled within it: strident and defensive, with everyone talking at once.

The KHTB team clearly relished the arguments that erupted at actual screenings of the film. Their letters back and forth between New York and Chicago are full of gleeful anecdotes recounting particularly pitched discussions in which the object is clearly not group understanding but victory in a battle of wits. "I was quite jovial and polite in kicking their asses," Ed Bland told fellow producer Mark Kennedy after a particularly heated discussion at the Playboy Jazz Festival.[56] In Bland's depictions, the discussions associated with the film were not so much an exchange of ideas as a heated battle between profoundly incompatible points of view. "When they went musical I scared them off and when they went cultural Mark scared them off + at times Mark and I switched roles," Bland wrote to Hill after a 1960 screening at the Cinema 16 art house in New York. "After a while [jazz historian Marshall] Stearns sat there mouth ajar as Kennedy and I poured point after point after point."[57] Approaching the concept of roles in discussion not as vehicles for increased interracial understanding but as tools for scoring points, Bland communicates the degree to which *The Cry of Jazz* mounted an elaborate spoof on, and intervention in, the discussion culture in which it was destined to circulate.

This evident enjoyment in provoking scenes of outrage among *The Cry of Jazz*'s white audience members suggests that the film was, in fact, an insurrectionist weapon aimed at liberal projects of media governance. It provided a means for avenging the toxic burden of exemplarity that white liberals frequently placed upon their black interlocutors. Indeed, it seems very likely that the audience whose consciousness was most affected by the film was ultimately other black people who, like the KHTB team, were getting very weary of being asked to set good examples. In a letter telling Bland he would try to come to Chicago for one of the film's premiere screenings, Kennedy registered his distaste at the idea of entering the screening space, a community organization on the South Side called the Abraham Lincoln Center: "Ugh! Horrid joint! Full of social workers and Unitarians, or is it the social group workers in the vineyard and fellowship for ethical reconciliation? We may be compelled to crawl, but must we actually creep, before walking?"[58] This dissatisfaction with the culture of liberal race relations was radicalizing black intellectuals elsewhere in the cultural sphere at the same time. Harold Cruse, with whom Bland and Hill co-authored a treatment for their never-produced second film, was one of them; Amiri Baraka was another. Interviewed in 1984, Baraka credited the film with raising his consciousness of the relationship between racial identity and aesthetics.[59]

## CULTURE TALK

As this praise suggests, *The Cry of Jazz* was not simply an effort to expose the presumptions of white liberal educational media. Its core principle, central as well to the work of Baraka, Cruse, and others, was the idea that arts and culture were vital for the development of black political consciousness. In this respect, it paid obeisance to another form of media governance common in the postwar period: the use of cultural programming to elevate the sensibilities and broaden the intellects of mass audiences. Alex's lengthy, often arcane disquisition on the progressive stages of jazz makes the connection clear, as it drew, with neither spite nor irony, from the conventions of the straightforward humanities lecture film, common throughout the period. These were films provided to educational and public service TV by such popular pedagogues as Frank Baxter, a Shakespeare professor from the University of California, or Professor Mortimer J. Adler, whose local San Francisco public service TV program, *The Great Ideas* (KGO-TV, 1952–53), was syndicated to educational stations throughout the 1950s. They too were produced with the idea of discussion in mind—especially Adler's program, which directly encouraged viewers to share their thoughts about the concepts he lectured them about, and to write to him with questions about their meanings.[60]

Indeed, the character of Alex, whose extended lecture on jazz as "the constant creation of new ideas" structures the film, often sounds a lot like a politicized, musicological version of Adler. In his TV program, Adler staged a series of Socratic dialogues for viewers at home, enlisting Lloyd Luckman, a dean at City College of San Francisco, to role-play the part of interlocutor. Luckman took to the part of the querulous sidekick with gusto, while Adler, a stocky, beady-eyed man with bee-stung lips, delivered erudite glosses on classic texts, always in complete sentences and without the benefit of cue cards. Unlike *Soap Box*, which used role play to replicate, if only awkwardly, the flow of everyday conversation, Adler and Luckman used the technique to converse on such Great Ideas as love, democracy, language, and leisure, demonstrating the "great conversation" of Western civilization

in action. In a program devoted to the question of how to learn from discussion, the two men showed viewers the right and wrong ways of conducting civil conversation. "Now Mr. Luckman and I aren't actors," Adler told the audience, "but I think we can show you what we mean. I make a long speech at you, Lloyd, not to you, but at you." Luckman squirmed theatrically as Adler talked, then said: "Yes, and while you're talking I'm waiting in a fidgety sort of way for you to finish, so that I can go on saying what I was saying before you started talking."[61] Adler even went so far as to lecture viewers about how to watch television, demonstrating it himself by looking at selected educational broadcasts on a TV in the studio and pointing out ways he and Luckman might discuss the programs with each other.

Like Adler, Alex adopts a professorial persona as he explains jazz and black culture in terms of abstractions—"the contradiction between freedom and restraint," "the Negro's eternal re-creation of the present." Like Adler, Alex categorizes and classifies ("two types of rhythm . . . exist simultaneously in nearly every bar of jazz"), drawing upon universals ("a rhythm of stress and one of length . . . characteristic of Negro music throughout the world"). And like Adler watching educational television with the viewer in order to compare different

His shelves laden with copies of the Great Books, Mortimer Adler provided viewers of *The Great Ideas* with written instructions on how to conduct themselves during group discussion.

styles of screen pedagogy, Alex invites the viewers of *The Cry of Jazz* to listen with him to the sounds of black jazz and white jazz, the latter a sprightly and soulless romp that sounds like the theme song from a game show.

Despite the obvious differences between the two philosophers, the film's art direction provides some grounds for drawing the comparison. Assuming that Parkwood is Hyde Park, the home of the University of Chicago and the milieu where Adler's Great Books schemes were hatched, it seems only fitting that the set decoration of the apartment (presumably it belongs to Alex) includes a shelf of identically bound and lavishly embossed volumes. Judging by their size, these were not actual copies of the *Great Books of the Western World*, a series compiled by Adler with former University of Chicago president Robert M. Hutchins and marketed to cultural aspirants by Encyclopaedia Britannica. Still, Alex's books, their embossed covers announcing their status as great works, signify culture with a capital *C*, along with the abstract art on the walls and the African statuette on the bookshelf. This décor materialized the aspirational approach to books and art associated with the Great Books movement. But as with everything else in *The Cry of Jazz*, Alex's Adlerian persona and the cultural

legacy he narrates is an inversion of white liberal axioms. If Adler's liberal education was an effort to resurrect the dead thinkers of centuries past, Alex's discourse ultimately advances the proposition that jazz, and the great Negro ideas it contains, is dead: "Jazz is dead because ... the strangling image of a futureless future has made the Negro a dead thing too." And while Adler spurned historical contexts in his exploration of ideas, Alex never fails to bring history back into the picture, speaking with devastating directness of "the outrageous savagery of white Americans." He focuses our attention on the future too: jazz, he tells the stunned white members of the Parkwood Jazz Club, "is merely a faint glimpse of something with colossal power which is arising."

The musical history recounted in Alex's lecture stands as a pointed retort to Adler's cultural pedagogy, as black figures were entirely absent from the intellectual and artistic legacy the latter devoted his life to preserving. Adler was conspicuously silent on matters such as racial prejudice and school segregation in the 1950s, even though he expended considerable energy fostering discussions devoted to education in that period.[62] He certainly had no time for the idea that black people might have contributed something to the Great Books and

Great Ideas projects. As late as 1990, Adler defended the total absence of black writers in a new edition of *The Great Books of the Western World*, making the preposterous claim that "probably in the next century there will be some black that writes a great book, but there hasn't been so far."[63] As this remark suggests, Adler's Great Ideas and Great Books projects instrumentalized culture and discussion in very particular ways. Unlike intergroup relations leaders, Adler quite explicitly eschewed the idea that concrete solutions to immediate social problems could emerge solely from the interactions of individuals exploring their commonalities. As Dana Polan notes, Adler was interested in the supposedly timeless universals of Western thought as a means for testing "the historically contingent issues of the day."[64] But he shared with the producers of *The Cry of Jazz* the powerful belief that culture could be an engine for social change, and that didactic explanations of its meanings might shepherd the development of individual consciousness.

Testing this belief through experiments in moving images was a goal not confined to Adler nor, for that matter, to the KHTB team. Cultural uplift was a key instrument in fantasies of governing by television in the postwar period, shaping in particular the experiments in arts and culture undertaken by the Ford Foundation through its Television-Radio Workshop. *Omnibus*, the workshop's ninety-minute arts and education program, exemplifies the postwar ideal of culture instrumentalized in the service of Cold War liberal fears and fantasies about the perils of the mass. It is hardly a coincidence that Dwight Macdonald, the most vocal postwar critic of mass cultural appropriations of arts and letters, deplored the earnest didacticism he saw in Adler's writings and in *Omnibus* as well as in *The Cry of Jazz*, which he called "a wretched little hymn of racial snobbery."[65] What Macdonald deplored in all three was the way they solicited their audiences as inferior kinds of publics, substituting what he saw as a phony-baloney, vulgarized avant-garde for the kinds of culture that he believed might actually promote truly individualized selves. (Macdonald certainly would have had no truck with the liberal pieties and wooden performances of civic programs using discussion and role play.) As the next chapter details, the Ford Foundation's *Omnibus* embraced the middlebrow disposition that Macdonald abhorred, using it as a resource for improving television (and by extension, its audience) by exemplifying the levels of excellence that the medium could achieve. But this philanthropic excursion into popular media activated some key contradictions in Establishment liberal thought, particularly, as we shall see, when shifts in postwar race relations began to place pressure on the high-minded pursuit of cultural edification.

| | |
|---|---|
| We dissolve to last of kids coming in the door to the classroom and we follow them as they take their seats. | No violence the first day stories for the newspaper Now the real problems beg |
| The teacher looks over his class. | An integrated class... |
| We see blocks of negroes together and blocks of whites together. | ...with the worst kind of segregation...self segreg |
| C.U. teacher. | What do you do?  Mix them Seat them alphabetically? Lean too far forward, or far backward? |
| We see the class waiting for the teacher to begin. | |
| Teacher sits on the edge of his desk. | TEACHER:  (lip sync)

This is Civics 1.  We're to be studying government local, state and national We're going to look at th under which we govern our in a democracy. |

issolve to last of kids
ng in the door to the class-
and we follow them as they
their seats.

teacher looks over his class.

ee blocks of negroes
ther and blocks of whites
ther.

teacher.

ee the class waiting for the
her to begin.

her sits on the edge of his
.

No violence the first day...no
stories for the newspapers...
Now the real problems began.

An integrated class...

...with the worst kind of
segregation...self segregation.

What do you do?  Mix them up?
Seat them alphabetically?...
Lean too far forward, or too
far backward?

TEACHER:  (lip sync)

This is Civics 1.  We're going
to be studying government --
local, state and national.
We're going to look at the rules
under which we govern ourselves
in a democracy.

*Chapter Three*
# THE ENDS OF THE MIDDLEBROW

PEOPLE HAVE been trying to reform television since practically the day it was introduced. The story of their efforts is, in some respects, the story of the wishful fantasy that how people think, behave, and conceive of themselves can be molded with the methods and content of TV programming. It is a powerful idea because it often feels uncontestable and true. For instance, I myself believe that American voting practices would change if campaign advertising were banned and candidates were granted equal amounts of free airtime, and I have yet to hear arguments that might convince me otherwise. However, in the first years of commercial television, liberal reform fantasies crystallized not around voting practices but around another aspect of citizenship, namely, the possibility that Americans were unprepared and uneducated when it came to meeting the challenges and responsibilities of the postwar world. Brooding over the possibility that escapist popular culture and narcotizing mass entertainment might fuel the insurgent, antimodern energies associated with American populism, many Cold War liberals believed that some kind of cultural readjustment was necessary to prevent mass culture from "paving the way for totalitarianism," as one critic hyperbolically claimed.[1]

Among the organizations that set about addressing this problem, the most prominent—and certainly the most capable financially—was the newly formed Ford Foundation. Its 1949 mission document, referred to as the Gaither Report (after RAND corporation head Rowan Gaither, who headed the commission that produced it), called on the Ford Foundation to use mass media for "the rapid and extensive education of adults about the world situation, the nature of the struggle in which we are engaged, and the heritage we are seeking to defend."[2] A classic text of Cold War liberalism, the Gaither Report asserted the interdependence of capitalism and democracy, proclaimed the sovereignty of the individual, and called urgently for action in the face of impending Armageddon. It recommended that the Ford Foundation invest its funds in five areas: "the establishment of peace, the strengthening of democracy, the strengthening of the economy, education in a democratic society, and individual behavior and human relations."[3] For the foundation's officers, a technocratic nongovernmental elite whom Dwight Macdonald called "philanthropoids," the future of global governance rested on the wide dissemination of the Gaither Report's internationalist vision.[4] "The American people are the most powerful in the world," wrote Ford Foundation officer Robert Maynard Hutchins in a letter to Hollywood producer Jack Skirball. "If they are unenlightened," he continued, "they will be the most dangerous people in the world."[5]

However, Hutchins and other advocates of preemptive television reform were not motivated solely by elitist anxieties about the popular classes. The push for early intervention also grew out of the negative example set by radio over the previous decade and a half. Proclaiming the industry's failure to provide educational programming in radio, educators went to battle against commercial broadcasters at the end of the 1940s, determined to secure from the Federal Communications Commission more frequencies for nonprofit TV stations.[6] Ultimately, their efforts to expand educational broadcasting were of limited success; in the face of FCC indifference, the Ford Foundation and other philanthropic organizations stepped in, allocating increasing levels of funding to the nonprofit educational stations that would later form the basis of the public television network. But the foundation did not abandon the possibility of reforming commercial television and its viewers. As a later chapter details, its independent subsidiary, the Fund for the Republic, devoted extensive resources toward reforming the coverage of civil liberties and civil rights in news and public affairs programming. And the foundation itself, at least in its early years, staked its reformist claim in the area of commercially sponsored cultural programming, hoping to raise levels of taste both in the audience and in the industry. The spread of consumer culture was a troubling phenomenon for philanthropoids, but for the liberal business leaders who sat on the foundation's first board of trustees it was also one of the signal achievements of the American free enterprise system. Rather than oppose the rise of consumer society, they sought to activate commercial TV's democratic promise. In 1951 the foundation's trustees authorized the establishment of its own Television-Radio Workshop, an agency that would produce commercial programming designed to encourage higher standards on for-profit channels, thus demonstrating that "educational and cultural values can achieve a large audience."[7]

The decision to commit extensive resources to a project aimed at improving commercial television from within was a curious one, given the despair surrounding radio. Some foundation officers questioned the wisdom of the workshop from the beginning. "To what extent are we committed to 'baby' the industry?" asked Hutchins. "The worst thing the Ford Foundation can do is to regard our relations with the industry as so important and delicate that we fail to promote competition with it and criticism of it."[8] Yet although such reservations would prove persistent, they did not interfere with the Television-Radio Workshop's ambitions in commercial TV, which crystallized in one notable and well-publicized intervention in mainstream programming practices: the ninety-minute arts and culture program *Omnibus*. A fixture of Sunday afternoon television throughout the 1950s, *Omnibus* aired on CBS between 1952 and 1956, moving to ABC and then NBC before its cancellation as a regular series in 1959.[9] Critics were full of praise for the program. Jack Gould of the *New York Times* called it "sweeping and imaginative," and Jack O'Brian of the *Journal-American* pronounced that "it might very well be the best television program ever produced."[10] To this day, *Omnibus* is remembered fondly as a symbol of the aesthetic ideals of early of television. In 1999, Hume Cronyn hosted a documentary on public television entitled *Omnibus: Television's Golden Age.*

The Television-Radio Workshop's head, Robert Saudek, announced his determination to set new standards for commercial television when, on the eve of its first broadcast, a workshop press release quoted from the Gaither Report to explain that the program was "the first major implementation of a mandate of the trustees that 'the Foundation will support activities directed toward the effective use of mass media for non-academic education and for better utilization of leisure time for all age groups.'"[11] The program was not, host Alistair Cooke firmly told viewers in an April 1955 broadcast, a program designed only for "a superior type of city person." Rather, he explained, "more people watch 'Omnibus' on the prairies and in the suburbs than in the big cities. We are very proud of that statistic and proud too that the pump priming of the classics that 'Omnibus' did three years ago has now made it a regular thing to see ballet and Shakespeare and classical tragedy on any network." *Omnibus* thus invited viewers to imagine not only how television might be better but also how they themselves might be better if only they seized the chance at self-improvement through culture that it offered.[12]

## THE POLITICS OF MIDDLEBROW CULTURE

It is in the halls and offices of the Ford Foundation, both luxuriously carpeted in a décor Dwight Macdonald mocked as "both sumptuous and democratic," that the story begins.[13] Paul Hoffman, the first president of the Ford Foundation and the former administrator of the

Marshall Plan, sounded very much like an activist for educational broadcasting when he called on the foundation to fund the Television-Radio Workshop. "It may not be too late to save television from the fate of radio," he wrote in a telegram sent to the trustees from the foundation's first headquarters in Pasadena, California. "In view of the tremendous power of the medium, the cultural and perhaps even the political fate of the country may be affected, if not determined, by what is done with television."[14] But although Hoffman's words were rhetorically similar to calls for educational television circulating in reform discourse at the time, the Television-Radio Workshop was conceived in explicit *opposition* to educational broadcasting. The workshop was the idea of an advertising executive named James Webb Young, a vocal ideologue for corporate liberal leadership. The founder of the Advertising Council and public relations advisor to Hoffman at the Marshall Plan (the two met as members of Roosevelt's Business Advisory Council), Young was greatly admired by businessmen and public relations professionals for his passionate speeches advocating "socially responsible capitalism."[15] He strongly opposed the allocation of broadcast frequencies to educational organizations, maintaining that educators, unlike commercial broadcasters, were not good at holding "non-captive audiences."[16] Young conceived of the Television-Radio Workshop as the solution to the aesthetic shortcomings of educational broadcasting. The trustees' funds, he argued, would contribute far more effectively to the reform of television if used to finance programming for commercial channels.

Young's argument for foundation involvement in commercial TV reflected his long-standing commitment to example setting as a mode of liberal self-regulation, a commitment manifested in his original vision for the Advertising Council as a means for demonstrating the spirit of voluntarism in American business (thus warding off direct government intervention and regulation).[17] By establishing a presence on the air, he reasoned, the foundation could "provide independent leadership, in the form of encouragement, example, and study, as a forceful means of supplying television with standards of service and performance."[18] The implication, of course, was that this would make government intervention unnecessary and disarm the educational television lobby. To run the workshop, Young hired Saudek, a former ABC public affairs producer. *Omnibus* was Saudek's idea, and he sought to embody Young's ideal of corporate liberal cultural leadership in its funding structure. The program's production costs were split between the foundation and a roster of commercial sponsors, in the hope that the harmonious collaboration between profit-making organizations and philanthropic ones would show the FCC, the broadcasting industry, and the viewing public that public service and commerce were not incompatible goals.[19]

In developing *Omnibus*, Saudek had in mind a kind of television that did not obey the rigorous segmentation and codes for continuity established by radio. Sometimes the program's entire ninety minutes were taken up by an opera; on other occasions, it presented several short segments of irregular length, often, but not always, linked by a theme. Film and live material were mixed together, with continuity provided by the program's host, British expatriate journalist Alistair Cooke, who introduced and commented on segments, occasionally participating in them. The idiosyncratic form of the program makes it difficult to write about, a problem compounded by the fact that copies of *Omnibus* are difficult to find today. Saudek's estate has placed restrictions on the show's commercial exploitation. Until recently it was only in archives, although a documentary produced in 1999 captures some of its flavor.[20] A further difficulty is the fact that the program covered an immense and diverse range of material; indeed, it is impossible to summarize in a few sentences the kinds of works it featured. A very partial list would have to include lectures on music from Leonard Bernstein, specially commissioned works by writers such as James Agee and William Saroyan, condensed versions of classic opera, and films and studio segments designed to expose American viewers to forms of culture from around the world: Indian music and dance, Japanese Noh theater, and Yugoslavian ballet, among others. *Omnibus* also featured scientific films on topics such as X-ray technology and undersea exploration (including the first American broadcast of Jacques Cousteau's film work) and, as a bonus for advertisers, five-minute "economic education" films that were essentially public relations commercials masquerading as industrial documentaries.

Its deliberate effort to appear different from other television programs, emphasizing cultural material that fell outside the broadcast mainstream, made *Omnibus* easy to mock. Radio comedian Henry Morgan captured the program's occasional pretensions when he imitated the stagey Britishness of host Alistair Cooke introducing "a Melanesian ballet based on the dithyrambs of Rabindrinath Tagore." Combined with spoofs of the show's commercials (ads for yogurt, pearl, and bacterial cultures), Morgan's send-up poked fun not only at the program's content but also at its uneasy synthesis of artistic expression and commercial speech.[21] The parody was also a razor-sharp critique of the sometimes tedious seriousness of "culture" as a category of TV programming. And indeed, it must be said that although some parts of *Omnibus* are riveting, especially when viewed in the solitary darkness of a media archive, others compel the viewer to grope guiltily for the fast-forward button. A hodgepodge of aesthetics and attitudes, the program moved, at times very self-consciously, between reverential museum pieces and the kind of formulaic eccentricity typified by Saroyan's dramatic style. It was overloaded with Americana (Agee's dramatized biography of Abraham Lincoln, Archibald MacLeish celebrating Grandma Moses, a ponderous documentary reenactment of the writing of the Constitution), while its segments showcasing overseas cultures sometimes came off as an invitation to wonder at the strange ways of foreigners. And, as advertisers never ceased complaining, it contained entirely too much ballet.[22]

But any individual's opinion of what was good or bad about *Omnibus* may differ sharply from someone else's, and this was in fact the point of the show. At the center of Saudek's vision was a determination not to appeal to all viewers at the same time but rather to provide—consistent with the meaning of the show's Latin title—something for everyone. And indeed, for every misfire there were plenty of moments that fulfilled the program's promise of a different kind of television: an excerpt from Roberto Rossellini's 1950 film *Flowers of St. Francis*, which used real friars as actors and had virtually no dialogue; a sequence in which

Gene Kelly worked with famous athletes, including Sugar Ray Robinson and Mickey Mantle, to turn actions such as throwing a punch or swinging a baseball bat into dance moves; a production of Oscar Wilde's *Salome* starring Eartha Kitt. Moreover, despite Morgan's comedic disparagements, there is something admirable about *Omnibus'* dogged insistence that commercialism and cultural uplift could coexist. While critics, notably Macdonald, railed against the dilution of high culture and its instrumentalization for self-improvement and profit, *Omnibus* flew the middlebrow flag with pride.[23] Saudek embraced the term, characterizing *Omnibus'* audience as members of the middlebrow, rather than the highbrow, in order to reassure the network and potential sponsors that the program would remain within the acceptable aesthetic boundaries of commercial television.[24]

Although identifying with the middlebrow was a convenient way to assuage fears about the program's appeal, the strategy made *Omnibus* subject to the political and aesthetic demands the period placed upon middlebrow culture. The middlebrow, as Marianne Conroy notes, was a hopelessly compromised mode of cultural consumption in the postwar years, required to be "at once politically effective, morally responsible, and culturally respectable."[25] Charged with the task of communicating the responsibilities of postwar citizenship to the populace while prevailing upon commercial television to be less commercial, *Omnibus* was squeezed into the shifting, contested space between popular and elite realms, and it was often compromised as a result. While comedians lampooned its pretensions, elite critics judged it to be facile and pedestrian; Macdonald, for example, observed that the program "has a disturbing habit of falling flat on its face when it tries to soar."[26] In many respects, the problem was similar to that faced by public television programmers a decade and a half later. As Laurie Ouellette notes, programs such as *Public Broadcasting Laboratory*, which tried "to fuse mass political enlightenment to the aesthetic cutting edge," inevitably found themselves without an audience, criticized from all sides.[27]

The comparison with public television is appropriate. *Omnibus* is often considered a template for the programming practices of PBS.

The latter also combined corporate and foundation funding, emphasized the presentation of great performances, and (in a more associative way) employed Cooke as an urbane, interpretive host (he was the *éminence grise* of *Masterpiece Theater*, a PBS staple throughout the 1970s and 1980s).[28] Both, moreover, were products of a cultural oligarchy committed, Ouellette points out, to making "elite culture and knowledge ... available to all Americans."[29] While the comparison makes sense, this should not obscure the ways that each was very much a product of its particular time. At the moment it was founded in the late 1960s, the public television system reflected the Great Society period's hospitality to federal involvement in culture. Moreover, its hopeful vision of the future was tinged with fears that the New Left and black power radicalism, if not contained within pluralist frameworks of representation, might demolish existing cultural hierarchies.[30] *Omnibus'* political motivation, in contrast, was to maintain the separation of culture and state; recall that for James Webb Young, reforming commercial television from within was a way of staving off government regulation. Moreover, if PBS looked toward the future, *Omnibus* looked back, with a certain amount of anxiety, at the past. For Cold War liberals, state-administered culture (at least within the borders of the United States) was associated with the threateningly redistributive energies of the New Deal. By including commercial sponsors, *Omnibus* affirmed the cultural values of capitalism in the wake of the Depression and in the face of communist alternatives. Although it shared some qualities with PBS, it was ultimately the product of a peculiarly postwar vision of a cultural front purged of its populism and restaffed with a Cold War liberal elite.

Another important distinction between the goals of *Omnibus* and those of PBS lies in the motivations behind its instrumentalization of culture. In the early Cold War period, culture was a tool of national security, valued for the connotations of freedom, creativity, national identity, and self-realization attached to it as a concept at the time. As a number of historical studies have shown, foundations, the State Department, and the CIA collaborated in promoting American arts and letters overseas, hoping to demonstrate the fertility of cultural life in the free world to European intellectuals who might be inclined to reject the ideological precepts of capitalist democracy.[31] *Omnibus* represents a less well-known form of interventionist culture: the privately financed domestic project that sought to complement these international programs in cultural diplomacy by refashioning the intellectual landscape of the American interior, attempting to make good on U.S. claims for the moral and cultural superiority of capitalist democracy.[32] Both categories were integral to the Cold War policy of containment. When containment's architect, George F. Kennan, advised the Ford Foundation on how to proceed in its goals of establishing peace, he recommended against any direct propagandistic offensives against communism or the Soviet Union. It would be far more helpful, he argued, for the foundation to initate long-term projects that were not overtly ideological. Cultural sponsorship was one component of this strategy, which he defined, according to foundation officer Dyke Brown, as "U.S. self-improvement [and] promotion of free inquiry and expression throughout the rest of the world."[33]

It was because of its emphasis on self-improvement that middlebrow culture became an important weapon in the cultural Cold War's home front.[34] Not simply an orientation toward arts and letters, the middlebrow is a philosophy of conduct that correlates closely with an ideal system of government through culture in which citizens strive constantly to improve themselves.[35] *Omnibus*, more than any other specimen from the archives of postwar uplift, was a concrete embodiment of the instrumental liberal philosophy of cultural consumption as a path to self-governance based in developmentalism, rationality, and balance. These values were amplified in contact with the structures of commercial broadcasting. Television was perceived as a medium in its "infancy," facing an important stage of development (a similar logic applied to its audience too); it was targeted by modes of reform that stressed the elevation of reason over mindless entertainment; and it was committed, ostensibly at least, to ideals of fairness and balance enshrined in its professional norms and enforced, supposedly, in federal policy. From its theme music, adapted from Bernstein's *Age of Anxiety*, to the economic education films through which the foundation's corporate partners spoke to its audience about the benevolent goals of North American capitalism, its meanings overdetermined by the psychological and economic demands of containment, *Omnibus* epitomized the cultural dimensions of Cold War governmentality.

The two kinds of reform the program was supposed to carry out— the liberal internationalist vision of U.S. self improvement through culture, administered in a top-down fashion by TV, and the corporate liberal faith in television's capacity to improve itself—were two fundamentally different approaches to television as a medium of unofficial governance. *Omnibus* could not help revealing their incompatibility. It was fairly easy to follow through on the goal of changing TV's aesthetic standards, and it was not too difficult to think about international cultural programming as a way of leading viewers away from populist positions such as isolationism. But trying to reconcile the

Initially, the Ford Foundation's media advisors conceived of commercial television as a way of fighting the Cold War on the home front, providing enlightenment and intellectual stimulation for a population they feared would be seduced by mindless entertainment and fall into an illiberal or hysterical populism.
*Image courtesy of the Ford Foundation Archives.*

hopelessly contradictory meanings of democracy circulating in official U.S. discourse at the time, most evident in the contrast between the ideals of the free world and the unfree realities of black Americans in the Jim Crow South, was another thing entirely. The language of television entertainment and the pedagogical address of the middle-brow were ill-equipped for the task, especially when rising voices of desegregation and decolonization promised to expose these contradictions on local and global levels simultaneously. Taken in turn, two segments—a dramatic rendering of agricultural reform in India, and an adaptation of *Uncle Tom's Cabin*—provide instructive examples of the ways that *Omnibus*, and the Television-Radio Workshop's staff, tried to negotiate the contradictions within the Cold War liberal project.


## VILLAGE INCIDENT: INDIA

Although they were rarely identified as such, *Omnibus* occasionally ran pieces that promoted the work of the Ford Foundation, and in the summer of 1953, workshop staff perused reports from the foundation in search of material for such a segment.[36] Their choice, a piece on agricultural development in India, was a timely one. Secretary of State John Foster Dulles had visited India and Pakistan in May, and the two nations' struggle over Kashmir was headline news. That fall, relations between India and the United States would become considerably strained after the *New York Times* reported that Washington was weighing the question of military aid to Pakistan, a nation strategically located in relationship to the Persian Gulf, China, and the Soviet Union.[37] Moreover, India's neutralism and its leadership in the growing nonaligned movement posed a potential threat to U.S. interests in the region and, more generally, to the efficacy of containment. The question of Indian morale and U.S. attitudes toward India was therefore of utmost importance in U.S. foreign policy circles. Given this situation, it was probably inevitable that the communist proclamation, attributed to Lenin, that "the road to Paris leads through Peking and

Calcutta" would become the ultimate Cold War cliché. Tirelessly repeated by men such as Chester Bowles, former U.S. ambassador to
India, it was a shorthand warrant for the argument that intensive philanthropic and government aid to India was the best way of turning the
nation against communism.[38] Ford Foundation officers and trustees
largely agreed with this view, awarding India more grants than any
other "less-developed" country in the 1950s.[39] Under Hoffman's leadership, the foundation granted $1.2 million to Jawaharlal Nehru to fund
rural development via a series of village-based projects in the state of
Uttar Pradesh. Administered by Douglas Ensminger, the foundation's
representative in India, these projects were collaborations—not always
smooth—between U.S. social scientists and representatives of Indian
universities.[40]

From the Ford Foundation's perspective, the goal of the village-level
grant initiative was to strengthen India's commitment to democracy
by raising standards of living and literacy levels. For workshop staff,
it was good television material. The story of the modernization of an
Indian village promised both to engage television audiences and to
impress upon them the geopolitical importance of international development. It was, in Saudek's words, "an interesting focal point . . . as
it personalizes a story, and gives Americans an idea of the relative position of such countries in the march of progress."[41] As they began to
develop the segment, the workshop staff turned to Bowles and Ensminger for advice. At Ensminger's suggestion, they hired a playwright
named Arnold Sundgaard to dramatize some aspect of Indian life in
the postindependence era.[42] It made sense that Ensminger would rec-
ommend Sundgaard for the job. Both men were former New Dealers;
Ensminger had worked in New Deal agricultural projects throughout the 1930s, and Sundgaard was a veteran of the Federal Theatre
Project. The short play he scripted for *Omnibus*, entitled "Village Incident: India," drew on the Federal Theatre Project's experimental
staging techniques to present a snapshot of Indian village life while
teaching audiences about such issues as literacy, religion, and land
reform. Described by workshop staff as a "dramatic documentary,"
the piece aired on March 1, 1954, as part of a program that included

two short films, a children's fantasy story from Denmark, and an adaptation of a John Steinbeck story starring Thomas Mitchell.[43]

Half lecture and half drama, "Village Incident" is a curious artifact of Cold War visual culture. This is in part because of its innovative staging, which lifted Popular Front techniques out of their original, politically radical context and adapted them for liberal internationalist pedagogy. But it is also because of the ambivalence it manifested concerning possible parallels between social progress in India and America. In part, this ambivalence stemmed from the way it represented racial otherness. In casting white actors to play Indian villagers, the production team could not hope to give viewers an accurate sense of the people whose lives were actually being changed by international development grants. Instead, they seemed to rely upon conventions for the representation of the Eastern Other that were then active in U.S. popular culture. When I first watched "Village Incident," I was surprised to find that elements of its mise-en-scène, most notably makeup, gesture, voice, and costume, were highly reminiscent of the pastiche science fiction serial *Captain Video and His Video Rangers*, which aired daily on the DuMont network between 1949 and 1955. The white actors in brownface who play the villagers do not try to approximate Indian accents. Instead, like the vaguely Orientalized space aliens of *Captain Video*, they intone their lines in a stiff, declamatory style. Sundgaard's dialogue adds to this impression. When a teenage boy played by Mark Rydell rushes on-screen to announce the arrival of Gandhian land reformer Vinoba Bhave (who had recently been featured in *Time* magazine and whose name they pronounce in Latinate fashion as "Baharway"), he declaims awkwardly: "Have you heard the news? Bhave is coming to town, this very day, I tell you!"

As this dialogue might suggest, "Village Incident" (like *Captain Video*) borrowed lightly from the conventions of the Hollywood middlebrow, particularly the epic genre. (Bhave, played by Everett Sloane, wears a biblical-looking headdress that certainly would not seem out of place in the epic context.) It was less indebted to contemporaneous representations of India in mainstream cinema—a lush filmic world of bodice-ripping bandits and British soldiers—although at times

Sundgaard's script seemed to draw on viewers' familiarity with these Hollywood versions of Indian history as well.[44] He rewrote a complex situation detailed in Ford Foundation grant reports that concerned farmers who refused to replace wooden plows with iron ones for fear of offending the carpenter caste making it into a scene in which a blacksmith won't touch a tractor because he believes it has been greased with animal fat.[45] This was clearly a reference to the bullets greased in lard that sparked the Sepoy Rebellion, a well-known event in colonial history that had been dramatized recently in a Warner Bros. film entitled *King of the Khyber Rifles* (1953)

Such moments of cultural license suggest that explaining India's developmental "challenges" for a U.S. audience in 1954 required some significant translation. To explain the issues at stake, Sundgaard drew, on the "Living Newspaper" technique associated with the New Deal's Federal Theatre Project, which presented research in public health

Playing land reformer Vinoba Bhave in *Village Incident: India*, an experimental live docudrama about post–independence India, Everett Sloane wore a headdress that seemed more Biblical epic than South Asian.
*Drawing by Bill Vourvoulias.*

and community government as experimental drama via stylized staging, projected images, and other innovative effects. Thus, in between scenes written in declamatory "Hail, centurion" dialogue, the de facto narrator of "Village Incident," Tarlok Bhajvar (played by E.G. Marshall), uses stylized slides projected on scrims in the darkened studio, giving viewers an informal lecture on the geopolitical and historical context shaping rural Indian life. Sundgaard also used a device unique to the television age: the voices of hypothetical viewers, who announce themselves as a husband and wife watching in Roanoke, Virginia, and who interrupt the action with questions about references they don't understand. But the kinds of issues raised by these viewer stand-ins required some delicate handling, as they invited an uncomfortable connection between the social hierarchies in faraway India and the racial hierarchies of the American South. When asked about independence from Britain, for example, Tarlok hesitates and replies that before 1947 India was "some say 'with,' some say 'under' the British."

E.G. Marshall, playing Tarlok, *Village Incident*'s narrator, spoke directly to the camera using a chalkboard and slides projected onto scrims to explain post–independence India to a hypothetical viewer asking questions from Roanoke, Virginia.
*Drawing by Bill Vourvoulias.*

This equivocal explanation of the relationship between British colonial power and the subjugated population of India reads as an attempt to be fair, accommodating imperialist ideology by presenting a "balanced" perspective—even though independence had surely rendered such judiciousness unnecessary.

For viewers alert to the demands for balanced viewpoints in broadcast news coverage, this presentation of "both sides" of the colonial argument might have recalled the language of balance and neutrality that television networks, anxious not to alienate Southern audiences, demanded of journalists covering civil rights.[46] And indeed, a subsequent scene demonstrates similar circumspection when parallels between caste in India and segregation in the United States insinuate themselves into the script. During a lengthy explanation of programs to increase sanitation, literacy, and life expectancy in India, Tarlok is interrupted by a member of the untouchable caste reluctant to enter

*Village Incident* used the projected image of a stick figure to explain literacy levels in India—the crudely drawn boots represent the proportion of the population capable of reading and writing.
*Drawing by Bill Vourvoulias.*

the village hall. Tarlok invites him in, saying, "There are no signs on these doors." Sangat replies, "There is caste, Mr. Bhajvar." In response, Tarlok gives him a little lecture: "There are no buildings you cannot enter now. But you have an obligation too. You must learn your rights! And practice them!"

This brief exchange, painting a somewhat rosy picture of the abolition of caste in postindependence India, makes the issue of U.S. civil rights impossible to ignore. Written signs forbidding entry were an institutionalized form of discrimination associated not with the caste system but with the Jim Crow South and South African apartheid. This reference, coupled with the fact that the segment has already explained the low levels of literacy in India (which would presumably make text an ineffective medium for demarcating caste-specific spaces), makes it clear that segregation is being invoked here as an oblique analogy to explain caste to Americans. But the analogy goes no further, despite the fictional viewer's request for more explanation. Tarlok merely explains that caste has existed in India for thousands of years, perhaps inviting comparison to the idea of segregation as entrenched Southern custom, and goes on to suggest that interested viewers seek out a book that explains it in detail. He produces a paperback copy of *In the Minds of Men* by sociologist Gardner Murphy, and holds it up to the camera so the audience can make a note of it. The choice of Murphy's book to explain caste politics is an interesting one; based on a UNESCO study commissioned by the government of India, it devotes an entire chapter to a forthright discussion of the similarities and differences between U.S. racial prejudice and the caste system. That "Village Incident" refers the viewer to a book rather than delving into the topic in detail suggests that primary responsibility for educating Americans about social inequality—whether at home or abroad—does not lie with the medium of television.[47]

This avoidance shows *Omnibus* uneasily skirting the contradictions between two narratives: the developmentalist story of the West's moral and material superiority, staged within the Cold War's international power struggles, and the decidedly regressive tale of U.S. racial politics in the twentieth century. "Village Incident" must represent

As if reluctant to discuss parallels between racial segregation in the United States and caste segregation in India, Tarlok responds to the hypothetical viewer's questions about caste by recommending a book published by the United Nations.
*Drawing by Bill Vourvoulias.*

India as a new state on the road to modernization and, implicitly, construct the United States as a nation that, because it is further along in the narrative of development, can help India along this path. If the analogy between race and caste were made explicit, then the developmental logic at work here would be reversed, clouding the optimistic, internationalist vision of postwar global order on which rested liberal aid policy. A sense of the undermining power of the race-caste analogy haunts another scene in which Tarlok holds up a text for the viewer to see. This time it is an issue of *Time* magazine from the previous year that features a cover story about Bhave. When I located the original issue, I discovered a diagonal strip on the left side of the cover announcing a feature story entitled "The U.S. Negro: A Decade of Progress." But the text was invisible on the cover shown in "Village Incident: India," at least in the videotape copy I viewed, leaving me wondering whether it had been covered over for the broadcast or whether the

Parallels between caste and racial prejudice haunted *Village Incident*. Tarlok held up to the camera a *Time* magazine cover featuring Bhave; obscured—possibly intentionally—is a diagonal banner announcing an article about racial politics in the United States.
*Drawing by Bill Vourvoulias.*

resolution of the kinescope was simply too poor. This small moment of undecidability is entirely appropriate, however, as it encapsulates the hesitancy with which the program hints at the race-caste analogy; still, even if it only hovers on the threshold of explicitness, it undermines the story of progress and democratization that "Village Incident" works so hard to tell.

It is thus fitting that "Village Incident" resolves the paradox that racial prejudice introduces into its narrative of progress by referring the viewer to further reading. The gesture at once fulfills *Omnibus'* avowed mission of reaching middlebrow audiences, a mission most closely associated at the time with the pursuit of learning through the great books program devised by Mortimer Adler, and allows the program to evade the question of race. But it is fitting in another sense too. The middlebrow ideal of self-improvement, in which individuals actualize their citizenship by making up their own minds through directed reading, mirrored the dominant ideology of U.S.-India relations, in which policy elites advocated an approach to economic development and bilateral geopolitics that affirmed India's right to determine its own destiny—making up its own mind through nonalignment—while working assiduously, through channels such as development, philanthropy, and international exchange, to turn it away from the communist cause.[48]

This strategy of guided sovereignty and managed choice turns out to be central to "Village Incident" in another way too, as it is the basis of its explanation of property distribution in Nehru's India. Bhave's philosophy of land reform (which contemporary critics are apt to interpret as political quietism) advocated individual actions, rather than state policy, as the basis for agrarian justice.[49] Thus, when Tarlok questions whether the equality outlined in India's new constitution can be achieved, Bhave tells him to have faith in the work of human beings, explaining that he has taken on the task of walking from village to village, convincing landowners to donate some of their property to the landless. The kind of equality that Bhave espouses, involving a massive redistribution of wealth, might have struck viewers in 1953 as uneasily close to Maoist policies in communist China. But "Village Incident" is careful to distance the inherent collectivism of Bhave's proposals from communism, portraying him instead as a New Testament–style evangelist. As Bhave tells Tarlok, "I have come to loot your village through love." This statement, and indeed much of Bhave's mystical dialogue, is taken directly from the *Time* magazine article Tarlok references early in the segment, which reassured readers that Bhave's voluntarist approach to land reform is a way of preventing communist penetration of village governance.[50] At such moments, the televisual middlebrow's emphasis on combining print and visual media works as a form of domestic containment, anticipating and preempting alarm on the part of the Cold War viewer that the Ford Foundation might be giving aid to people working to destroy the private property system.

The tightly constrained treatment of collectivism in "Village Incident" illustrates the distance between the Cold War cultural governance of *Omnibus* and the Popular Front performance sensibilities it tried to adapt. If Federal Theatre Project performances dealt with "neglected publics"—workers, black Americans, ethnic minorities— and sought to raise issues for discussion, "Village Incident" addressed the generic mainstream that was signified in the very concept of the "television audience" and alluded to risky subjects in order to manage them rather than motivate further questions.[51] It even asked the questions itself. Still, there is no guarantee that such efforts at textual containment succeed. The hesitant and uneasy treatment of caste prejudice and race might prompt viewers to think about forms of internationalism quite removed from the kind the Ford Foundation's philanthropoids had in mind. Desegregation activists had already established connections with India's nonviolence movement through movement leader Bayard Rustin, who traveled to India in 1945 to observe civil disobedience in action. Moreover, Tarlok's reference to a book based on the UNESCO study of caste might easily recall controversies around national systems of racial discrimination that occurred in the first years of the UN's founding. Most notably, it might recall India's 1946 complaint against the treatment of Indian laborers in South Africa, which led the South African government to appeal to an embarrassed U.S. delegation for support, citing their mutual interest in containing the "race problems" within their borders.[52] In short, the segment's discussion of the social revolution in India could raise the possibility of further revolution, perhaps an international movement of angry global citizens of color. Such a possibility might have occurred to viewers who tracked down the issue of *Time* in which Bhave appeared, reading in the threatening conclusion of the article on "Negro progress" that "the majority of the world's peoples, whose skins are colored . . . judge the U.S. very largely on evidence drawn from the 'Negro Problem.'"[53] Two years later, when the Bandung conference in Indonesia brought international visibility to the nonaligned movement, this statement would be confirmed.[54]

It is impossible to know whether the workshop was actively attempting to avoid the implications of such judgments by submerging parallels between caste and civil rights in "Village Incident." Most likely it sought to avoid controversy, and indeed, regardless of intention, the segment was well received as an example of innovative television. Elizabeth Forsling, a critic hired by Saudek to write weekly reviews of the program for the workshop's self-assessment, praised it for its "enlightening experimentation." "India is a problem both to itself and the rest of the world," she wrote. "'Village Incident' was a lucid and gripping explanation of some of these problems and of some work toward their cure—told in a manner new to television."[55] But if Forsling failed to discern a civil rights parable on this occasion, it is interesting to note that a little over a year later she was more than ready to read one— and denounce it—in her review of the *Omnibus* adaptation of Harriet Beecher Stowe's *Uncle Tom's Cabin*, calling it "the most notable piece of Northern propaganda ever written."[56] This broadcast, which aired in April 1955, was arguably the most controversial segment *Omnibus* aired, and it is certainly the closest the program came to a direct statement about Southern race relations. If, as I have suggested, the effort to create a global civic awareness in "Village Incident" foundered upon the contradictions of domestic race relations, then the *Uncle Tom's Cabin* adaptation is an opportunity to examine what happened when *Omnibus* looked back on the history of those relations through the prism of a text that was itself a cultural artifact of governance, its status as such assured by the oft-repeated anecdote of President Lincoln greeting Stowe as "the little lady who started this great war."

## REWRITING *UNCLE TOM'S CABIN*

Professional adaptations of *Uncle Tom's Cabin* were scarce in the 1950s, even though the decade marked the one hundredth anniversary of its publication. This no doubt reflected increasing unease with the degrading minstrelsy of the Tom show that remains the novel's most enduring theatrical legacy, as well as growing resistance among black Americans to Stowe's depictions of slaves. In his 1949 essay

"Everybody's Protest Novel," James Baldwin condemned the book for its "self-righteous, virtuous sentimentality," seeing the emasculated and dehumanized figure of Tom as evidence of the extent of white racial fear.[57] Baldwin's assessment marked, as Linda Williams points out, "the definitive end of the popular appeal, to blacks or whites, of a novel whose martyred main character's name had now become an epithet of servility."[58] Aside from the *Omnibus* production, written by Ellen M. Violett, only one other new adaptation appeared in U.S. popular culture in the 1950s (as far as I can tell): the "Small House of Uncle Thomas" number in the 1951 Rodgers and Hammerstein musical *The King and I*.[59] The number clearly owed more to the tradition of the Tom show than to the original novel, although it was also very much a product of its time.[60]

In the fall of 2008 I met with Violett, who was in her early twenties when she wrote the script, to discuss her motives and goals in adapting the novel for television. As she explained, her goal was to exclude the more sentimental moments by confining the narrative to the middle section of the novel, which focuses on Tom's time with the St. Clare family. The action begins with Tom meeting little Eva on the steamboat (in the original she falls overboard and he rescues her, but this does not happen here). The remainder of the adaptation covers three major narrative events in the novel: Eva's death from consumption and St. Clare's promise on her deathbed that he will free Tom; St. Clare's sudden death in a tavern brawl shortly thereafter; and his wife Marie's decision to sell their slaves, culminating in the auction at which Legree buys Tom. Violett's adaptation deliberately omitted the sensationalist set pieces of the novel's theatrical history. There were no bloodhounds chasing terrified Eliza across the ice. The notorious whipping scene was omitted.[61] And Topsy, as Michelle Wallace has pointed out, was played "by a little black girl of about ten, quite convincingly, . . . with none of the comedic business of most prior Topsys."[62] Instead, the script stressed the interpersonal tensions within the St. Clare household. It focused on Marie's malingering and her callousness toward the household slaves, and it devoted extensive screen time to St. Clare's arguments with his abolitionist cousin Ophelia, for whom he purchases Topsy (partly out of pity for Topsy and partly out of a desire to unmask Ophelia's hypocritical aversion to the slaves whose freedom she advocates). A coda shows Shelby, Tom's first master, on a steamship accompanying Tom's body home to his plantation in Kentucky.

The idea of an unsentimental *Uncle Tom's Cabin* may seem unlikely, but it was nevertheless what Violett had in mind as she drafted the script. She had first encountered the story as a theatrical production for children, but after rereading the novel at the invitation of *Omnibus* producer Paul Feigay, the segment's originator, she found the novel to be "extraordinarily good social comment on human beings."[63] As she explained to Feigay, she had removed the "excesses in sentimentality" in order to reclaim *Uncle Tom's Cabin* from the canon of children's literature and foreground the psychological dimensions of slavery developed in the book. If previous stage adaptations used the character of Legree to convey the immorality of owning slaves, Violett located the moral problem in the character of St. Clare, the benevolent but ineffectual and dissolute master whose inaction and untimely death send Tom to the auction block and from there to Legree. For Violett, the sensationalist scenes of violence associated with Legree distracted attention from the horror of "the thing itself"—slavery— which depended for its existence "not only on the brutish tyrant, but on the most civilized, intelligent, and generous of the white masters."[64] The great-granddaughter of a New Orleans slaveowner who had freed his slaves, Violett was interested in the moral corruptness of the St. Clare figure, a man who knew that slavery was wrong but did nothing to end it. She saw the story of his inertia as an opportunity to debunk the myth of the kindly slaveowner, and thus to speak to contemporary audiences about the perniciousness of ongoing illusions about race in American culture.[65]

The removal of sentiment from *Uncle Tom's Cabin* was, in several respects, the embodiment of midcentury ideas about how people's exposure to culture could shape their conduct and attitudes. To begin with, it brought the novel in line with Cold War liberalism's dominant literary aesthetic, a system of moral and artistic values that is

-2-

▉ think most of her plot twists are concessions to the periodical she published it in. But if the emphasis was properly construed again, it seems to me, the book could be removed from the class of children's fiction where it does not belong (children would have no use for anything in it but the angels and the sadists). I have always heard it spoken of as a sort of Negro "Black Beauty" Whereas it is really extraordinarily good social comment on human beings -- at its best.

Violett was insistent in articulating her vision of a de-sentimentalized, and thus more timely, adaptation of *Uncle Tom's Cabin*.
*Image courtesy of Ellen M. Violett.*

most famously embodied in the writings of Lionel Trilling and which orbits somewhat obsessively around the question of how good literature might teach self-governance, or as Trilling called it, "moral conscience." As Trilling argued across the essays collected in the 1950 volume *The Liberal Imagination*, literature's capacity to stimulate moral conscience lay not in muckraking genres, nor in the social realism of a Dreiser, but rather in the psychological complexities associated with writers such as Henry James.[66] *Uncle Tom's Cabin* is often considered the epitome of the didacticism that Trilling despised, although his brief assessment of the novel, a breezy encyclopedia entry, was relatively mild compared to George Whicher's 1948 dismissal of the book as "Sunday school fiction."[67] Baldwin, of course, was the most vocal critic of the book's political and aesthetic values, charging that it, and all "protest novels," rested on an "ideal of society [as] a race of neatly analyzed, hard-working ciphers." The protest novel's failure, he concluded, lay "in its rejection of life, the human being, the denial of his beauty, dread, power, in its insistence that it is his categorization alone which is real and which cannot be transcended"—an assessment that had an obvious affinity with Trilling's views on literature.[68] Vio-

OVERALL NOTE

I have attempted the treatment so ewhat in the style of the
original, barring only the real excesses in sentimentality
for which the book is already too well known.

What it not known for, at least not to me, is the high
level of its observations on the effect of slavery not only on t
negro, and not only on the brutish tyrant, but on the most
civilized, intelligent, and generous of the white masters.

om's first master was an inept farmer who could not make thing
and thus sold Tom to clear his mortgage. He no more wanted
lose Tom than he wanted to lose his only plough; additionall
nd his wife were distressed at parting this way with this
of whom they were fond. But, Tom belonged to Mr. Shelby
erefore pressed to the wall Mr. Shelby could sell Tom.
om's last master, Simon Legree, could kill Tom. And d

In Ellen Violett's *Omnibus* adaptation of *Uncle Tom's Cabin*, the moral dilemma of the story revolved around the delusions of kindly master Augustine St. Clare rather than vicious sadist Simon Legree, turning the play into a commentary on postwar "gradualist" philosophies of integration.
*Image courtesy of Ellen M. Violett.*

lett's antisentimental adaptation of *Uncle Tom's Cabin* can be seen as a recuperation of the novel, bringing it in line with the values that Baldwin and Trilling espoused, although she insists to this day that her script's stripping away of the novel's sentiment merely revealed the psychological complexity inherent in the original work—a justified assertion in terms of its middle section.[69]

Violett's elevation of psychology over sentiment in *Uncle Tom's Cabin* made the book more relevant to the period's arguments about the origins of racism, which often turned on the problem of individual and group psychology, as we saw in the previous chapter. Violett drew an explicit parallel between the two periods in her notes to Feigay: "The same arguments seem to be going on today between St. Clares and 'Vermonts'" (St. Clare's abolitionist cousin Ophelia is from Vermont). In focusing on St. Clare's failings and his flawed, "too little too late" benevolence, she signaled her adaptation's connection to sentimental political education strategies employed by the abolitionist movement, and in so doing she also mounted a rebuttal of arguments for gradual reform that would try to address the excesses of Jim Crow while preserving its essence. At a time when racism became increasingly defined as a "psychological and interpersonal challenge . . . that was irrational and would surrender to logic," Violett's depiction of white southern interiority as painful and contradictory would have been recognizable to the liberal viewer as a parable and a warning.[70]

I was that viewer when I watched Violett's adaptation at the Library of Congress, and I could see that it would be easy to interpret the play as an indictment of Jim Crow. It begins with a male voice on the soundtrack singing a spiritual accompanied by a guitar—an instrumentation that recalls the folk music of the mid-1950s—followed by a sequence in which a female voice reads from Stowe's original introduction over shots of a hand writing. She mentions the importance of states' rights and worries that "this matter is dangerous to investigate." I also felt that the adaptation largely succeeded in its antisentimental aesthetic. Boosted by the strong performance of James Daly, who played St. Clare, it struck me as a spare, tightly structured psychological portrait of a man in the grip of self-deception. Only Lynn Loring's performance, which brought a saccharine touch to the role of Eva despite Violett's efforts to make the character "slightly more of this earth than the original," recalled the conventions of the novel's dramatic history.[71] Tom, played by John Marriott, has far less screen time than the white characters, his marginality perhaps an acknowledgment of the character's problematic status as a figure of black masculinity.

On the night that the segment aired, Cooke's short introduction was clearly intended to anticipate and defuse strong reactions among viewers. Calling the book "violent . . . sentimental and . . . one-sided" the acknowledgment that there was another "side" was surely inserted for the benefit of Southern patriots—Cooke reached into the middlebrow vocabulary of cultural authority to legitimize the broadcast, describing the novel three times as a classic. The point of reviving it, he told the audience, was not to "pump up any emotion left in a political issue [i.e., slavery] that is surely dead" but rather "to show you another side, to get away from the melodrama of this great classic." Violett's adaptation, he explained, was simply "a little psychological drama about a Southern family and their real troubles." The eradication of sentiment thus allowed Cooke, speaking as the official voice of *Omnibus*, to tell the viewer that the broadcast was not a political statement but rather a pedagogical opportunity, an invitation to see what happens to the familiar melodramatic story of *Uncle Tom's Cabin* when it is adapted to fit the realist conventions of "quality" television drama.

Violett did not intend her exploration of psychological realism to draw upon the didactic resource of the middlebrow, an endless reserve of comparing and contrasting. But the segment's aesthetic distance from both the original and its theatrical history, creating opportunities for pedagogical reflection, provided a useful justification for the workshop's decision to take *Omnibus* on an allegorical foray into the political challenges of the period. This what-if approach was characteristic of many *Omnibus* segments, which often strove to give people a fresh look at the classics. (A striking one, included in the 1994 documentary, has Leonard Bernstein corral a cast of professional musicians on a floor-size enlargement of the score of Beethoven's Fifth Symphony, demonstrating to viewers what an earlier draft of the symphony, incongruously featuring a flute, would have sounded like.) Racial politics, it seemed, could only be presented to *Omnibus* viewers via a process of cultural discernment, in the interests of making good television—"let's see what an unsentimental version of *Uncle Tom's Cabin* would look like" (as opposed to Violett's more politicized "look how even the best and most liberal Southern slaveowners fed the corruption of the system"). The impossibility of a more direct approach was made clear in late 1954, in the workshop's response to a program suggestion from the American Jewish Committee. The committee had requested that *Omnibus* address the "psychology of race prejudice" in a panel discussion about "the problems that will be posed, and the scars that will be inflicted, during the struggle to implement the desegregation decision of the Supreme Court," but Saudek flatly refused. His reasoning, as another staff member explained, was that "*Omnibus* is primarily entertainment and has been from the beginning."[72] Saudek was wary of the "pious sermon," and although he did admit to feeling "an obligation to do something in this field," Violett's version of *Uncle Tom's Cabin* was the closest that *Omnibus* ever came to fulfilling that obligation.[73]

This disavowal of politics in the face of obvious political allegory highlights the exceptional nature of the *Uncle Tom's Cabin* broadcast. It would be unusual for any entertainment program to address the desegregation struggle in the South—even allegorically—in early 1955, during national anticipation of the *Brown II* decision calling for "all deliberate speed." But it is especially notable that the program in question should be *Omnibus*, with its high-profile foundation sponsor. Philanthropic organizations were even more avoidant than commercial television when it came to political controversy. Quietism was voluntary on the part of the networks (and economically expedient in relation to sponsors and Southern affiliates), but it was a legal mandate for philanthropies. The Revenue Act of 1934, restructured in 1954, prevented tax-exempt organizations from engaging in activities that sought to influence legislation, distribute propaganda, or express support for a particular political candidate. In the summer of 1954, when workshop staff planned the upcoming season and contracted Violett to write her adaptation, the second of two congressional hearings into the influence of foundations on the American way of life was in progress. The investigation, led by U.S. Representative B. Carroll Reece (a Republican from Tennessee), focused intensely on the Ford Foundation. Although the commission and its charges of subversion eventually would be discredited, the hearings were under way as Feigay and Violett worked on the *Uncle Tom's Cabin* draft, and one of the commission's targets was foundation activity in U.S. race relations, specifically the Carnegie Corporation's hiring of Swedish sociologist Gunnar Myrdal to study the forms and consequences of racial segregation in the South.[74] *Omnibus* was the public face of the Ford

Foundation for many Americans, and steering clear of any material that could be interpreted as propaganda was surely a priority.[75]

If Cooke's nervous disclaimer was intended to counter any suggestion that the Ford Foundation might be trying to influence the government of race at this critical juncture, it could not forestall audience outrage. During rehearsals, in anticipation of negative reactions from black viewers, the production team had excised the word *niggers* from a line uttered by Simon Legree. John Marriott, who played Tom, had suggested substituting *blacks*—according to Violett, the term was at that time almost as offensive—but at the insistence of a workshop staff member, most likely producer William Spiers, the line was cut altogether.[76] Given the novel's reputation as a source of racial stereotypes, however, the very fact of the broadcast was enough to prompt complaints. When Frederick O'Neill, founder of the American Negro Theater, found out about the production (he was originally offered the part of Tom, Violett speculates), he tried to convince Feigay to abandon it. On the day the show aired, he assembled a large group of black actors at his home in Harlem to view the broadcast. As it turned out, their reactions were largely favorable. One member of the group, actress Rosetta Lenoire, wrote a note to Violett praising her "divine adaptation."[77] In the end, the most vocal protests against the broadcasts came from other fronts. Ford Motor Company dealers protested after the program aired, presumably because they thought it would hurt their sales, and Saudek's in-house critic, Elizabeth Forsling—taking it upon herself to speak for the South—reacted with fury that *Omnibus* would choose to air the segment "at a time when the Negro problem, in the segregation issue, is so much before us again, at a time when old, old wounds are about to break open again."[78]

The most vigorous protest against the broadcast came from the Daughters of the Confederacy. Hearing of the segment in advance, President General Mrs. Belmont Dennis sent a telegram to Henry Ford II asking that he cancel it, claiming that the book "slanders the South."[79] Mrs. Beale J. Faucette of the New York division wrote in also, predicting that if the show aired, it would "cause ill feeling and resentment against the Ford Foundation and Ford Motor Company that might never be erased."[80] Saudek explained to them both that the drama was a "newly written" and "carefully edited" version, reassuring them that a "clarifying statement [placing] the story in its proper historical context" would precede the play.[81] Tellingly, he also indicated that the workshop had taken extra measures to defend against charges of propaganda. Reminding them that *Omnibus* had recently broadcast a segment entitled "The Four Flags of the Confederacy," paying "tribute to the courage and gallantry of the South and its heroes," Saudek hinted that *Omnibus* had strived to present a balanced viewpoint on the historical question of slavery.[82]

Decades later, during the recording of his Ford Foundation oral history, Saudek was asked about the segment on the history of the Confederate flag, and he denied that the piece was meant to balance *Uncle Tom's Cabin*. But the records of the workshop indicate otherwise.[83] In December 1954, the workshop staff seemed to be considering the idea of canceling the Stowe adaptation. In his letter rejecting the proposal for a panel on desegregation from the American Jewish Committee, staff member Max Wylie explained that "it is our present fear that over the segregation problem now so quickly developing that extremists will take a real tough look, no matter how it were written—of anything that we put on the air in the way of 'Uncle Tom's Cabin.'"[84] However, the following February, a little over a month before the adaptation was scheduled to run, Wylie sent Saudek a memorandum entitled "the saving of UNCLE TOM (via a pro-confederate feature)." Saudek's penciled marginalia on the memo indicate the lengths to which he felt prepared to go in the effort to appease white Southern audiences. Attached to the memorandum were some suggestions from historian Milton Meltzer about possible visual material that would "make today's television audience eyewitness to the Confederacy's side of the battlefront." Next to the suggestion that the segment focus on the battle of Gettysburg, Saudek wrote, "But CSA lost!" On the front of the memo, his annotations suggested that the staff explore the possibility of featuring "a conf. bk or something . . . cf-able [comparable] to Uncle Tom?"—a somewhat unworkable suggestion, as such a literal "balancing" of *Uncle Tom's Cabin* with a book that was comparable to it would mean giving credence to the proslavery position.[85]

The impulse to balance the political viewpoints contained in a century-old novel speaks not only to the book's continued relevance in the 1950s but also to the complex political work carried out by the concept of balance in postwar public culture. The archival record does not reveal the source of the idea that *Uncle Tom's Cabin* required balancing, although it is clear that the decision to run the piece on the Confederate flag was made in a hurry (the segment aired with only a month's planning). It is possible that foundation officers or a sponsor insisted on it, but there is no evidence to suggest so. The order is equally likely to have come from CBS, although the creation of balance was certainly not a regulatory requirement in the context of *Omnibus*: the 1949 Fairness Doctrine, which mandated that broadcasters cover controversial issues and air opposing viewpoints, applied at the time to news and public affairs programming, not entertainment.[86] Still, as Violett pointed out to me, there would not necessarily *be* any evidence. "Kowtowing to blacklist pressure was *routine* and *secret*," she stressed, suspecting that the balancing acts required by the *Uncle Tom's Cabin* adaptation were also likely to have been performed under deep cover. Political censorship, she explained, "didn't just vanish with McCarthy's disgrace, not with Richard Nixon around and JFK's attorney general, Bobby [Kennedy], having been former minority council at McCarthy Committee hearings."[87]

Ultimately, the source of the directive to balance *Uncle Tom's Cabin* is less important than the assumptions about racial politics that it reveals. Under the Fairness Doctrine, balance involved the presentation of contrasting views on controversial issues and its purpose was to create an informed citizenry. Programming a segment on the history of a flag's design was a curious interpretation of the principle—how, exactly, would it provide a counterweight to a polemical work of literature? The flag and the book were cultural forms identified with historically opposed political positions, but they were not in any sense representative of a dialogue, and their juxtaposition was less an application of a rule than a kind of preemptive effort to avoid alienating Southern segregationists. Moreover, the controversies in which the book was embroiled went beyond two sides, its depictions equally reviled by blacks and by pro-Confederate whites. Any adequate means of balance would not only have to voice the Confederate position, it would also have to address the contemporary black critique.

Saudek's misguided interpretation of the concept of balance highlights the generative inexactness of cultural forms as resources for civic pedagogy. The vague, pro forma nature of the balance supplied by the flag segment freed *Omnibus* to speak about contemporary race relations in a progressive political voice. "The Four Flags of the Confederacy" looked backward, pandering to Southern nostalgia and memorializing those who suffered in a bloody war, whereas *Uncle Tom's Cabin* allegorized the racial struggles of the past as lessons that might apply to the present. Although the two might seem to balance each other, their juxtaposition created a forward-looking sense of political change. Yet the terms in which this vision could express itself ultimately were dependent upon the mutual compatibility of middlebrow cultural formulae and the system of commercial television. Like commercial TV, the middlebrow was bound by a logic of equalization. As cultural historians have noted, it strived constantly to mediate between impossible positions, "to balance demands for accessibility with quality and to reconcile authority with democracy," and stressed such ideals as fairness and objectivity in the assessment of literary works.[88] Because it was interested in demonstrating the compatibility of culture and commerce, *Omnibus* reinforced rather than challenged the political quietism inherent in network television's preoccupation with balance; if the adaptation of *Uncle Tom's Cabin* managed to make a covert statement about racial politics, the conditions of its broadcast foregrounded the limits of the workshop's vision of change from within.

The balancing of *Uncle Tom's Cabin* is instructive because it points to the continuities between strategies for governing television and strategies for governing the nation. After all, in the postwar period the metaphor of balance was not simply part of the self-regulatory framework for commercial broadcasting, it was also central to the rhetoric surrounding the new mandate of racial integration in public education. The balanced viewpoint was an ideal frequently invoked by segregationists and their gradualist allies, no doubt because it provided a way of factoring their views into the calculus of interest group politics, premised on the idea that balancing extremes ensures an even distribution of power favoring the center.[89] But it was also an integral part of the executive approach to integration; appointees to Eisenhower's 1957 civil rights commission, for example, were drawn from "both sides" of the segregation issue.[90] As this might suggest, Eisenhower tended to honor the segregationist point of view even after segregation was declared unconstitutional, and despite the fact that its supporters increasingly resorted to violence. *Brown* lawyer (and later Supreme Court justice) Thurgood Marshall wrote to Eisenhower in 1956 to point this out, complaining that the president's characterization of anti-integration violence as the responsibility of "extremists on both sides" equated "lawless mobs with federal courts." These, he explained acidly, were the "only two [sides] involved."[91]

Thus, although the "balanced viewpoint" sought by the workshop may have been an effort to keep the Ford Foundation out of politics, it depended, ultimately, on a rhetorical strategy that was deeply embedded in the political culture of the period, a culture in which—paradoxically—the language of fairness and consensus was also the language of conflict. This politicized strategy of depoliticization may seem like a contradiction, but it is more properly understood as a marker of television's unsettled place in the peculiar form of nongovernmental governance that characterizes philanthropic work. Restrictions separating philanthropies from the political sphere do not so much keep foundations out of politics as they enable them to serve as institutions of "unofficial government," as one turn-of-the-century civic leader put it.[92] Analogous to the separation of powers through which the state regulates itself internally, the restrictions on tax-exempt organizations define the complementary fields of governance in which philanthropic and state power operate. Put another way, the tax law's demarcation of the point at which private activity begins and state power ends creates a symbolic threshold in a broader continuum of rule.

The equivocal treatment of racial politics on *Omnibus* highlights television's ambiguous place on this continuum. Although the rhetoric of the Gaither Report may have positioned the medium as a conduit between official and unofficial government and between state authority and civil society, *Omnibus* demonstrated that TV's civic capacity was stretched to the limit by the national crisis of racial inequality.

The constraints on *Omnibus'* ability to speak about racial politics were symptomatic of the quandary surrounding governing by television in which the workshop staff found themselves. In trying to balance *Uncle Tom's Cabin* and hinting hesitantly at an analogy between Jim Crow and the Hindu caste system, *Omnibus* was also trying to balance divergent conceptions of nongovernmental governance associated with philanthropy and commercial broadcasting. Each obeyed a distinct sense of how to inhabit the thin space of rule between state and private sectors. Ruled by the demands of sponsors and affiliate stations in the South as much as by federal regulation, broadcasters' expectations of neutrality conformed closely to the centrist logic of the Eisenhower administration's inertial racial politics. This accommodating stance was compatible with the Ford Foundation's interests insofar as it provided protection against charges of political interference, but it was fundamentally incompatible with the foundation's direct, top-down ideal of changing the nation by changing commercial television. The representation of racial injustice in *Omnibus* was shaped by inchoate tensions between visions of governing by television in the philanthropic and broadcasting professions that would ultimately make that mission impossible to sustain.

## "IT AIN'T THAT GOOD AND NEVER WAS"

Throughout its existence *Omnibus* was plagued by conflicts between the industry-oriented focus of the workshop staff, committed to the idea that commercial television could be made better, and the philanthropic vision of Ford Foundation officers, whose approach to media reform reflected broader ideas about how to remake the American citizenry, ideas derived from the foundation's technocratic liberal model of citizenship education. Television production required, by necessity, a commitment to concreteness, a willingness to work within the confines of narrative and visual conventions. It was a form of public communication constantly balancing technical possibilities, budgetary limits, and a practical awareness of how audiences might think and react. Philanthropy, on the other hand, spoke to its public via a language Dwight Macdonald called foundationese: "a dead language, written rather than spoken, and designed for ceremony rather than utility. Its function is magical and incantatory—not to give information or to communicate ideas or to express feelings but to reassure the reader that the situation is well in hand."[93] Television, in the Ford Foundation officers' minds, was a conceptual instrument for assuaging elite fears about the inertial obstinacy of those they considered the masses, conveniently graspable in the collective noun of the mass audience, and not an ongoing form of cultural practice.

A deep-seated form of organizational culture clash ultimately undermined the process of bringing about edification through culture in the Ford Foundation's commercial television work. Saudek and his staff would endeavor to fulfill their obligations toward the foundation with segments such as "Village Incident: India," which combined formal experimentation with liberal internationalist didacticism, but they had little use for the officers' abstracted vision of television. Correspondingly, the kind of television they wanted to make, television that would break boundaries as an art form, had little relevance for the philanthropoids. Each group viewed the other with suspicion. Workshop staff members were uncomfortable with the high-minded organizational culture of the foundation. They parodied foundationese and its constant invocation of community and individual rights in their routine office communications—right down to the aggrieved "who ate my lunch?" kind of note.[94] And they invented their own names for the various divisions within the organization, calling the Fund for Adult Education, for example, the "Fund for Grown-ups."[95] Programming suggestions from foundation officers, especially when too overtly colored with Cold War ideology, were often peremptorily dismissed (someone, possibly Alistair Cooke, reacted to the suggestion that *Omnibus* present an adaptation of Orwell's *1984* with a scrawled note: "My idea of horrible").[96] The officers, in turn, were wary of ceding autonomy to Saudek in determining the direction of the Ford Foundation's television work, viewing the workshop as an anomaly in the foundation, an awkward reminder of the short-lived tenures of Young and Hoffman. They were also concerned that the existence of the workshop countermanded foundation policy, which stipulated that funds should be spent on grants rather than on operating programs.[97]

Indeed, although popular memory often enshrines *Omnibus* as a durable artifact of television's golden age, its future was threatened by foundation officers' ambivalence from very early on. Preparations for discontinuing *Omnibus* began in October 1953, as it entered its second season. Rowan Gaither, recently appointed foundation president, voiced his doubts about the program in a confidential memorandum to high-level officers, suggesting that they reach a decision about the workshop's future in three or four months.[98] In January 1954, foundation officer Milton Katz began the long process that would result in *Omnibus*' termination. He appeared at a meeting of the workshop's advisory board, directing a surprised Saudek to ask that its members discuss whether "*Omnibus* has met its objective of proving that middlebrow programs are commercially feasible" and suggesting that the program had reached "the point of diminishing returns."[99] In 1955, Saudek began negotiating the terms of *Omnibus*' separation from the foundation.[100] The deal would take another two years to finalize, a period in which relations soured considerably. In a set of handwritten notes jotted in preparation for the final meeting to decide the program's fate, foundation officer William McPeak wrote a biting assessment of the workshop on the back of a canasta score sheet, his anger apparent in the holes his pencil left in the paper. Describing Saudek as a careerist working not for the Ford Foundation but "for Saudek and the Saudek objectives for TV," McPeak concluded with a damning jab at the show itself, lapsing into colloquial language to emphasize his disgust: "Let's don't be beguiled with the omnipotent influence of Omnibus. It ain't that good and never was."[101] The foundation finally issued a terminal grant to Saudek for a new production company, Robert Saudek Associates, in 1957. *Omnibus* managed to find sponsors and a shared network time slot for another year, but after that it would appear only as an occasional Sunday special on NBC, finally disappearing from the air in 1961.[102]

*Omnibus'* cultural reform agenda drew on the principle of leading by example, and in this respect it seemed compatible with a broader postwar ethos, one that encompassed divergent political motives. Exemplarity was, as we saw in the previous chapter on intergroup discussion, a complicated realm of political action and rhetoric in this period. It was part of a pious white liberal discourse on black citizenship abhorred by J. Saunders Redding and others, but at the same time, it was central to the nonviolent movement's activist strategy.[103] It was also an integral motivation for Cold War liberalism's modest assault on the color line. Leading by example was a linchpin in the doctrine of containment—"to lead the Free World," notes John Fousek, "the United States would have to set a moral example the world could follow"—and the Eisenhower administration's minimal concessions to civil rights legislation were an effort to legitimize the nation's claims to geopolitical virtue.[104] Although workshop staff and foundation officers had divergent agendas when they conceptualized television as a vehicle for setting good examples, each understood the relationship between culture and citizenship in a kind of political vacuum, and their visions of governing by television thus failed to anticipate the challenges of postwar political culture.

The challenges were very apparent to Robert Hutchins, who never quite subscribed to the idea that improving television's cultural offerings or raising its audience's levels of taste was a legitimate civic practice. Hutchins' skepticism might be surprising—he was a long-standing admirer of, and collaborator with, Mortimer Adler, perhaps the most vocal exponent of the middlebrow cultural ideal in this period—but it is best understood as a reflection of his concerns about the postwar situation. Hutchins had no quarrel with cultural education, but he felt that the period's political problems demanded a more direct approach.

William McPeak was one of several Ford Foundation officers opposed to funding *Omnibus'* fifth season, jotting a damning assessment of the show on the back of a Canasta score sheet. *Image courtesy of the Ford Foundation.*

A less conciliatory stance toward the television industry, and a commitment to changing the terms in which it represented civic struggle, was vital. To the degree that he was interested in commercial television, Hutchins saw it as a crucial tool for raising awareness of the ongoing erosion of civil liberties precipitated by domestic anticommunism, and for educating citizens about the issues at stake in the ongoing fight for racial justice in the South. In 1954, when he left the

Ford Foundation to become head of its "wholly disowned subsidiary," the Fund for the Republic, he turned to television sponsorship as a vehicle for concrete intervention in the public debates about these controversial issues. Although the next chapter will raise questions about his commitment to the struggles of actually existing black people, there is no doubt that he thought it was crucial to remind American television audiences of the constitutional issues at stake, and to use the medium as an instrument for rethinking the mechanisms of democratic rule.

### Roll # One, Two and Three    (Talk)

ne One -- TALK BY CHAIRMAN OF STATE PUBLIC SERVICE COMMISSION WADE O. MAR'

REGARDING HIS VIEWS ON HOW TO ENFORCE SEGREGATION IN LOUISIANA.

### ROLL # 4 TRI -X

NE 2 -- SHOTS OF POLICEMAN CHECKING SIGNS AT BUS STATION

NE 3 -- SHOTS OF SIGN " WHITE WAITING ROOM "

NE 4 -- POLICEMAN CHECKING SIGN ON DOOR ENTERING WAITING ROOM.

NE 5 -- SIGN COLORED WAITING ROOM.

NE 6 -- SHOT OF BUS STATION SIGN.

NE 7 -- SHOTS OF BUS STATION BUILDING

NE 8 -- SHOTS OF BATON ROUGE SIGN.

NE 9 -- STREET SCENES AT BATON ROUGE.

We'd better got both sides

*Chapter Four*
# LIBERAL MEDIA

MANY AMERICAN intellectuals greeted the rise of commercial television with dark prophecy about the decline of civilization, but few
were as acidulous in their condemnation as University of Chicago
president Robert Maynard Hutchins. In 1951, as he prepared to leave
the university for his new post as an officer of the Ford Foundation,
Hutchins delivered a farewell address to undergraduates that warned
of "the horrid prospect that television opens up before us, with nobody speaking and nobody reading." Television, he predicted with characteristic hyperbole, would usher in "a bleak and torpid epoch . . . which,
if it lasts long enough, will gradually, according to the principles of
evolution, produce a population indistinguishable from the lower forms
of plant life."[1] Hutchins held to this opinion during his brief tenure at
the Ford Foundation, where he urged the trustees to invest in alternatives to network television, most notably nonprofit and educational
broadcasting. But his contempt for television was nothing compared

to his horror at what was happening to U.S. political culture in the early 1950s. While many liberal intellectuals and public figures were paralyzed in the face of congressional Red-baiting and the poisonous spread of the blacklist, Hutchins was unafraid of expressing his outrage—often in intemperate terms—at the unchecked disregard for civil liberties he was witnessing in government and in the media.[2] As soon as he arrived at the Ford Foundation he proposed that it establish a quasi-autonomous nonprofit organization to carry out research and to promote education in civil liberties and civil rights. The Fund for the Republic was incorporated in late 1952; in May 1954, Hutchins was appointed its president. By then he was convinced that some kind of mass media intervention was necessary in order to preserve the democratic freedoms enshrined in the Bill of Rights. Despite his continued distaste for TV, one of his first actions as head of the Fund was to appoint a television consultant.

Between 1954 and 1959, when it moved to Santa Barbara, California, to become the Center for the Study of Democratic Institutions, the Fund for the Republic spent around $9 million of its $15 million Ford Foundation allocation. Around $700,000 went toward its television projects.[3] These included a script competition, grants to independent producers and community organizations sponsoring local public service programs, and an array of television ventures that its officers commissioned themselves. In his uncompromising commitment to changing the political culture of the postwar United States, Hutchins did not hesitate to define the Fund's mission in terms co-extensive with that of American democracy: "We regard the sphere of operation of the Fund as including the entire field of freedom and civil rights in the United States and take as our basic charter the Declaration of Independence and the Constitution."[4] This mandate required a drastic overhaul of the country's media system, and from early on Fund officers envisioned their television work as a way of reforming the industry's existing methods of covering civil rights and civil liberties. Their first request to the board of directors for television funding explained that the money would be used not only to sponsor programs educating the public about "the contemporary situation with regard to civil liberties and racial and religious discrimination" but also to provide "assistance to networks and stations in the presentation of programs . . . that might not otherwise be shown," *assistance* being a politically safer term for a nonprofit's activities than *pressure*.[5]

For the officers of the Fund, the challenges posed by the Cold War and the color line made interpreting the Constitution, and the rights and responsibilities of citizens, a matter of immense moral and geopolitical consequence, and it was vital that the television industry fulfill its public service commitments in the realm of civic education. The failure of democratic institutions to protect civil liberties was, Hutchins declared, "a sickness afflicting our country." As is often the case with reform rhetoric, Hutchins considered the media industries to be both a cause of and a solution to the disease. "If our hopes for democracy are to be realized," he told an audience at the Sidney Hillman Foundation awards in 1959, "the media must supply full and accurate information on which the people can base their judgment on public affairs, and they must offer a forum for the discussion of those affairs."[6] The Fund under Hutchins pushed for educational programming in commercial TV that moved beyond the safe realms of religious and cultural affairs to address matters that concerned the very definition of democracy, and it tried to work with institutions of television news to incorporate a constitutional angle into coverage of political controversies.[7]

Broadcasters were disinclined to comply with Fund officers' reform agenda. The problem was not simply the Fund's place on the margins of the industry's power structure, it was also Hutchins' public persona. He frequently came off as dogmatic, inflexible, and elitist, leading Dwight Macdonald, himself an incurable snob, to conclude that Hutchins' effectiveness as a liberal advocate would always be compromised by his personality traits: "great verve and courage in pushing unorthodox and in general sensible ideas, combined with superficiality, arrogance, poor judgment about people, and a congenital lack of maturity both in understanding specific situations and effectively dealing with them."[8] The projects for promoting civic education through television that would prove to be the most innovative were grassroots local programming initiatives with which Hutchins was barely involved.

But while the history of the Fund for the Republic's television projects does not contradict Macdonald's assessment of Hutchins' fatal flaws, its telling will bear witness to the conceptual and institutional circumstances, more powerful than personality, that defined national liberal realpolitik in this period, blocking its progressive possibilities. Hutchins described the Fund as an "anti-absurdity project," implying that its target was antidemocratic extremism, although the absurdity it tackled was integral to mainstream politics. The protection of the free world provided a ready rationale for the suspension of democratic freedoms, while a distorted language of freedom was central to segregationist arguments for the preservation of the color line.[9] For the Fund, intervening in this pernicious discourse required more than simply promoting a return to the conceptions of liberty on which the Republic was founded. It also involved pointing out the hypocrisy of those perpetrators and apologists who invoked democratic freedoms to justify the blacklist and Jim Crow. This concern with unmasking hypocrisy fueled a sense of moral righteousness at the Fund, but it was an ill-conceived strategy for public education. Even though Fund officers turned to television as a means of making contact with the people, they were unwilling to relinquish the idea that the people were part of the problem. Ultimately, their experience with television shored up their sense of the liberal political project as a stance against irrationality, rather than a means for facilitating broad-based coalitions mobilized for social change.

Given the political climate of the mid-1950s, it is surprising that Fund officers ever entertained the possibility that television might help restore fading democratic principles. Tellingly, they spoke of hiring a "TV infiltrator, who might influence for the better programs now being produced, or the handling of issues by such programs, and who would remind people in the industry that the Fund was ready to provide assistance to programs in our field of interest."[10] As the espionage language indicates, broadcasting was not a hospitable institution within which to promote civil liberties and civil rights. Networks required loyalty oaths of their employees and accepted the tyranny of the blacklist with craven alacrity; voluntary self-censorship and military collaboration were the norm in television war reporting (the news department of at least one network, CBS, had close ties to the Central Intelligence Agency); and national coverage of emerging civil rights struggles conformed to invidious standards of "balance," in part because networks were concerned that Southern affiliates would refuse to carry such programs.[11] But these endemic problems in the television industry only increased the feeling among officers of the Fund that the medium was essential to their mission of educating Americans about the current crisis in American democracy. The goal, as one TV consultant put it, was "dropping an occasional idea into the kitchens of folks like my neighbor, who rarely, if ever, thinks about the Bill of Rights but who regularly watches her television machine."[12] Despite their own misgivings about the medium, Fund officers recognized that it was the most expedient and wide-ranging vehicle for spreading information about the causes supported by the Fund.

Publicizing these causes was important, Fund officers felt, because they were often ignored or distorted in mainstream media. Many of the organizations that received financial support from the Fund were considered controversial. In addition to television production, the Fund made large grants to the Southern Regional Council, an Atlanta-based civil rights organization, and financed the formation of a commission on race and housing. It also commissioned several studies, among them a two-volume account of blacklisting in the entertainment industry, a research project focused on federal loyalty programs, a study of right-wing extremism, and an analysis of fear in education. The Fund supported the American Friends Service Committee's legal defense fund for conscientious objectors and the Common Council for American Unity's work protecting the legal rights of noncitizens. It also ran a program for the widespread distribution of books and pamphlets on civil liberties. All of these projects dealt with matters of heated public debate, and after their first few board meetings the Fund's directors grew concerned that the kinds of appropriations Hutchins was asking them to authorize crossed the already blurred line between education and propaganda, jeopardizing the organization's tax-exempt status. The Fund's lawyers reassured them that convincing "large numbers of people that American concepts of freedom and democracy are as important in 1954 as they were in 1776" was not a violation of the tax law.[13] But moral righteousness was no guarantee against controversy, and indeed, for Hutchins and his staff it was a necessary by-product of their efforts to clarify the constitutional principles at stake in anticommunist ordeals and Southern segregation.

As it turned out, Hutchins overestimated the protective strength of the democratic truths he sought to revive, at least in the context of Cold War politics. From its inception, the Fund was the target of right-wing attacks. Hearst columnist Westbrook Pegler railed against its first president, a Republican congressman from New Jersey named Clifford Case, claiming that he was part of a "mysterious group in president-elect Eisenhower's headquarters" conspiring "to defeat anti-Communist candidates and all who stand against unrestricted immigration."[14] Radio commentator Fulton Lewis Jr. regularly assailed the Fund in his weekly broadcasts, and *Firing Line*, the American Legion newsletter, called the Fund "a huge slush fund for a full-scale war on all organizations and individuals who have ever exposed and fought Communism."[15] For years congressional investigations into the activities of tax-exempt organizations targeted the Fund. When Hutchins took office, the Reece Commission, led by Republican Congressman B. Carroll Reece of Tennessee, was already under way. A man who felt no need to disguise his deep animosity toward the Ford Foundation and the Fund for the Republic, Reece identified the Fund as a "king-sized Civil Rights Congress," trotting out the curious theory that that "Communists and Socialists seize control of fortunes left behind by capitalists when they die, and turn these fortunes around to finance the destruction of capitalism."[16] Hutchins' record as a supporter of academic freedom and his public statements defending the rights of individuals to join the Communist Party were, for Reece, confirmation of the Fund's subversive intent. "Since we know Hutchins' attitude towards communism and we know that his conception of civil liberties is similar to that of the communists," he argued, "we can be sure that the new Ford Foundation project will aid the communist conspiracy and will try to discredit all who fight it."[17] Hutchins did little to deflect such attacks. A year and a half into his presidency, he announced his principled stance on civil liberties in an appearance on NBC's *Meet the Press*, declaring that he would have no qualms hiring a communist "for a job he was qualified to do."[18] Shortly afterward, the House Un-American Activities Committee announced that it would begin investigations into the Fund's tax-exempt status. The investigations would come to nothing, but they would greatly influence the form and nature of Fund advocacy in television.

## CITIZENSHIP FOR DUMMIES

Hutchins turned to television upon arriving at the Fund in 1954 in part because he saw it as the only means of bringing civics lessons to more intractable pockets of the population, but it was also a move toward direct action that countered the moribund state in which he found the organization. Under Case, the Fund had focused primarily on backing academic studies. When Hutchins took over, he immediately changed its focus to include more direct forms of intervention in problems of civil liberties and civil rights. As his assistant, Hallock Hoffman, explained, the Fund "has determined to change bad practices and to instigate good practices in as direct a manner as possible. While some of our projects are studies, we embark upon studies only when this appears to be necessary to action, or the only practicable means of action."[19] Brought in to replace the existing staff hired by Case, Hoffman was one of several freethinking liberals chosen by Hutchins to run the everyday affairs of the Fund. Along with other members of the new staff, he exhibited an energetic commitment to direct intervention in the political crises of the day that matched the unbending liberalism of the organization's leader. Hoffman, the Quaker son of Paul Hoffman, had abandoned the business world a few years earlier to work for the American Friends Service Committee. The father

of five children, he held to the credo that the personal is political, saying, "The peace making you can achieve at home forms the nucleus
for peace making outside the house."[20] To run the New York office
Hutchins hired W.H. "Ping" Ferry, a former public relations director
for the CIO's Political Action Committee. A bearded nonconformist,
Ferry habitually wore a button in his lapel that said "Think Free."[21]
Both men were closely involved in the various television projects the
Fund initiated or supported over the years. Hutchins may have galva-
nized the use of television as a vehicle for public education, but for
most of the Fund's life span, oversight of its television projects was
largely left to Hoffman and Ferry.

In their initial efforts to find a voice on television for the Fund's
mission, Fund officers considered a variety of genres and modes of address, commissioning proposals from several sources. Their responses
to these story ideas, and to the members of the industry with whom
they interacted, provide a revealing view of their beginning expectations
concerning the broadcasting profession and its audience. Evaluating
one proposal for a half-hour dramatic series, television consultant
Howard Chernoff offered Hutchins and Ferry his blunt assessment:
"It is corny enough to appeal to the people we are trying to reach."[22]
The proposal in question, which came from Hollywood producer Jack
Skirball, outlined a series about a Midwestern family, the Stewarts,
who "represent the finest in the middle class American group; with
all of its virtues and a few of its vices." Skirball envisioned the show as
a sugarcoated civics lesson, stressing that its goal was entertainment
rather than propaganda. It should look like "the same kind of family
series as a producer would make even if it weren't sponsored by the
Fund for the Republic," he argued, although he added, contradicto-
rily, that its story lines would address "problems brought about by the
anti-democratic forces in American life [such as] fear in education,
blacklisting, discrimination, censorship, injustice"—a rather uncon-
ventional set of topics for family television back then.[23]

Perhaps aware of the difficulty of balancing entertainment and
political education, the Fund did not pursue Skirball's proposal, choosing instead to develop pilot episodes of a series that would take a more

direct approach to the issues via the biting humor of *Li'l Abner* cartoonist Al Capp. The program featured commentary from Capp on civil liberties and civil rights issues, interspersed with scenes in which actors demonstrated—supposedly comedically—the absurdity of prejudice and narrow-mindedness.[24] Capp's caustic jibes were undoubtedly closer to the sensibilities of Fund officers than Skirball's preachy drama was, and the acted scenes of clueless bigotry surely resonated more strongly with their own feelings about the unenlightened American public. But when the Fund sought airtime for the pilot episodes, it became clear that there was a sharp disconnect between its officers' ideas of progressive television programming and those of the networks. In early 1955 Ping Ferry made plans to screen them to NBC executives, expecting to be offered a time slot and assistance in finding a co-sponsor. "We can pay for the room and the drinks and invite our friends," he told his colleagues in a burst of enthusiasm, although he worried that it would not look good to have the Fund "appearing to make a vigorous effort to 'sell' its first TV show."[25] Reactions from NBC, however, made it apparent that the show was unlikely to make it to the air, let alone find a sponsor. Sylvester "Pat" Weaver, the network's programming head, reacted with clear distaste. A Fund staff member reported that Weaver found the humor highly inappropriate, and had advised that the program's candid approach violated NBC policy, which required an indirect mode of representation when it came to controversial issues: "In the case of discrimination, for example, to use Negro actors wherever they should be used without any emphasis on the actual fact of their use."[26] This was NBC's well-publicized "integration without identification" philosophy, which the network claimed would help raise the visibility of black performers on television.[27]

The discrepancy between the Fund's approach and that of NBC lay in their respective models of viewer responses. Both Weaver and the Fund officers believed in example setting, but their goals and objects were different. Fund officers focused on cognition and behavior in the examples they tried to set, seeking to normalize liberal attitudes in the minds of the average white viewer. Weaver, on the other hand, focused on the positive representation of black people as a way of normalizing *them* in the white mind. The policy was undoubtedly a strategic effort on the part of NBC to sidestep potential controversies. Although "integration without identification" was lauded among Negro leaders, at least according to *Variety*, Weaver's reference to it in response to Capp's direct indictment of racial prejudice highlights the policy's utility as a form of self-censorship.[28] At a time when the nation awaited the *Brown II* decision, which would determine the timeline for desegregation, "integration without identification" kept entertainment programming that explicitly addressed matters of discrimination off the air, allowing NBC to avoid taking a stand and potentially alienating Southern audiences.[29] NBC's effort to promote the visibility of black people on television was thus also a vehicle for network accomodationism at the same time. Fund officers saw the Capp pilot as a way of changing such mealy-mouthed or avoidant approaches to civil liberties and civil rights, but they seem not to have anticipated the possibility that the networks would be resistant to change.

The distance between Fund officers' ideas about the appropriate method of fighting discrimination via TV and those of the networks did not prevent the Fund from continuing to seek access to network television throughout 1955. Indeed, judging by the program ideas they proposed, it seems that Fund officers had not learned very much about the industry from their encounter with NBC. They commissioned *Westinghouse Studio One* veterans Rod Serling and Reginald Rose to script a pilot episode for an anthology drama about civil liberties, a program promoted as the first of several "'open ended dramas' . . . primarily concerned with freedom in our time, and [which] will present more than one side of situations."[30] Fund officers sent the resulting script, entitled "The Challenge," to several consultants for comment. It was not favorably received. Public relations consultant Reggie Schuebel noted that the script was simplistic in its representation of the right-wing characters. "I'm afraid," she wrote, "these disciples of liberalism underrate the brain power of the right wing so that intolerance bounces back upon itself."[31] The Fund was undeterred by Schuebel's criticism. It shot the script, which Ferry referred to as a "civil liberties soap opera," with Sidney Lumet producing and *Studio One* director Worthington Minor directing, then sent it to the networks in the hope that the all-star production team would attract a sponsor for the series. Although CBS was initially interested, no sponsor was forthcoming despite the program's illustrious credits. The film was eventually re-edited as an educational short to be shown to civic discussion groups.[32] A second program, *Herblock's Week*, was similarly compromised by Fund officers' inability to judge the appropriateness of the programs they commissioned. Featuring political cartoonist Herb Block, it was developed for possible network broadcast but ended up being cancelled while still in production. As a press release explained, Block's "effectiveness as a news commentator would depend in large part on his complete freedom to discuss current issues and particular legislation . . . it would not be practical to limit Mr. Block's field of discussion to the boundaries set by the charter of the Fund."[33]

This sheepish retraction suggests that the Fund's failure to secure network airtime for these projects might have stemmed from its officers' unfamiliarity with the conventions of the formats they chose. Although they were aware that nonprofit organizations were prohibited from trying to influence legislation, they shortsightedly invested in a program based upon polemical commentary on public affairs. And while they stressed that "The Challenge" would be open-ended and show both sides, this disclaimer, referencing the norms of professional journalism, was a somewhat incongruous note to sound in the context of anthology drama, a format defined by codes of artfulness and psychological realism. It was also a somewhat self-defeating gesture given that the issues the program was supposed to demonstrate were drawn from the supposedly inarguable tenets of the Constitution.

As network sponsorship opportunities dwindled over the course of 1955, Fund officers shifted their funding focus away from program ideas they commissioned themselves toward ones that were initiated and developed by independent producers. This focus on funding (rather than commissioning) was also a shift toward closer collaboration with community organizations and local media producers, as opposed to the large media organizations centered in New York and Los Angeles. These arrangements came with some problems, however, because they required that Fund officers relinquish a certain amount of control over the treatment of issues they wanted to see covered. Perhaps the most successful example of community-based television supported by the Fund was *A City Decides*, the documentary reenactment of events surrounding the integration of the St. Louis public school system (discussed in more detail in Chapter Two). In 1955 the Fund granted $35,000 to Fleishman-Hillard, a St. Louis public relations firm, to produce the film. Made with the cooperation of the National Council of Christians and Jews, the Urban League, and other civic bodies, it circulated widely in nontheatrical film circuits, and would eventually secure Sunday public service airtime on NBC in 1957. Despite no evidence of theatrical release, it was nominated for an Academy Award in 1956. The Fund intervened in the content of the film once, at the end of the process. On the advice of their public relations firm, they asked for a reshoot of the final scene, a rapprochement in which a black student shares his work with an unprepared white student, to avoid giving tacit approval to cheating.[34]

*A City Decides* was noticeably different from the Fund's previous network television projects, marking a change in tone that accompanied the shift to locally based independent productions. While these earlier programs relied on ridicule, polemic, and sentiment to communicate the issues at stake, *A City Decides* asked viewers to identify with the experiences of an "actual" person: a civics teacher in a newly integrated classroom, played by a Washington University English professor. The film was still uncomfortably pedagogical at times: questioning its truthfulness, a British reviewer complained about the final scene's suggestion that "a classroom exercise in citizenship symbolically healed the one ugly incident between white boy and colored."[35] But these preachy moments were offset by documentary techniques, such as the use of nonprofessional actors to re-create the events surrounding integration, which gave a sense of concreteness and historicity to the action onscreen. The film placed the necessary "both sides" perspective in the mouths of actual people, and its moral authority—the teacher—is presented as a participant in the desegregation process rather than a media figure or a member of the East Coast intellectual elite.

Its conformance with the familiar (and, at the time, authoritative) conventions of the re-enacted documentary made *A City Decides* eminently suitable for network public service time, allowing NBC to clear it for broadcast on forty-five stations. However, the film's success was not only the result of its documentary form. It was also facilitated by the Fund officers' long-standing relationship with Martin Quigley of Fleishman-Hillard. Quigley was a media professional—he had previously served as station manager of KETC, the St. Louis educational television channel—but he was also a former Ford Foundation staff member who had worked closely with Hutchins. He served as a trusted intermediary between the Fund and director Charles Guggenheim, and his efforts in involving grassroots organizations in St. Louis were crucial for the film's subsequent distribution on television, leading to NBC's National Conference of Christian and Jews' Brotherhood Week broadcast. The benefits were reciprocal; by getting these groups involved, Quigley also provided them with opportunities for networking around the cause of civil rights. Only six of the stations that aired the film were in the South, but the Southern Regional Council nevertheless used the opportunity to mobilize its members across the region, asking them to call their local NBC stations to find out whether the film was being broadcast and to encourage them to program more material on integration.[36] The Fund also coordinated a broad-based publicity campaign, asking churches, labor unions, and educational groups to send out postcards announcing the screening to their mailing lists.[37] Although many of the people who received these mailings would have discovered that the program wasn't broadcast in their area, the mere fact of its broadcast was nevertheless a valuable occasion for organizing the local, grassroots networks so vital for civil rights activism in the period.

Among Fund television projects, *A City Decides* was somewhat exceptional in its capacity to aid local groups to coordinate around civil rights issues on a national level. The results were far less impressive when Fund officers had to negotiate directly with media producers, especially when the programs in question pushed the boundaries of educational and public service programming conventions. As was the case with their failed efforts to establish relationships with the networks, these local negotiations provide illuminating examples of how Fund officers approached the challenge of participating in democratic governance through television. Forced to articulate what exactly they thought civic education should look like on-screen, they revealed some of their assumptions about viewers, and about how audience attitudes or behaviors might be translated into practices of citizenship. A particularly telling example was an episode of the nationally syndicated series *Confidential File*, a sensationalist investigative series that combined documentary footage and live studio interviews conducted by *Los Angeles Mirror* columnist Paul Coates. *Confidential File* was a risky project for the Fund because it took a somewhat prurient approach to controversial subjects that were only occasionally, and then indirectly, linked to the question of civil rights.[38] The series frequently disguised the identities of those Coates interviewed, and this was likely the case with the episode in question. Entitled "Daytime Whites," it featured "Negroes who pass as whites during the day in order to get better jobs than would otherwise be open to them."[39]

Although the Fund had agreed to cover its production costs, the *Confidential File* episode became the subject of debate within the organization after it was broadcast. A Fund employee named Elizabeth Huling recorded her reaction in a condemnatory memo that circulated among the officers. Describing the interviewees as "ill at ease" and "stilted," Huling declared: "I was embarrassed for them and disgusted with the show's producer. Ten times as much pain would have been lavished on the mouthing of the cheapest commercial."[40] At the heart of Huling's critique was the idea that the episode failed to establish an affective bond between the interviewees and thus did nothing to advance the cause of civil rights. Although it might seem reasonable to assume that sympathetic reception required some kind of identification between viewer and subject, Hoffman was unwilling to consider such a possibility. Angered by Huling's reference to advertising, and perhaps also by her forthrightness, he scrawled his response on the cover memo: "She's nuts. What a comparison! People have long learned to turn off their minds when the slick commercials come on. Let's make up our minds on the basis of the kine[scope], and fire Miss Huling if her opinion is as bad as I think." Despite this reaction, however, Hoffman himself was uneasy with the way the program handled the issue of discrimination. "The feeling of the injustice practiced on the people before your camera was clear and compelling," he wrote in a tactful letter to Coates. "The other feeling, that the society was denying itself able, creative work from able, creative people by discrimination, was not as clear."[41]

The terms in which Hoffman envisioned the program's educational impact are illuminating. Whereas Huling focused on the *affective* connection to viewers, Hoffman was concerned with whether the program engaged their capacity for reason, allowing them to draw conclusions about the social impact of discrimination. His criteria for television's success or failure in civic education thus seemed to turn on a program's ability to lay out a positive course of action, and he conceived of the viewer as a rational citizen merely awaiting information that would make him or her aware of the objective social costs of irrational phenomena, such as discrimination. Hoffman was initially interested in funding further episodes of the program, drafting an excited memorandum that listed possible topics: "American Indians, Stool Pigeons, Wire Tapping ('they are against it'), Wet-backs . . . Chain gangs, Mixed marriages."[42] But after viewing the program, he seemed to lose interest, perhaps recognizing that the sensationalist context in which these issues were treated would not foster the rationalist viewing sensibility—or attract the rational viewers—that he had in mind. In a sense the disagreement reprised the split between Fund officers and Weaver occasioned by the Capp pilots. On one side, there was the liberal faith in the inherently persuasive power of a rational argument, whether couched in Capp's commentary on the absurdity of prejudice or Coates' (unrealized) demonstration that discrimination was detrimental to "society as a whole." On the other side, there was the professional awareness of the power of unconscious and emotional reactions to media rhetorics, and of the importance of the framing discourse in any effort to persuade.[43]

Given this persistent tension, it makes sense that the television projects Hoffman championed at the Fund mostly fit into the news and public affairs category. The format best exemplified the possibility of separating rationality from sentiment within the institution of television, and it was governed by professional codes that extended beyond the industry's borders. Hoffman strongly supported the idea of funding a local San Francisco television program called *Barrier* (KRON-TV, 1956) produced by Edward Howden of the San Francisco Council for Civic Unity. A tireless community relations advocate, Howden became a civic celebrity in 1957 when he convinced a reluctant white homeowner to sell his house to black San Francisco Giants outfielder Willie Mays.[44] His agenda in reporting on civil liberties and civil rights in the Bay Area was "to inform the viewer concerning, and to stimulate his active interest in, affairs coming within the two subject fields."[45] It was the same goal he had in mind with his radio news program *Dateline: Freedom*, also produced with grant money from the Fund, which was premised on the idea that educating the public on racism required formats, such as news, that were marked by "the absence of preachment, of an underlying attitude of moral superiority, or of other emotionalized and opinionated approaches commonly associated with the field of intergroup relations."[46] Hoffman and other officers were impressed by Howden's ideas. They allocated $60,000 for the production of *Barrier* and speculated the program "might set a model for similar programs in other areas."[47] This never happened, however. In 1957, a year after *Barrier* went on the air, the Fund's educational mission abruptly changed direction away from direct funding of community projects. Other television projects were affected too, including one that also arose from Hoffman's interest in using local news as a venue for civic education and which is worth examining in more detail despite its abrupt foreclosure. Known as the Newsfilm Project, its history—more properly its downfall—played an interesting role in the Fund's change in course, and it aptly illustrates the promise, and the shortsightedness, of the Fund's vision of governing by television.


## BALANCING ACTS

In 1954, shortly after arriving at the Fund, Hoffman inaugurated a pilot program for distributing film clips and scripts for stories related to civil liberties and civil rights to local Los Angeles news stations. The idea was a simple and ingenious one, as it adapted for the Fund's purposes a public relations format created by corporations. As the original unsigned proposal explained, "Los Angeles TV news editors currently receive considerable film furnished by commercial firms with public relations objectives. This material is used in substantial quantity on news programs with established audiences [and] this same approach would be valid and effective in publicizing news stories of interest to the Fund for the Republic." The proposal's inside knowledge of the industry suggests that its author was likely George Martin, a Los Angeles news producer who would become the project's director. It outlined a news-gathering operation in which events "would be covered on film at the scene and, where desirable, in the words of the people involved." It also stressed newsworthiness, taking into account the requirements of local news editors: "Stories would be based on some concrete, timely news event. Film, edited to between forty-five seconds and two minutes, would be serviced to local television stations along with a script prepared to be narrated with it by the station's newsmaster."[48] A forerunner of so-called advocacy journalism, the Newsfilm Project appropriated for progressive ends a PR tool that would evolve into today's insidious video news releases, or VNRs—vehicles through which drug companies (and, as we learned in 2005, the presidential administration of George W. Bush) use the news environment as a vehicle for promotion, publicity, and propaganda.[49]

In its concreteness and industry savvy, the proposal for the Newsfilm Project was strikingly different from most of the Fund's other television proposals. Instead of trying to work against the professional practices of the industry, it took advantage of a perennial need in local television news at the time—free footage—and conformed to industry norms for the gathering and packaging of stories. Like *A City Decides*, it did not try to reinvent existing television formats and conventions; rather, as Hoffman put it, the Newsfilm Project modeled itself after "programs which have audience acceptance."[50] The project also, in its very nature, limited the prospect of self-sabotage by Fund officers. The emphasis on timeliness, and the need for ongoing coordination of camera crews in the field, made their day-to-day involvement logistically impossible and kept them from direct, potentially abrasive contact with the media workers who used the Fund's material. Although the officers fretted over the risks involved in giving Martin free rein, they recognized that he needed a relative degree of autonomy to run the project. As Hoffman explained to Fund officer Edward Reed, Martin's "regular personal visits with our consumers—the working news show producers and editors—will assure us that we are providing the kind of material they want, and guarantee its use."[51] Martin was an employee of the Fund, but only he had the expertise to choose the project's staff, engaging union cameramen to shoot stories locally, and to negotiate contracts with news syndicates to distribute clips to stations that signed up for the Fund's newsfilm service.[52] The hands-off approach that the Newsfilm Project required was risky, given the controversies surrounding the subjects the project covered, but the potential for intervening in the dominant televisual discourse on civil rights and civil liberties was immense.

Only a few examples of Newsfilm Project footage appear to have survived into the present day. All are from its pilot year in California television news markets. But these extant examples give us a sense of the materials that stations received when they subscribed to the service. The story would arrive as a can of film containing silent B-roll footage and some short sound-on-film segments, usually interviews or statements. The B-roll set the scene: shots of signage, perhaps some footage of the town in which the story took place, and other more clearly pointed shots designed to communicate a broader liberal message. This celluloid material would be accompanied by a suggested voice-over script; the point was to give stations leeway in how they edited the film. Although Newsfilm Project camera crews were careful to present more than one point of view when they shot footage for the Fund, the material sent to stations was structured so that the Fund's liberal agenda would be clear. A good example is the film package the Newsfilm staff put together for a story covering efforts to desegregate the El Centro, California, school system in 1955. It included a synch sound segment in which a school board official read a gruff and defensive statement denying that schools were segregated, but the bulk of the footage was devoted to shots showing the contrasting conditions of black schools and white schools—the former shown to be overcrowded and dilapidated, the latter consisting of modern buildings and grassy outdoor spaces in which contented-looking teenagers gather for horseplay and gossip. The film package also showed plaintiffs in a law suit against the school district. Shot with stark

company, which has had to raise fares and curtail service because of the drop in patronage, says it cannot comply with the Negroes' demands without violating state segregation laws.

Efforts to mediate the dispute by groups like the Alabama Council on Human Relations, an inter-racial conciliatory organization, continue. But so far the opposing factions remain far apart and tension continues in Montgomery.

The film supplied you herewith shows scenes of the main bus station, a downtown parking lot where Negroes gather for rides, and a statement on the situation by the Rev. Robert Hughes of the Alabama Council on Human Relations. You may wish to file the film for later use as stock footage.

SUGGESTED FILM SCRIPT FOLLOWS:

When the Fund for the Republic's Newsfilm Project sent footage covering civil rights and civil liberties to local TV news departments, it provided a suggested voice-over script in an effort to guide the meaning of the footage when aired.
*Image courtesy of Princeton University Library.*

lighting so that they resembled iconic figures from the photographic archives of the New Deal Works Progress Administration, their visual presence communicated dignity, determination, and moral clarity.

After a year in California the Newsfilm Project went national, adding a New York office in November 1955 to facilitate East Coast coverage and distribution. For a little over a year it existed as an ambitious, and potentially radical, effort to coordinate local and network news coverage of issues pertaining to civil liberties and civil rights across the country. Summarizing the project at its conclusion, Martin explained that its aim was to counter prevailing approaches to these topics in the industry: "Since the regular news media were covering the sensational aspects of the problem, most of our material dealt with efforts, successful and otherwise, toward communication between the races and with examples of peaceful segregation."[53] During its seventeen months of operation the project produced around one hundred clips, which were distributed by the United Press Movietone News syndicate to its subscriber stations and by the New York office directly to the networks.[54] The clips covered topics that ranged widely in their focus and timeliness. Ones focusing on the desegrega-

Newsfilm Project footage documenting the struggle to desegregate the E1 Centro, California, school system included scenes, clearly inspired by New Deal–era federal photography, in which plaintiffs suing the town's school board explained to the camera segregation's negative impact on their children's education.

tion of the Louisville, Kentucky, school system and the Montgomery, Alabama, bus boycott, for example, were widely used by local stations and the networks. Others—bystander attacks on a pacifists' parade on Armed Forces Day, the firing of a white Florida county health department doctor for dining with a Negro midwife—did not achieve significant airtime.[55] Although net usage figures over the course of the project's operation are hard to gauge with any accuracy, the files indicate that NBC used around fifty-five clips in total and that United Press Movietone News estimated that "any given clip will be seen by 5% of total viewers in UPMT areas."[56]

Despite its innovative approach and its promising distribution record, the Newsfilm Project would end up a casualty of Hutchins' reckless career as a television figure in this period, a career marked by persistent cluelessness about the medium's possibilities and limits as a vehicle for advocacy. After his disastrous appearance on *Meet the Press* led to multiple government investigations of the Fund's tax-exempt status, the activities of the Newsfilm Project were severely curtailed, greatly reducing its capacity to educate and organize, particularly around issues of desegregation and civil rights. But although the Newsfilm

Project was a short-lived venture, its story deserves to be told. More than an example of a lost opportunity for media advocacy in the early civil rights movement, the project provides a rich and multilayered picture of the relationships between grassroots organizations and national and local media institutions at a time when each was in the process of radical transformation. As part of the ongoing campaign to make the issues at stake in the civil rights movement a matter of ongoing extra-regional and national significance, the project took the Fund's educational mission into the arena of advocacy, if not activism. It was unique in its efforts to rebalance television coverage to include forms of inequality less visible than moments of direct conflict and violence (a story on segregated voting booths in the South, for example) as well as instances of peaceful integration (a story on the unchallenged removal of segregationist signs in the Dallas bus system) and, perhaps more unusual for the time, a number of stories about discrimination against Mexican-Americans in California.

The project's history also provides valuable perspective on the rationalizations broadcasters used to explain their approaches to civil rights coverage. As the civil rights movement and the segregationist "massive resistance" campaign both gained momentum, news editors

FROM: George Martin, Jr. *[signature]*                                    | THE FUND FOR THE REPUBLIC |

SUBJECT: Newsfilm Project Progress Memo through January 1, 1957

NEWSCLIPS RELEASED:   New Board Members:  Incoming Board Chairman Elmo
(New York)            Roper introduces three new Board members and comments
                      on the current state of American freedom.  To local
                      stations in New York City, Washington, D. C.,
                      Arkansas, and Los Angeles.  Estmated audience: 908,500.

                      Negroes Vote:  Scenes in Cuthbert, Georgia, as
                      Negroes exercise their franchise there for the first
                      time.  Estimated audience:  555,500.

                    · Bus Boycott Ends:  Negroes begin riding busses in
                      Montgomery, Alabama, on unsegregated basis, ending
                      their long boycott of the bus line following
                      Supreme Court decision in their favor.  Estimated
                      audience:  1,458,000.

NEWSCLIPS RELEASED:   Statues:  Beverly Hills art dealer seeks injunction
(Los Angeles)         permitting him to display in his window nude
                      replicas of famous statues, including Michaelangelo's
                      "David".  Police had ordered the figurines removed
                      as "obscene".  To Los Angeles stations.  Estimated
                      audience:  555,500.

                      Jo-Ann Allen:  Interview with Negro girl, student at
                      Clinton (Tenn.) high school during integration

**The Newsfilm Project's monthly progress reports detailed a range of approaches to civil
liberties and civil rights coverage and relayed information on audience numbers and network
exposure to Fund officers.**
*Image courtesy of Princeton University Library.*

at the networks and local stations justified the levels of coverage they
gave to the struggle over integration in terms of budgetary choices. After meeting with network news editors, a Newsfilm Project consultant
reported back to the Los Angeles office that an NBC staffer had confessed that the network had not covered the Atlanta Board of Education's August 1955 decision to permanently revoke the teaching license
of any teachers affiliated with the NAACP because "distance and expense... didn't warrant NBC sending out a crew."[57] By engaging
stringers, news syndicates, camera crews working for Southern stations, and occasionally church media groups such as the Methodist Radio and Film Commission, the project effectively subsidized network
coverage of civil rights issues.[58] The record of its efforts is the story of a
sustained attempt to push local struggles surrounding rights of citizenship across the shifting threshold of media gatekeeping defined by bud-
gets, determinations of newsworthiness, definitions of local and national
interest, and other forms of professional rationalization.

The Newsfilm Project's successful negotiation of the gatekeeping process depended upon the extensive channels of communication Martin established with media workers, and these ongoing professional relationships mark another important difference between the Newsfilm Project and other Fund television activities. From the start, the project was crafted using feedback from the industry. In early 1956, when the Fund considered expanding the project to a national scale, Martin sent questionnaires to station managers throughout the country asking them whether they would use clips from the service and soliciting their interests and concerns about covering civil liberties and civil rights stories. These private communications provide a glimpse of the ways that news professionals at the local and network levels understood the terms in which the early civil rights movement would be represented, and of their attitudes toward the civil liberties that the industry to which they belonged had been so willing to violate. They also illustrate the ways that regional identity shaped how these issues looked to local news managers, most obviously in Jim Crow states, but in other regions too. William Ekberg of KFYR-TV, in Bismarck, North Dakota, wrote, "We have a special Indian problem, but it is difficult to see how you could concentrate releases to aid in the solution"; Jim Maize, of KOA-TV in Tucson, requested coverage of "anything you may possibly have on Spanish-American violations." Harry Reasoner, then news director of KEYD-TV in Minneapolis, asked for film on "incidents outside the South, housing, any material on freedom of the press."[59]

The questionnaire provides particularly useful insight on the ways that Southern news editors approached civil rights. The response provided by Dick Sanders of WLBT-TV in Jackson, Mississippi, is particularly interesting given the station's notorious history. Its unbridled editorial support for segregation and its persistent violation of the Fairness Doctrine led to the revocation of its license in 1969 (by an appeals court, after a protracted battle by civil rights groups). But Sanders responded to the questionnaire enthusiastically, suggesting a laundry list of possible topics: "stories on academic freedom, guilt by association, segregation, actual beliefs and feelings of Southerners, pointing out if possible the varying degrees of feeling among both races."[60] Unlikely as it might seem, given the uncompromising stance of his employers, Sanders was a liberal integrationist from Chicago. His call for more varied representations may have reflected his belief, expressed in a 1987 oral history, that television's focus on the most pitched battles of the civil rights movement worked "to galvanize the white opposition."[61] Indeed, the reference to "actual beliefs and feelings" was likely both a coded complaint about the stereotypical portrayal of white Southerners in national news coverage and an appeal for the visibility of Southern moderates. In the words of Steven D. Classen, the author of a nuanced and detailed history of the WLBT case, Sanders' story "points to the limitations of well-intentioned and principled journalists working in contexts where they are not truly free."[62] Sanders' enthusiasm for the Newsfilm Project communicates how important the service must have seemed to journalists working under those sorts of conditions.

Other Southern station staff, however, used the questionnaire as an opportunity to voice opposition to Northern liberals. This often took the form of a concern that Fund clips would not present balanced viewpoints on the stories they covered. Gene Lewis of KWTX-TV in Waco, Texas, wrote on the Newsfilm Project questionnaire that he was only interested in "objective" stories, and Conrey Bryson of KTSM-TV in El Paso, Texas, took the occasion to issue a blunt statement of the gradualist position on desegregation: "We don't want to appear to be carrying on a crusade for civil liberties. As far as we're concerned here in El Paso, we don't need such a crusade . . . if a story has real news significance, we'd like to have it, but we believe the achievement for greater civil liberties calls more for patience than for crusading."[63] Martin took note of this kind of feedback as he developed strategies for the effective placement of clips. In May 1956, after receiving the questionnaire responses from these and other Southern stations, he sent clips covering a recent civil rights rally in New York's Madison Square Garden to one hundred stations "everywhere except the deep South," theorizing that "a non-racial story would be a better first offering to them."[64]

The issue of objectivity and balance, and the desire to avoid the appearance of "crusading," was a perennial concern among many broadcasters with whom Newsfilm staff interacted, not only those in the South. The television news directors canvassed by Martin and Hoffman before launching the California pilot indicated that acceptance of Fund clips would depend on their freedom from bias, even if the issues they covered were a matter of constitutional law. In part this concern was a matter of professional standards in journalism. Some station news directors were willing to risk controversy—John Thompson of the NBC-owned-and-operated KRCA-TV (Los Angeles) avowed that "controversy is the heart of news"—but others, such as Claud Mann of KSBW-TV in Salinas-Monterey, California, feared that "the clips might get them into controversial areas."[65] News directors and station managers often cited the balance issue in comment cards supplied with each clip package when they returned them to the Fund. Some of these were Southern stations; WSLS-TV in Roanoke, Virginia, rejected a clip covering the NAACP convention in 1956 because of its "non-objective job of reporting the convention," but concerns came from other regions too.[66] Yet many stations also praised Fund stories for their objectivity, even when the clips seem, from their descriptions at least, to have been highly vulnerable to the "unbalanced" charge. "Very timely and unbiased," remarked the employee of KVEC-TV (San Luis Obispo, California) who filled out the comment card for a clip that showed the efficiency with which forty thousand black citizens of Montgomery, Alabama, organized alternative transportation during their boycott of the city's segregated bus system and which neglected, as most Fund clips did, to provide the segregationist point of view.[67]

Such affirmations of the Fund's unbiased approach helped get clips on the air, but they also point to the compromises that Martin and his staff had to make in order for this to happen. A glance at the suggested voice-over script supplied with the clip praised by KVEC-TV illuminates the elements that would have made it acceptable to television news editors who might otherwise balk at covering controversial issues. After explaining the situation, the script introduced a statement by Robert Hughes of the Southern Council on Human Relations with the following lead-in: "Hughes says there is a large group of middle-of-the-road whites in the South, midway between *extremists of both sides*, who have not yet spoken out on racial problems" (emphasis added). Sixteen words of Hughes' statement followed, but they said nothing about extremism and merely called for a bridge between "our Negro and white population."[68] The reference to "extremists on both sides" was quite possibly the key to the clip's acceptance. The phrase anticipated word for word Eisenhower's public statements later that year in response to segregationist violence during the integration of the Mansfield, Texas, and Clinton, Tennessee, school systems.[69] This spurious language of parity, as detailed in the previous chapter, was not uncommon in the public speech on segregation in this period. The rhetoric of "both sides" seemed to apply a democratic principle of fairness, but when it came to network coverage of civil rights, at least prior to the Little Rock crisis of 1957, its meaning was often about as democratic as the de facto meaning of the word *equal* in the phrase "separate but equal" in that it equated segregationist violence with black Southerners' efforts to claim their legal rights. Arguably, attributing this rhetoric to a civil rights leader was a strategic move, a way of getting the clips shown while promoting the idea of the movement as an organization of moderate and rational individuals. At the same time, it furthered the legitimacy of the rhetoric and put it into wider circulation.

The "both sides" rhetoric was one way that broadcasters' accomodationism and federal quietism supported each other, and its presence in this script indicates the limits of the Newsfilm Project's ability to carry out the Fund's mandate in the field of civic discourse, described by Hoffman as "changing bad practices and instigating good practices."[70] But it is important to note that these limits were not so much ideological as they were legislative. Because federal law prohibited nonprofits from trying to influence legislation or spread propaganda, the rhetoric of parity served as a shield to protect the Fund from investigation. Production materials for another story suggest that the "both sides" approach in the project's clips was motivated as much by awareness of this legislative limit as by as journalistic convention. Some time in early 1956, a Movietone News cameraman went to Baton Rouge, Louisiana, to shoot Newsfilm Project footage that would be released to stations in April of that year. The occasion was likely the state legislature's recent passage of a statute mandating segregated waiting rooms for public transportation users, as the shots logged on the cameraman's "dope sheet" focused on segregationist signage

A 1956 HUAC investigation into Fund activities made the Newsfilm Project staff highly cautious in their coverage of the civil rights struggle in the South and more inclined to give equal time to the segregationist point of view, as the handwritten note at the bottom of this footage log attests.
*Image courtesy of Princeton University Library.*

in a bus station, and included synch sound coverage of a speech by the chairman of the state's Public Service Commission.[71] Someone, most likely Martin or the New York office manager, Herbert Bernard, penciled "We'd better get both sides" at the bottom of the sheet. Given that the only opinion directly represented was that of a state official in charge of enforcing the segregationist statute, the annotation might seem to call for inclusion of the perspectives of those who opposed it. But as the clip's subject was the state's legislative affirmation of the legality of segregation, it is just as likely that this call for "both sides" was meant to caution against creating the impression that the story was criticizing the law.

Undoubtedly, this imperative came from the Fund itself. Officers were acutely aware of the delicate legal circumstances surrounding the Newsfilm Project's coverage of the ongoing struggles against Jim Crow in the South. In October 1955, Hoffman had consulted with Fund attorney Harrison Harkins to ascertain whether the recently revised Revenue Act regulations covering nonprofits might pose a problem for the project. Harkins was reassuring, reminding Hoffman of court rulings holding that "the collection and dissemination of information on so-called 'controversial' subjects were still within the scope of the term 'educational purpose,' particularly if an attempt was made, or an opportunity was afforded, to present the facts on both sides of the question." He concluded by sanctioning the Newsfilm Project, "as long as it doesn't influence legislation, is fair and balanced, and doesn't advocate for the election of a candidate."[72] But despite this reassurance, the project was destined for more active forms of self-censorship over the course of 1956. The House Un-American Activities Committee (HUAC) and Treasury Department investigations prompted by Hutchins' defense of Communist Party membership on *Meet the Press* the previous year made Fund officers increasingly worried that the Newsfilm Project would fuel governmental hostility toward the Fund, and after the Treasury Department identified three pieces of film as examples of possible bias, they moved to restrain the activities of Martin and his staff.

The circumstances surrounding this intervention in the Newsfilm Project reveal the contingent nature of the Fund's commitments when it came to civil rights. HUAC's primary focus was the Fund's civil liberties work, most notably its two-volume study of the blacklist, but the Newsfilm Project's ongoing contribution to the visibility of the civil rights movement sustained lasting collateral damage. The Reece Commission had seen fit to investigate the Carnegie Endowment's funding of Gunnar Myrdal's study of race relations in the South the previous year, but the Fund news clips deemed suspect by the Treasury Department focused not on racial struggles but rather on the civil liberties issues at stake in state and popular forms of anticommunism. The first was a report on postal censorship, which detailed the U.S. Postal Service's decision to confiscate copies of the *Moscow Gazette* ordered by a retired schoolteacher trying to learn Russian. The second was the aforementioned footage covering attacks on pacifists protesting on Armed Forces Day. The third was a report covering a meeting of the right-wing Congress of Freedom, which the investigators claimed intentionally sought to make the participants look ridiculous.[73] Of course, civil liberties and civil rights were intertwined. But the latter defined a mass movement for massive social change and thus was more widely controversial. Even though none of the stories under investigation by HUAC covered civil rights topics, the Fund's general counsel, Bethuel Webster, instructed Martin to curtail the Newsfilm Project's coverage of the struggle in the South. In an August 1956 phone call, Webster explained that "for the moment we've simply got to play possum to a great extent and not get engaged in things which our enemies could cite against us as being outside of our charter powers and our tax exemption." When Martin pressed for examples, Webster replied, "Specifically I think it applies to the Fund chaperoning this trip of Negroes and whites into Louisiana." Martin protested that the planned trip would not be chaperoning—"we'd be merely following them and reporting what happened"—but Webster insisted: "It helps not to prejudice our whole program in order to get an exciting picture of race relations in Baton Rouge." Martin deferred to the new policy, agreeing that "except for fairly innocuous things in which we can do a thoroughly balanced job we ought to lie low for the time being."[74] He was not aware of it at the time, but this withdrawal from the sphere of active political struggle was a harbinger of the policy shifts at the Fund that would eventually lead to the Newsfilm Project's demise.

The immediate impact of this new policy was to create confusion. Most of the stories covered that year were related to civil rights, so it was unclear how the Newsfilm Project would continue to operate.[75] As he pulled back on any future civil rights coverage, Martin looked to the project's past in his efforts to fight the Treasury Department charges. He wrote letters to network news directors soliciting written testimony that the project's stories "provided fair, professional reporting on newsworthy civil liberties issues," volunteering that it would greatly help the Fund's case to be able to show that "a major, reputable news dissemination organization uses our material and finds it in conformance with its own standards of fair and informed reporting."[76] Martin's staff found themselves working in a state of beleaguered uncertainty, regularly pressing him to specify whether a story was appropriate to cover.[77] Fund legal consultants urged caution above all else; when queried about a seemingly uncontroversial story about a Negro attorney's election to, and immediate ouster from, the position of Justice of the Peace in a Florida county, the response was "Only if we can make it educational."[78] The remainder of the project's activities prior to its closing in April 1957 were greatly shaped by the climate of fear created by HUAC. Looking at the self-censorship practices they involved conveys the paradoxical nature of the political rationality linking the Cold War and the color line. If the exigencies of Cold War geopolitics, particularly the need to combat the nation's international image problem, motivated federal action on civil rights, domestic anticommunism served as a means for containing civil rights advocacy and activism on local and grassroots level.

The work of self-censorship is most readily apparent in the records surrounding the final film project undertaken by Martin and his staff, a documentary film that incorporated library footage from the networks, existing footage from the Newsfilm Project, and some new material provided by Jim Peck, a filmmaker hired by Martin to direct

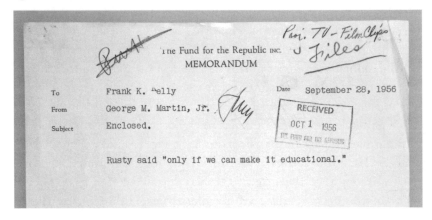

**Making a Newsfilm Project story "educational" was an effort to avoid propaganda charges during the HUAC investigation.**
*Image courtesy of Princeton University Library.*

the production. The film, originally entitled *Crisis in the South*, aired in ABC's Sunday public service time in June 1967, with the title *Segregation and the South*. The Fund's files do not contain a copy of the proposal for the film, but it seems that the rhetoric of parity was liberally applied throughout; after reviewing the proposal, Frank Loescher, the Fund's intergroup relations consultant, wrote to Martin approving of the film but advising that he "watch out for the 'plague on both your houses' reaction if you equate White Citizens Councils and [the] NAACP." The latter, he reminded Martin, was "on the side of the Supreme Court."[79] The Newsfilm Project's staff did not seem to follow this advice, however. After reviewing a final print, another Fund staff member, Paul Jacobs, faulted the film for committing this very error:

> Specifically, there is one scene in the film which alternates shots of the KKK and the NAACP, A. Philip Randolph and Martin Luther King. At this point the narrator states "But in spite of the hateful words and bitter charges from both camps, the Supreme Court decisions were bringing desegregation to the South." I believe that this is factually incorrect

and certainly places the NAACP, Randolph, and King at opposite ends of a continuum from the KKK. I believe that posing these two forces in this way is a bad distortion of the situation in the South. The fact is that the NAACP and the Negroes leadership have behaved with a great deal more restraint in attempting to get the law inforced [sic] than was believed possible at the time.[80]

Martin's stubborn attachment to the "both sides" rhetoric that Jacobs criticized likely sprang from his desire to get the film shown in the South. This would prove to be a wishful delusion, and it led to significant, deeply undermining concessions in the film's treatment of its subject matter. Apparently unmoved by Loescher's warning, Martin pursued opportunities to include the segregationist point of view. Through Peck, he engaged Hal DeCell, the public relations director of the segregationist Mississippi State Sovereignty Commission, as an advisor on the film. It was DeCell who proposed that Martin change the film's title from *Crisis in the South* to *Segregation and the South*, and his involvement in the production process greatly compromised its value as a tool in the Fund's mission of educating the public about the civil rights granted by the Constitution.

As Yasuhiro Katagiri recounts in his study of the Sovereignty Commission, Peck approached Governor Coleman of Mississippi to request DeCell's services as a consultant in November 1956, suggesting that DeCell could help the Fund "in accurately presenting the point of view he represents."[81] Ironically, given Jacobs' critique, DeCell complained that the final version of the film did not include any coverage of "negro extremists" and suggested that it be re-edited to include them. Martin did not grant this request, nor did he make any changes after DeCell objected to "the use of the term 'when' rather than 'if' in connection with the ultimate desegregation in Mississippi."[82] But as Katagiri notes, DeCell had apparently instituted some significant changes earlier in the project. He boasted to the commission's director that he had persuaded the Newsfilm Project to remove segments covering the 1955 murder of Emmett Till, and to include footage "giving our side of the situation," including the views of Klan

MISCELLANEOUS
ACTIVITIES:

Southern Documentary: Work continued on the
documentary treatment of inter-racial communication
in the South. After screening by James Peck in
New York, the Project purchased film from NBC and
CBS to augment our own footage. Scripting and film
editing are now under way and the Project hopes to
have a completed version of the film available for
viewing by mid-February.

As part of the preparation of the film, Peck and the
Project Director conferred at length with Harold
DeCell, public relations director of the Mississippi
State Sovereignty Commission, who came to Los
Angeles for the purpose. He contributed many
suggestions which he felt would improve acceptance
of the film in the South, and promised to assist
in distribution. During his visit, the Project also
arranged a meeting with Mr. DeCell, Mr. Hutchins,
and Mr. Hallock Hoffman.

In an effort to secure airtime on Southern stations George Martin, the Newsfilm Project
director, engaged a consultant from the segregationist Mississippi Sovereignty Commission for
*Segregation and the South.* The final cut of the documentary included a number of accommodations to the segregationist point of view instigated at the consultant's request.
*Image courtesy of Princeton University Library.*

members and of Conwell Sykes, chairman of the Greenville, Mississippi, White Citizens Council.[83] Still, DeCell's involvement did not
help the film clear Southern stations. Only eleven of the thirty-one stations to air it were in Southern states, and none were in the battle-
ground states of Louisiana, Mississippi, Alabama, and Arkansas.[84]
Nor did it forestall network concerns about balance. NBC refused the
film because it "insults Southerners as villains [and] might offend . . .
Southern station managers," a remark that raises the question of how
the film would have been received if DeCell had not been involved in
its production.[85]

More crucially, this remark suggests the possibility of reading
the film as something other than a capitulation to the appeasing ideal
of representing both sides. Although DeCell saw himself as a pro-
segregation censor, it is conceivable that in his desire to get the anti-
integration view represented, he unwittingly assisted in the development
of a technique that would become a key element of network documentaries on the civil rights movement at the end of the decade: the use of
segregationists' own words to undermine their stance. Sasha Torres

notes this technique in her reading of "Sit-in," a 1960 documentary
about the Nashville lunch counter protests that ran as an episode of
the NBC series *White Paper*. Narrated by Chet Huntley, the documentary is notable in its unvarnished representation of segregationists,
who speak candidly and use the word *nigger* freely. Noting that the
documentary presents segregation in Nashville as a fait accompli, Torres suggests that the retrospective viewpoint allows the filmmakers to
represent segregationists without compunction "as inarticulate, il-
logical, mendacious, or self-aggrandizing."[86]

Although they did not have the security of a retrospective viewpoint, Martin and his staff used this hanged-with-their-own-rope approach throughout the Newsfilm Project, most notably in the piece
about the Congress of Freedom that Treasury Department officials
charged was not objective because it made its subjects appear farcical.
Martin was quick to deny this charge to Fund officers, pointing out
that "it is not the function of objective reporting to keep people from
looking ridiculous" and reminding them that Eric Sevareid of CBS
had used the clip.[87] It is impossible to judge (at least until a print turns
up) whether Martin hoped to make segregationists look ridiculous in
*Segregation and the South*, but the *New York Times* review that ran
after it aired suggest that it is conceivable. Noting that the film "did
not gloss over the unpleasant side of the situation," reviewer Jack Shanley remarked upon the extensive sequences in which segregationists
spoke: Georgia governor Herman Talmadge, Ku Klux Klan members,
and "a white student expelled from the University of Alabama [who]
indulged in a sardonic and irrelevant denunciation of Mrs. Franklin
D. Roosevelt," the last characterization suggesting that the film allowed the ugliness of illiberal language to speak for itself.[88] The Newsfilm Project had little in common with cinema verité and other forms
of political documentary that would emerge at the end of the decade,
but this treatment of its subjects' speech, coupled with the Treasury
Department's accusations of ridicule, suggests one way that the project presaged the emergence of later rhetorical modes. Although it was
a short-lived endeavor, the Newsfilm Project enacted a unique vision
of governing by television, one in which the promise of documentary

news film allowed the more progressive facets of the liberal establishment agenda to emerge.

As it turned out, the Fund's decision not to renew the Newsfilm Project in April 1957 had nothing to do with the activities of the project itself. Increasingly convinced that the Fund had failed in its efforts to clarify the principles of civil liberties for the public, Hutchins had begun to formulate a radical change of direction. The Fund, he claimed, "has for the most part assumed that everybody understood civil liberties and was in favor of them. It has supposed that the disclosure of failures in this field would result in efforts to remedy them. It has not sufficiently reckoned with the proposition that one man's failure is another man's success." The solution, he argued in a series of memoranda circulated to Fund officers and trustees throughout 1956, was to create an institute devoted to "prolonged discussion of principles" in order to "promote coherence and intelligibility in the program of the Fund."[89] Hutchins claimed that the timing of his proposal had nothing to do with the HUAC controversy. Still, the investigations, although widely discredited, made it easier to convince the trustees to back the new plan. The institute he proposed would remove the Fund from community group involvement, as it would be "directed and conducted by a group of men of the highest distinction, aided by assistants and consultants, who will devote full time over a period of years to examining the state of the free man in the United States and ideas and institutions associated with the terms 'liberty' and 'justice.'" Nor would it involve grant making, which Hutchins felt did not conform to "intelligible standards of action" and would distract the officers from the task of analyzing the "basic issues" at stake in the protection of civil liberties.[90] Two officers, Dave Freeman and Adam Yarmolinsky, protested the shift, arguing that grant making was crucial in the civil rights arena, where "no individual or group of individuals can find *the* answer to the problem, but . . . many groups, with different approaches, will help to work out common sense solutions."[91] But ultimately, Hutchins prevailed, and the board tentatively approved the plan at meetings in November 1956 and May 1957.

Although the Fund would continue to support some of its ongoing grant projects, its focus from then until its 1959 transmogrification into the liberal Santa Barbara think tank the Center for the Study of Democratic Institutions would be "inquiry into the basic issues of civil liberties and individual freedom."[92] With the adoption of this new mandate, the organization began to foster a more centrist advocacy, mainstreaming its once radical mission. The group counted among its founding ideas for discussion such well-worn topics of interest group pluralism such as "the role of the corporation" and "the role of the trade union" as well as Cold War foreign policy. These concerns, coupled with the increased involvement of corporate liberal business leaders and mainstream policy intellectuals, brought the Fund's projects in line with centrist establishment organizations such as the Americans for Democratic Action. It would still address issues related to civil rights, but its involvement in the movement was over.

The shift to the Basic Issues program was, ultimately, a reflection of Hutchins' own racial politics. In 1972, Ping Ferry—by then an éminence grise of the New Left—reflected on Hutchins' uneasy relationship with the civil rights movement. "Bob . . . always wanted to treat the black issue at the level of Supreme Court decisions," he recalled, "not what was happening in the streets and so on." In the end, Ferry surmised, "it just plain made him uncomfortable."[93] Ferry stayed with Hutchins for many years, but radical politics remained part of his agenda. After he left the Center for the Study of Democratic Institutions he became a trustee of the Daniel J. Bernstein Foundation, where he made a point of financing causes "generally ignored by conventional foundations . . . GIs, deserters, and draft refusers; black, yellow and brown groups; convicts and ex-convicts—all those habitually neglected or picked on by authority."[94] But for Ferry, as for Hutchins, mainstream media would no longer be a tool for intervening in dominant discourses of citizenship. Hoffman would continue to work in broadcasting, becoming president of California's listener-supported Pacifica radio network in 1964. Still, his experience with the Fund had clearly altered his opinions of mainstream news media. In his work at Pacifica, Hoffman devoted sustained attention to the "problem of balance," arguing that the principle was best fulfilled when nonprofit media outlets provided alternative viewpoints to those articulated in commercial news formats.[95]

## SURVIVAL AND FREEDOM

The end of the Newsfilm Project was not quite the end of the Fund's involvement in television. One of its final commercial television projects, an interview program it called *Survival and Freedom* (1958), encapsulated the organization's rejection of the grassroots.[96] A Sunday night program hosted by Mike Wallace on ABC, the program was intended to serve as publicity for the Basic Issues concept.[97] The show was a version of *The Mike Wallace Interview*, a series of intense encounters between Wallace and often controversial guests that benefited from Wallace's emerging reputation as a sensationalist and probing interviewer.[98] In sponsoring the program, the Fund sought to capitalize on this reputation while bringing in a roster of guests whose high profile might encourage "opinion leaders" to watch the show.[99] This interest in addressing not the so-called masses but the elites within their ranks who might, as sociological studies at the time proposed, shape opinion, marks the shift in media policy that came with the new focus on Basic Issues.[100] With the sponsorship of *Survival and Freedom*, the Fund's trajectory in the media environment of the 1950s becomes clear. It followed a path that led from an eclectic, varied approach engaged in sponsoring small-scale efforts to bring about concrete change on the local level to a more nationally identified and abstract set of discussions staged among elites.

In its visual presentation and conceptual orientation, *Survival and Freedom* was the antithesis of the Newsfilm Project. The latter showed black people involved in actual struggles, facing racial injustice and terror in the concrete spaces of everyday life. *Survival and Freedom*, in contrast, took place in the abstracted space of a darkened

TV studio, an appropriate milieu given the generally abstract nature of the questions Wallace posed. Its guests, all white men, included such well-known liberals as Justice William O. Douglas, public intellectuals such as psychologist Eric Fromm and author Aldous Huxley, liberal business leaders such as Cyrus Eaton of Republic Steel and NBC's Sylvester "Pat" Weaver, and prominent foreign policy figures such as Henry Cabot Lodge Jr. and Henry Kissinger. The program used a minimal set: armchairs for Wallace and his guest, and a small table between them on which sat a sheaf of paper, some water glasses, and an ashtray the size of a dinner plate. Wallace is generally framed in medium shot, while the guest is framed either from behind Wallace, in an over-the-shoulder long shot, or (more usually) in a medium close-up. The conversation was uninterrupted by advertisements, which was no doubt a relief to viewers; prior to the Fund's sponsorship, Wallace did on-camera commercials for Philip Morris cigarettes. Wallace's questions seem to have involved some kind of consultation with Fund advisors. Several guests, for example, were asked to respond to the question "Is freedom necessary?"[101]

Considered in terms of access to network audiences, *Survival and Freedom* was the Fund's most successful foray into television. Its guests' statements frequently made headlines, and although it was initially contracted for only thirteen episodes, ABC extended the Fund's sponsorship run for another six.[102] However, tensions around balance and the definition of news emerged in the Fund's relations with ABC that were similar to those played out in the Newsfilm Project. As with the latter, the costs of the Fund's uneasy relationship with mainstream media were heaviest in the area of civil rights coverage. *Survival and Freedom* did not steer clear of civil rights issues, but the spokesmen for the cause who did appear on the show were Harry Ashmore, a white integrationist newspaper editor from Arkansas, and James McBride Dabbs, the white president of the Southern Regional Council. Both men spoke fervently; Dabbs was particularly outspoken, speaking candidly about the relationship between class and race in white Southern identity and indicating his acceptance of intermarriage. The use of white spokesmen for the civil rights cause was not the Fund's decision. Ted Yates, the show's producer, was a man committed to bringing black voices to mainstream TV (a few years later, while working at the independent New York station WNEW-TV, he made an effort to program the controversial film *The Cry of Jazz*, discussed in Chapter Two).[103] He tried to book Martin Luther King Jr. as a guest, but ABC refused to allow him on the show, arguing that Ashmore had already represented the civil rights cause on the program. Yates protested, pointing out that "in the interests of balanced programming it would seem sensible to me to have an important Negro on the series. In the year-plus that we've been on the network we have not interviewed a Negro. And in the presentation of the integration issue we have interviewed Governor Orval Faubus, the Imperial Wizard of the Ku Klux Klan, and Senator James Eastland, all segregationists."[104] Although this would seem like a persuasive argument within the terms of "balanced viewpoints," ABC stood firm and refused to allow a black interviewee.

The network's decision no doubt had something to do with a fear of alienating Southern audiences. But it might also have reflected wariness about the Fund among network personnel, who may have feared exposure to bias charges. This wariness seems to have led to some serious clashes between Hutchins and ABC executives. In one highly publicized case, the network refused at the last minute to air Wallace's interview with UN ambassador Henry Cabot Lodge Jr. because the Fund had allowed Lodge to edit and reshoot his comments, violating its code of objectivity for public affairs programming. Hutchins protested, claiming that the program was not news but rather an "educational interview" and that editing merely reflected a desire for conceptual clarity.[105] John Daly, the ABC news director who cancelled the broadcast, noted that Hutchins' letter of protest to the network misquoted *New York Times* columnist Jack Gould's assessment of the controversy. As he pointed out, Gould did not support the Fund's position, although Hutchins had claimed he did. Gould, Daly noted, was highly critical of the Fund's description of the programs: "I quote: 'under Dr. Hutchins' novel concept of the 'educational interview,' genuine reportorial independence becomes mere camouflage for a handout.'"[106] Undeterred, the Fund filed a claim against the network with the

ACLU, but it found no support. ACLU executive director Patrick Malin and radio-TV representative Tom Carskadon reviewed the case for Hutchins and agreed with Daly. In their words, "since the program is offered to the public as a news interview, the audience assumes it will see the give-and-take of a regular journalistic interview in which the subject presents his opinions in direct response to the questions. This is particularly true in view of the wide and deserved recognition that Mr. Wallace has won because of his penetrating television technique."[107]

Ultimately, what is significant about the Lodge controversy is neither the validity of the network's (and Gould's) arguments about journalistic integrity nor Hutchins' educational defense but rather its implications for the Fund's ongoing mission. In its efforts to alter the program, the Fund had violated the credos of free expression that it was established to serve. That Hutchins was unwilling to see the argument in these terms only confirmed Dwight Macdonald's damning 1952 assessment of Hutchins' educational philosophy, as embodied in the Great Books program: "There is a difference between informing the reader and telling him what to think that seems to escape Dr. Hutchins, possibly because in his case there isn't any difference."[108] The incident encapsulated the irreconcilable ideas about media and democracy that lay at the heart of all of the Fund's media projects. Ultimately, the organization's effort to translate democratic principles into the language of television only exposed and heightened the fundamental contradiction between the suggestible masses and the discerning rational citizen that lay at the heart of Hutchins' conception of the governed classes. The retreat from activism represented by the Basic Issues program resolved the contradiction by severing contact with the mass public. Although Hutchins was probably correct in his diagnosis of the Fund's shortcomings—namely, its assumption that everyone knew and approved of civil liberties—the Basic Issues program proposed a solution that, in advocating retreat rather than public engagement, only further entrenched the problem.

The contrast between the direct action agenda of the abandoned Newsfilm Project and the cerebral orientation of its effective replacement, *Survival and Freedom*, exemplifies the limitations of liberal thinking about media in the postwar years. George Martin's written communication with his employers at the Fund shows him adopting the tone of an underling charged with the futile task of satisfying a willful and impetuous child emperor. Hutchins was impatient to see the minds of Americans swing open, and regardless of whether Ferry's assessment of his racism is correct, it is certainly the case that his relationship to the Newsfilm Project betrayed an unrealistic understanding of the timeline and the effort involved in both civil rights activism and media reform. Perhaps the starkest example of this shortcoming is the fact that Hutchins demanded regular progress reports from Martin almost as soon as the project went national. The very idea of a "progress report" indicated his remove from the South and its struggles. It revealed his belief that civil rights was a finite goal, its achievement close at hand, and betrayed his naive impatience about the pace of its fulfillment.

Because of its abrupt, and arguably premature, cancellation, the Newsfilm Project stands as a tantalizingly unrealized possibility in the history of grassroots media. It was the product of diverse alliances between intergroup relations organizations, labor unions, church groups, and other protoactivist organizations, and in that capacity serves as an unacknowledged template for the kinds of activist media that would emerge in the 1960s. The latter are usually described, in technologically determinist framings, as a revolution brought about by the introduction of small-scale equipment: light film (and later video) cameras, increasingly portable sound recording apparatuses. But conceptions of technological possibility are always constrained by the political culture in which they emerge, and the studio-based, scripted efforts of individuals such as Edward Howden, who hosted the Fund-supported civil rights program *Barrier* on local San Francisco television (or, for that matter, the earnest Parent-Teacher Association role players of St. Louis, discussed in Chapter One), are not so much inadequate or insufficiently radical as they are indices of the limits of allowable media activism in the two decades between the end of World War II and the introduction of the Sony Portapak in 1967. The Newsfilm Project was a top-down effort insofar as it channeled Fund officers' concerns about the civic ignorance of the television-viewing public, but it also contained within it the seeds of a media organizing practice that would try to bring about national change on a local level, through institutions of public communication located within particular communities.

The Newsfilm Project was not the only postwar effort to manage populations and their opinions through nationally coordinated campaigns targeting local media outlets. Although their agendas were quite distinct from the Fund's, national labor organizations, as well as antiunion groups, were also heavily involved in local public affairs programming. Labor leadership's use of the medium to claim a voice in industrial and economic policy and to manage its relations with the movement's rank-and-file population is a field of governing by television that this book has yet to examine. In turning to it, the next (and final) chapter revisits the scene of economic activism detailed in Chapter One's account of DuPont's television work. Like the most politically innovative television projects of the Fund for the Republic, labor television in the 1950s spanned national and local scales, and it too sought to shape the meaning of balance, both as one of the period's core political values and as a principle of legitimation and access within the institution of television. Unlike the officers of the Fund, the labor leaders who initiated the programs discussed in the next chapter were by no means anointed members of the Establishment. But they were, increasingly, an elite group separated by bureaucracy and political aspiration from the rank and file they represented, and their experiments with governing by television were forms of elite communication insofar as they endeavored to appropriate the language of individual sovereignty, self-actualized rule, and maximum freedom that provided access to the forms of power and legitimacy authorized within postwar governmental reason.

New Board Members:   Incoming Board Chairman Elmo
Roper introduces three new Board members and comments
on the current state of American freedom.   To local
stations in New York City, Washington, D. C.,
Arkansas, and Los Angeles.   Estimated audience: 908,500.

Negroes Vote:   Scenes in Cuthbert, Georgia, as
Negroes exercise their franchise there for the first
time.   Estimated audience:   555,500.

Bus Boycott Ends:   Negroes begin riding busses in
Montgomery, Alabama, on unsegregated basis, ending
their long boycott of the bus line following
Supreme Court decision in their favor.   Estimated
audience:   1,458,000.

Statues:   Beverly Hills art dealer seeks injunction
permitting him to display in his window nude
replicas of famous statues, including Michaelangelo's
"David".   Police had ordered the figurines removed
as "obscene".   To Los Angeles stations.   Estimated
audience:   555,500.

## Chapter Five
# LABOR GOES PUBLIC

POLITE HOSTILITY is an art, and George Meany, president of the American Federation of Labor, demonstrated his mastery of the form in a brief note to CBS president Dr. Frank Stanton in September 1953. Meany's ostensible purpose was to thank the network for broadcasting *Labor '53*, an AFL-sponsored documentary film that aired in public service time on Sunday, September 6, the day before the Labor Day national holiday. But the word *thank* did not appear in Meany's letter. Merely expressing his "appreciation" for CBS' "interest in presenting" the program, Meany used the occasion to inform Stanton of television's poor record covering organized labor—"this is the first time such a program was presented on the networks"—and to spike the reproof with a boast: "You might be interested to know that we have received quite a bit of favorable comment on the program, not only from our people but from the general public."[1]

Stanton, however, proved to be an equally skillful player in the game of feigned cordiality. "It was thoughtful and extremely considerate of you to take time out from your busy day to write me about Labor '53," he wrote, laying it on thick with the redundant combination of "thoughtful" and "considerate." Stanton responded to Meany's dig about network television's meager labor coverage with the reassurance that CBS was "always willing and eager to schedule programs such as this," although he undercut the affirmation with a proviso: "when they are in the broad public interest and serve to inform and educate the tremendous audiences which the CBS networks reach."[2] With these politely pointed words, Stanton insinuated that the AFL did not commonly speak in the public interest, whereas CBS, the arbiter of neutrality, served its innumerable viewers by protecting them from the incursions of "special" or "vested" interests—a category in which, for Stanton at least, organized labor presumably belonged. Underneath the courteous language was the ill-concealed conviction that labor could not be trusted to honor the fancied distinction between propaganda and public service on which rested the television industry's claims to mediate and represent the interests of the nation.

This barbed exchange, with its veneer of civility, not only captures the tenuous nature of labor's relationship with commercial television in the 1950s but also indicates, in its concern with "public" (and, by implication, "special") interests, the degree to which labor's pursuit of TV sponsorship was closely entwined with its postwar struggle to participate in national governance. Ira Katznelson has succinctly described this moment as a transition "from labor as political opposition to labor as interest group."[3] The transition was a product of Cold War political culture, in which the spread of anticommunism dissolved previous activist alliances between liberals and the working classes, demanding a new political identity for labor. Trade unionists took steps to integrate labor into the political mainstream, embracing anticommunism and endeavoring to control grassroots actions among workers, especially after 1946, when a strike wave powerfully demonstrated the insurgent potential of the rank and file.[4] Detailing the agenda for labor in his 1947 Labor Day message, AFL president

William Green railed against the devastating Taft-Hartley Act passed that year, but he cautioned against a "spontaneous surge" of resistance. "We must fight our enemies not with ill-considered strikes," Green argued, "but with ballots, in the peaceful, democratic, and American way."[5] With these words Green, like many other labor leaders in the postwar period, articulated a vision of labor as a participant in pluralist governance, part of a polity increasingly understood as, in the words of one historian, a "roiling inconclusive contest of interested groups."[6] Signaling the extent of his commitment, Green also hitched the movement's future to the postwar economy's promise of endless, sustainable growth: "For our own good and the welfare of our country, we must keep production going at full blast."[7]

Over the remainder of the decade, television sponsorship would prove vital for disseminating this vision of labor's place in governance, providing a forum in which to confront trade unionism's enemies and to promote its contributions to postwar prosperity. Public service programming was a particularly crucial venue, even though it attracted a negligible audience and was a marginal format within the commercial institution of television. This was because the National Association of Manufacturers (NAM), long considered one of the most vehement and mudslinging business lobbies in American politics, was a prominent public service sponsor. The NAM's syndicated documentary film series *Industry on Parade* ran on local stations across the nation throughout the decade, winning critical praise and a number of Peabody Awards for its triumphant depictions of American industrial production. The program's address to the public was carefully crafted. As publicity director G.W. "Johnny" Johnstone explained in an internal memorandum, its "non-commercial, non-controversial, educational, and entertaining" approach strived "to create atmosphere and not debate," although he could not help boasting that "we go as far as we dare . . . under 'public service' time."[8] In taking viewers inside the factory and showing them how mass production created the economic freedoms enjoyed by American citizens, *Industry on Parade* perfected the art of the industrial film as a form of public relations and an outlet for Cold War economic nationalism.

The educational approach of *Industry on Parade* also gave NAM a powerful visual and rhetorical repertoire for countering negative perceptions that might have arisen from its invective-laden radio programming of previous decades, and consolidated the new "pro-public" identity it had begun to fashion in 1947 with its massive campaign for the passage of Taft-Hartley.[9] Characterizing the bill as an "impartial" and "improved" law "primarily designed to advance the interests of the whole public while still safeguarding the rights of all employees," NAM's Taft-Hartley activism laid the groundwork for a postwar media strategy that would relegate labor, as William L. Bird notes, to "extra-public status."[10] Faced with the NAM's colonization of the public interest, organized labor sought access to public service television in order to assert its political legitimacy and balance the management viewpoint. The icy exchange between Stanton and Meany was thus far more than a tussle between a haughty professor and a cheeky plumber; it was, rather, a pitched moment in the ongoing conflict over labor's claim to occupy a place in the pluralist schema of postwar politics. The conflict would continue throughout the 1950s, especially after the merger of the AFL and the Congress of Industrial Organizations fueled antiunion campaigns to instill public fear of "big labor."

The television projects of the newly formed AFL-CIO were conceived as a vehicle for battling negative public opinion and challenging *Industry on Parade*. Much as business groups used television as a means of "humanizing" the corporation, a process detailed in Chapter One's analysis of DuPont institutional advertising, the AFL-CIO used television to present the people of the labor movement to the public. As Meany explained when the federation announced the launch of its syndicated public service documentary series *Americans at Work* (1958–1961), "Much has been filmed of the gigantic machines that produce the goods used by everyone, everywhere. But the people who man these machines, the people who keep the products flowing, are more interesting than machines . . . we want our fellow Americans to take pride in our nation's workers and their contribution to the free enterprise system in a democracy."[11] With the reference to machines, Meany pointedly placed *Americans at Work* in opposition to the vision of industrial

As one executive at WGBH in Boston recognized, the AFL-CIO's *Americans at Work* was a vehicle for talking back to the corporate triumphalism of *Industry on Parade*, produced by the National Association of Manufacturers in the same period.
*Image courtesy of George Meany Memorial Archives.*

progress in *Industry on Parade*, although the populism of his statement was leavened with a Cold War economic rhetoric hardly distinguishable from that of NAM.

As this uneasy combination of populist and capitalist rhetoric might suggest, *Americans at Work* provides rich material for exploring the continuities between the televisual representation of working people and their economic governance.[12] As an effort to govern by television, the program is important today not only because it bears witness to labor's struggles as an interest group but also because of the stories about the economy that it tells, and the forms of economic citizenship it envisions. Scrutinizing the scripts, films, and other production materials housed in the George Meany Memorial Archives in Silver Spring, Maryland, one sees clearly that labor's sponsorship of public service programming was also the sponsorship of new conceptions of the individual, as a particular kind of laboring being, that were emerging in the postwar political economy. This chapter explores the visual and verbal counterpoint through which this occurred, examining how particular episodes of *Americans at Work* embody the transition from one mode of labor's visual representation to another, and how they register the internal contradictions of labor's postwar political and economic strategy in the process.

With production costs of over $300,000 and distribution reaching one hundred stations, *Americans at Work* was labor's largest television venture in the 1950s.[13] Its producer, Philip Martin, was a veteran of Popular Front–era documentary. The founder of Norwood Studios, a large industrial film producer in Washington, D.C., Martin worked with renowned New Deal documentarian Pare Lorentz in the 1930s. He won an Academy Award in 1946 for editing the now-classic anti-prejudice film *The House I Live In*, which starred Frank Sinatra and was directed by Albert Maltz, one of the "Hollywood Ten" blacklisted by the studios during and after the McCarthy era.[14] Martin's crew for *Americans at Work* included Boyd Wolff, one of the founders of the United Nations Film Division, as head writer.[15] Wolff was connected to the Federal Writers' Project in the 1940s, and the episodes he scripted bear the residual imprint of Popular Front–era aesthetics.[16] A jovial, bearded man, he quoted liberally from poetry, particularly Walt Whitman ("when the materials are all prepared, the architects shall appear"), and he worked hard to connect the stories of labor told in *Americans at Work* to broader economic processes, a method reminiscent of Karl Marx's explanation of the workings of capitalism through an analysis of a single commodity such as wheat.[17] (In one notable episode on workers in the cereal industry, Wolff wrote of a flake of milled grain: "This, in effect, is a picture of politics and economics held in the palm of a man's hand.")[18] Although Wolff died in 1964, I was able to track down his colleague S. Paul Klein, who served as the second writer on the series. Klein described Martin and Wolff as "strongly pro-union men ... filmmakers of the thirties and forties who understood the [political] importance of what they were doing,"

*Americans at Work* writers Paul Klein (left) and Boyd Wolff (right) wore luxuriant beards, marking them as a breed apart from their clients and colleagues in labor film production. *Image courtesy of S. Paul Klein.*

and who saw the television film as a format in which to extend their Popular Front sensibility into postwar visual culture.[19]

If *Americans at Work* is a fertile case study for exploring labor's vision of governing by television, it is in part because the Popular Front voice that found expression in Wolff's scripts was fundamentally at odds with the dominant rhetoric of national labor organizations in this period. Indeed, at times media workers within official labor federations actively silenced this voice, as the production records of *Operation Entertainment*, a pre-merger program sponsored by the AFL, make evident. A one-hour tribute to the USO co-sponsored with the U.S. Army in September 1954, its scripting process quite literally excised thirties-style verbal iconography from the AFL's public relations text. The first draft of an AFL sponsor announcement featured documentary images of bridge construction and farm work, accompanied by narration that described AFL members with modernist verbal imagery evoking the physical power of human work: "From the sweat of their toil emerge cities and skyscrapers . . . highways and the homes we live in." The visual imagery remained in the final version, but someone, likely Morris Novik, the federation's radio-television consultant, deleted this evocative sentence and substituted one that replaced references to working bodies with the consummately technocratic language of Cold War political economy: "They create the material of our standards of living, and the weapons to protect it."[20] This small redaction, combining impersonal, rationalist markers of economic well-being and nuclear scaremongering, suggested a new use for images of working people in labor media. In previous decades, documentary footage of workers at work had played a key role in labor's visual culture, its physical concreteness and human specificity providing an insistent, if romanticizing, iconography for radical articulations of solidarity rooted in the idea of the people. Now the purpose of such images was to anchor the abstraction of the Cold War–era economy, the people they displayed serving as ciphers of consumption-oriented economic citizenship.[21]

Against the Popular Front era's affirmation of working *people*, this new language of labor publicity presented the *population* as the basic economic unit of democracy, stressing workers' place in an economy of scale over their individual stories. *Americans at Work* readily incorporated this new language. In Klein's recollection, Novik rarely intervened in the writing process for the series; however, the "teaching points" he and other union officials provided for each episode stressed not the might and rights of labor but rather, via abundant facts and figures, the immense productivity of the workers on-screen and its relation to the standard of living enjoyed by all Americans. Like *Industry on Parade*, the series relied heavily on astonishing statistics and whimsical metaphors: "thousands of tons of ink . . . supply the thirsty presses of magazines, newspapers, and other publications" (*Industry on Parade*); "it takes four thousand meat packers to ship sixty-six million pounds of meat to over three hundred thousand stores in the

United States every day" (*Americans at Work*).[22] Indeed, encountering them together today, it is striking to see how much the two programs resemble each other, at least on first viewing. Both focus on the hidden world inside the factory, structuring each episode as a macroeconomic parable in which the production and consumption of commodities ensures economic growth.[23] The similarity extends to encompass the moral meanings implied in these narratives. In each program jaunty voice-over narration characterizes consumer goods as vehicles of the public good, registering the formidable demands of consumers as the basis for the overall wealth of the nation. Matching the hyperbolic economies of scale described in the voice-over, each program uses camera setups that stress the serial sameness of the items that rolled off endless conveyor belts, as if their perfect uniformity were evidence of the democratic equality of the Americans who produce and consume them.

This embrace of the conventions of corporate industrial film was a new media strategy for the labor movement, one quite distinct from the methods and styles of previous decades. It might be tempting to interpret the formal and rhetorical similarity between *Americans at Work* and *Industry on Parade* as merely an obligatory gesture, on a par with the strategic depiction of "both sides" in the Fund for the Republic's civil rights news films, discussed in the preceding chapter—an unpleasant but necessary ritual of access required by the conservative institution of broadcasting. But such concessions were a departure from the labor media activism of the 1930s and 1940s, and they had as much to do with changes in the labor movement, and the political climate in which it operated, as with the demands of television. In these prior decades, as Elizabeth Fones-Wolf has shown, unions used radio to "challenge the capitalist broadcasting system" as well as to organize and recruit members.[24] Although these strategies continued into the television age, particularly in highly industrial areas such as Detroit, where unions used local airtime as an effective means of communicating with their members, labor television sponsorship on the national level embraced to a hyperbolic degree the ideas of balance and fairness implied by interest group governance.[25] This concern with balance affirmed the power of corporate activism around Taft-Hartley, a bill premised on the idea of balancing the interests of labor and management, and indicated labor's consent not only to the discursive rules of public service broadcasting but also to the terms of postwar antiunion activism. Gerald Pomper, a political scientist conducting doctoral research at the AFL-CIO at the end of the 1950s, noticed the similarity between *Americans at Work* and institutional advertising produced by business, worrying about its implications: "When they perform their tasks properly," he pointed out, "unions by their very nature are disturbers of the status quo."[26] In adopting the industrial film format, Pomper suggested, the AFL-CIO conveyed the impression that its political goals were consonant with, rather than a challenge to, corporate power.[27]

This worrisome symmetry with management media strategies did not originate with *Americans at Work* but rather was the culmination of a trend in national labor television programming that began soon after Taft-Hartley's passage, particularly in the sponsorship practices of the AFL. Although Meany and other AFL leaders pressed for the repeal of the bill, the sponsored speech of TV programs such as *Operation Entertainment* advanced the bill's ideological vision of economic governance as a form of reciprocal partnership, heralding the postwar economy as the end of class struggle. The extent of this conciliatory approach is evident in the AFL-sponsored Sunday afternoon discussion program entitled *Both Sides*, which adopted an ostentatiously neutral approach to matters of controversy. It aired in unpaid public service time on ABC in 1953 and 1954, but the adherence to the principle of balanced viewpoints signaled in its title went beyond the basic convention of allotting equal time to guests with opposing views. The program featured commercials that purposely avoided commentary on the issues under discussion, stressing instead, in Novik's words, "the public service character and community interest of the labor movement."[28] However, the scripts for these commercials, filed among Novik's papers at the George Meany Memorial Archives, indicate that this identification with the public interest also involved identifying the interests of labor with those of capital. "The American Federation of Labor believes in free enterprise—for private capital as well as workers and farmers," one commercial's script reads. "This is the only country in the world where organized labor upholds the free enterprise system, where class hatred and class warfare are absent, where trade unions are willing to cooperate with private business to produce prosperity for all."[29] Such appeasing rhetoric was not altogether new in AFL media work, but its language of total collaboration was a consummate postwar invention, a product of Taft-Hartley–era industrial governance.[30]

More than a concession to TV's conventions, this language of partnership and teamwork was central to trade unionists' quest for a place in the postwar political order. Labor leaders in the 1950s assented to the period's prevailing reverie of an economy managed by "countervailing powers," as J.K. Galbraith's classic macroeconomic treatise described it—a vision in which unions and employers figured as complementary (rather than opposed) entities, united in their shared pursuit of national prosperity.[31] Labor was at best a "junior partner" in what Robert Griffith has called Eisenhower's "corporate commonwealth," but unions nevertheless demonstrated their appetite for pluralist teamwork in the collective bargaining process, pursuing contracts that reaped "the benefits of productivity."[32] The result was a superficial alliance between labor leadership and management in the 1950s, a "limited and unstable truce" that, notes Nelson Lichtenstein, was "the product of defeat, not victory."[33] In reality, the confrontation between labor and management moved from struggles over production to struggles over consumption, as manifested in the rise of contracts that emphasized the rights of workers to a portion of the economic gains from increased productivity.[34] Affirming consumption as the production of both national wealth and human capital—in Michel Foucault's words, "an enterprise activity by which the individual . . . will produce something that will be his own satisfaction"—the new language of labor activism in the 1950s anchored a macroeconomic vision fundamentally at odds with New Deal ideals of economic justice and redistribution.[35]

Although the language of cooperation seemed to hold the key to labor's political and economic citizenship, the effects of postwar industrial pluralism on the future of American trade unionism would prove to be grave. When World War II ended, union membership was at 35 percent of the U.S. workforce; by 1983, it was down to 20 percent, and in 2007 it was at 12 percent.[36] The ideology of industrial cooperation could not prevent the foment of antiunion sentiment throughout the 1950s, as ongoing congressional hearings on labor racketeering and the electoral advance of the right-to-work lobby provided plenty of evidence that labor was under attack within the political system. And the terms of the so-called truce greatly benefited management in the long run. Over the course of the prosperous 1950s and most of the 1960s, union leaders sacrificed their say in the quality of work life and their long-term control over the production process in favor of the wage increases associated with productivity. For industry, wage accords did little to interfere with long-term strategies of automation and plant relocation, the latter a tactic increasingly exploited as states adopted right-to-work laws.[37] The tenuous terms of labor-capital cooperation disintegrated with the economic crises of the 1970s, as corporations and government took decisive steps to disempower and defund organized labor.

On the surface, at least, there is no hint of this grim future in the cheery tales of industrial production told by *Americans at Work*. But although the program's public story of economic life was suffused with the affirmative language of growth and cooperation, the residual trace of earlier ways of imagining work and workers remained. A closer examination of the program, particularly those episodes authored by Wolff, illuminates the ways that retooling the imagery of laboring Americans for national media audiences was a process haunted by the past—and the future—of working-class politics in the United States. Indeed, through careful scrutiny, it becomes clear that the AFL-CIO's efforts to use the documentary format as a vehicle for explaining the relation between union membership and economic citizenship was a process that ultimately showed more than it was meant to reveal.

## DOCUMENTARY SURREALISM

The most obvious manifestation of the Popular Front aesthetic in Wolff's *Americans at Work* scripts is the use of imaginative language—mystical, psychoanalytically inflected, and sometimes even spiritual—to characterize the world of work. In an undated episode about workers in the paper industry, for example, the fanciful narration accompanying images of women working in an envelope factory asked viewers to ponder the fact that that "for an instant, this girl's fingertips touch the lives of countless unknown people in events yet to be unfolded," while the narration of a February 1960 episode featuring the United Packing Workers union poetically described the one hundred pounds of sugar consumed by each American every year as "a light snowfall blanketing the country."[38] But it would be an oversimplification to view this language as by itself a manifestation of the Popular Front sensibility. Indeed, it affirmed the consumption politics that cemented the labor-management truce, rendering the shop floor as the portal to a magical realm of circulation and exchange—the "enchanted, perverted, topsy-turvy world" wherein, Marx famously noted, the capitalist mode of production reproduced itself, via "the conversion of social relations into things."[39] The deeper sense of politics in Wolff's scripts emerges instead from the juxtaposition of word and image, each telling a different story, so that the narrator's hymns to the benefits of productivity-based industrial pluralism often anchor an image track that says something quite different. Visual representations, especially images of everyday life, are unruly vehicles for governance, and in their counterpoint with Wolff's narration, they illuminate the contradictions within the regime of economic accumulation to which postwar labor leadership subscribed.

The story these scripts tell is the story of labor's unwritten future. Automation loomed on the horizon, and beyond it lay the globalized offshore production schemes of the future, already in motion in the 1950s with the southward migration of key American industries.[40] In the aforementioned episode about sugar workers, for example, the narrative credited organized labor for the commodity's sweet abundance, but most of its footage of people working was shot in prerevolutionary Cuba, and the machete-wielding workers it showed were neither American nor AFL-CIO members. Seemingly aware of the problem this might pose, Wolff's voice-over script alluded to the setting simply as "one of the islands off the shores of the continental United States," but scenes of palm-lined Plaza Havana give away its location. The image track continues to reveal more than it is supposed to in the scenes shot in the United States. In the stark, antiseptic confines of the processing plant we see only one or two workers, their bodies dwarfed by the enormous sugar refinery equipment; the disjunctive scale makes their labor seem marginal to the production of sugar. Although the packing union is the focus of the episode, only one member of the union appears on-screen over the course of the program: a woman who patiently guides packages of sugar, filled by a machine, as they turn the corner on a conveyor belt. The shot is repeated several times, and this editing pattern creates the sense that her labor is largely symbolic—that it is the *image*, not the person it represents, that counts. What's more, the repetition of the shot only emphasizes the repetitiveness of her labor, suggesting that not just her image but also her job can be mechanically reproduced, through automation.

Although *Americans at Work* was the product of a time when labor's political strategy centered on the right to participate in consumption rather than on the right to govern the process of production, such views of the factory's interior documented the shop floor's continued, if disavowed, relevance as a realm of class conflict. Regardless of what the narrator said, the visual track testified to the costs involved in labor leaders' commitment to an economic order that defined the empowerment of workers in terms of purchasing power in the market rather than control over the conditions of the workplace. Indeed, the narration's lyrical language, replete with fantastic metaphors and arcane references, often seems to compensate for, or smooth over, the inadequacy of the image alone as a vehicle for conveying the centrality of union workers to the continuation of postwar abundance. When I interviewed him, Klein characterized Wolff as a man with vast knowledge and education, explaining his tendency toward lyricism as an effort to rise above the conventions of the factory film. "We wanted people to enjoy the process [and] bring a little elegance," Klein explained, implying that the goal was to transform the factory film into a vehicle for broader cultural education. This motivation is certainly evident in the episode about sugar making, which reaches back to ancient texts, quoting from the Bible and from Hindu and Buddhist scripture, to highlight the enduring human connection to sugar's "crystallized sunlight." But Klein's explanation doesn't account for the moments when image and word contradict each other. In this episode, the high-flown language only accentuates the abjectness of the scenes unfolding before the camera: shots of tractors and dirt, of desolate cane fields where workers in ragged clothing hack away at the densely planted shoots under the beating sun. Indeed, at times, the narrational hyperbole is so great that it reads as ironic. Over shots of brutal field work, hardly paradisiacal, the narrator declares: "From semi-tropical regions that are the nearest things on earth to paradise that we can know comes what poets have called 'angels' bread,' 'manna,' and 'nectar of the gods.'"

As Chapter One detailed, DuPont advertisements of the late 1950s sought to address viewers' "irrational" fears of business with techniques such as gigantism, and *Industry on Parade* certainly used fanciful analogies, as in an episode comparing the loading of cargo onto a freighter to passengers boarding a luxury liner.[41] But Wolff's scripts for *Americans at Work* take dreamlike and surreal imagery to new heights. Clearly familiar with both Marx and Freud, he introduced playful free association into the narrations he scripted, often with notably comic results. Personification—endowing the commodity with anthropomorphic qualities—was one of Wolff's favored techniques; he also displayed a taste for the incongruously absurd simile, proposing comparisons reminiscent of the aesthetics of the historical avant-garde. The narration of a film about upholstery workers declares that "furniture is the confidante and mute witness of all the intimate details of family life," a characterization that recalls the celebrated explanation of commodity fetishism in volume one of Marx's *Capital*, structured around the metaphor of a table that begins to think and "evolves out of its wooden brain grotesque ideas."[42] And jarring imagery evocative of Dada performance suffuses a film about meat cutters, in which the voice-over tells us that women workers preparing sausages for the smoker "gather up the links in seemingly endless chains, like necklaces."[43]

This promiscuously surreal imagery abounds in the scripts authored by Wolff, enacting the aesthetic of the grotesque that Michael Denning has identified as a signature of the arts of the Popular Front era. In opposition to conventional arguments that name social realism and documentary as the period's primary aesthetic modes, Denning cites examples as diverse as "the distended vowels of Billie Holiday's 'Strange Fruit'" and "the gargoyles that open *Citizen Kane*" to propose that "this proletarian grotesque is a plebeian appropriation of the avant-garde hostility to 'art,' the anti-aesthetic of Dada and surrealism."[44] The "contradictory fusions" of the grotesque are not inherently revolutionary; as Sharon Ghamari-Tabrizi has demonstrated, the grotesque's "ambivalent and volatile" voicing proliferates in Cold War nuclear culture.[45] Ghamari-Tabrizi's Cold War grotesque is epitomized in the figure of the Rand Corporation's nuclear expert Herman Kahn, who "jumbled together ordinarily segregated kinds of speech into a mishmash of expressions high and low, exalted and vulgar, scientific and uncouth" in his efforts to render tangible the perversity of trying to plan for a future after the unspeakable horror of thermonuclear war.[46]

The intrusions of the grotesque into Wolff's *Americans at Work* scripts synthesize both its proletarian and apocalyptic dimensions, injecting an aesthetic of shocking, even macabre, incongruity into the fabled abundance of postwar consumer society.[47] TV viewers in the early morning hours allotted for public service programming may not have recognized the surreal world of sausage necklaces, bewitched envelopes, and sugar blizzards created in Wolff's scripts as the dark side of the sponsor's optimistic vision of economic citizenship. But historians of the present, turning their attention to the stylistic and semiotic palette of the postwar industrial film, have made it increasingly clear that the genre, in the words of Edward Dimendberg, "rewards close reading with a veritable return of repressed geopolitical relations."[48] Expressing an ambivalence that could not be spoken directly, grotesque imagery in *Americans at Work* hinted at a repressed past and an unimaginable future that are recoverable now through the methods of close analysis the genre was never supposed to sustain. One episode in particular, a documentary about doll making, supplies richly suggestive material for thinking about the forms of citizenship that labor could articulate through television, as well as those waiting on the other end of the postwar trajectory of economic growth proposed in *Americans at Work*.

## DIALECTICAL DOLLS

July, 1959. Imagine awakening early one Saturday morning and turning on the television set. One channel is showing an installment of *The Christophers*, a filmed program teaching principles of Christian anticommunism through drama, reenactment, and panel discussions. On another channel, the arts program *Camera Three* features an opera singer warbling in a darkened studio. The third channel yields more promising material: an episode of *Americans at Work* shot inside a doll factory.[49] The film exploits its subject in striking ways. Shot after shot highlights the uncanny attributes of half-made dolls, looking horrifyingly like lifeless white babies. As incongruously cheerful music swells on the soundtrack, we see a man pump liquid plastic into the molds where dolls' heads are made. The egglike crania, just about life-size, go to an oven to incubate. When they are done the worker stabs each one with scissors, then quickly and efficiently uses forceps to pull it free. This violently corporeal image, the head stretching and twisting as if reluctant to leave the mold, is only one of many nightmarish images that appear in this film. In another sequence, tiny arms and legs travel along an assembly line and tumble off the end into a pile of severed limbs. An extended series of shots carefully documents the dolls' gradual acquisition of human features. Their blank, white faces stare eyelessly into space as a black woman in cat's-eye glasses gives them finely arched brows, rendering their perpetually surprised expressions with a delicate brush. In the hair department, women in lab coats perforate the dolls' vulnerable scalps with a stitching machine. Another worker uses a wicked-looking probe to puncture the dolls' eye sockets. It crumples their faces for an instant, leaving hard plastic eyes behind.

Entitled "Doll and Toy Makers" and scripted by Boyd Wolff, this episode of *Americans at Work* seems to have been filmed at a factory owned by the Ideal Toy Company of New York. Although the name of the manufacturer is not mentioned, the episode features a doll identical to the company's popular Betsy Wetsy model, and its footage is very similar to material included in a Betsy Wetsy promotional film made at around the same time.[50] "Doll and Toy Makers" is one of the most visually striking episodes of the *Americans at Work* series. It is also one of the most rhetorically adventurous, its voice-over continually using fetishistic language to animate the inanimate. The dolls, Wolff's script suggest, are not inert commodities but rather plastic

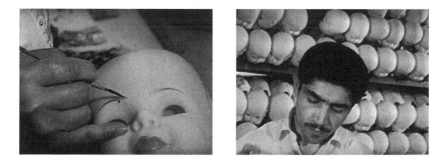

In an episode of *Americans at Work* featuring workers in the doll-making industry, the contrast between the faces of black and Latino workers and the icy white sameness of the dolls called attention to the racial divides of the postwar economy and the labor movement more generally.

homunculi that are, if we choose to believe so, *alive*: "Another doll is born as arms, legs, and head are joined to the torso. While no doll is childproof, the doll maker will give each one the best possible chance for a long and happy life." With such turns of phrase, the narration characterizes workers as the midwives and guardians of the commodities they produce, often to ironic effect: in one scene, we see women diaper and dress the dolls, carelessly flinging them onto a conveyor belt, while the narrator describes them as mothers lovingly tending their infants. The sense of subversive irony surfaces most clearly in the places where Wolff loads the parenting metaphor with sexual innuendo. The narration tells us that the design process takes place in a room reached by "a passageway known only to a few," followed by shots of a long injection rod rhythmically squirting white plastic into the head molds. Voice-over accompanying a shot of a worker tending the molds explains that "a new family of identical brothers and sisters is in creation. The stuff that is to become a doll must . . . spend a certain amount of time in the oven for curing."

In establishing a connection between obstetric and organized labor, the episode's fanciful tale of dolls gestating in the unionized factory told a larger story about the economy, forming an analogy between

the inhuman baby boom documented by the camera inside the factory and the explosive reproductive rates that fueled the postwar consumer society: "The modern toy factory is a far cry from the traditional Santa Claus workshop, which could hardly fill today's need." Watching this sequence today, it is astonishing to think that its eroticized depiction of plastic babies maturing in womb-kilns made it through the approval process, which involved vetting not only by representatives of the AFL-CIO but also by union officials and management from the factory featured on-screen. If the double entendre of Wolff's script was not apparent to these gatekeepers, it may have been because such off-color moments are eclipsed by the parable of citizenship the episode narrates, an elaborate tale in which dolls and the workers who make them are integral to the proper psychological development of the Americans of the future.

This proposition is established at the beginning of the episode, in a scene of little girls playing with dolls. The narration proclaims that the pleasures of doll ownership reside in the ability to choose your own doll and create a world with it, a description that links the imaginative activity of play to the utopian promises of postwar consumption: endless variety, maximum choice, and (because the narration

will subsequently highlight the miracle of mass production) technological advancement. Later, the script returns to the point, suggesting
that toys are crucial for the formation of the well-developed individual, a category of personhood that was central to Cold War citizen
talk and which anchored the developmental narratives of the period's
child psychology: "the outright creations of fancy that we call toys are
needed to allow full play for youthful imaginations [and] help children cut life down to their own size."[51] Wolff's narration is careful
to affirm the place of the unionized workforce in the process of indi-
vidualization, explaining that the tough treatment dolls receive as
they aid their owners' journeys of self-discovery means that they must
be unbreakable, made by skilled workers from the most advanced
materials.

With its allusions to child psychology, the developmental narrative of "Doll and Toy Makers" blends seamlessly into the racial politics of the period. The visual and psychological relationship between
children and dolls was a serious matter in the 1950s, providing a key
framework for thinking about the corrosive effects of segregation. In
a series of studies conducted in the 1940s, psychologists Kenneth B.
Clark and Mamie Phipps Clark had used dolls to evaluate children's

self-images, asking black and white children to choose between two dolls, one black and one white, with a series of commands culminating in "give me the doll that looks like you."[52] This last question prompted high levels of emotional distress among black children, a response that aided the Clarks' conclusion that segregation bred a sense of inferiority. In 1954, Kenneth Clark testified before the Supreme Court in *Brown v. Board of Education*, and the studies were quoted in the text of the decision.[53]

The Clarks' studies might seem tangential to the story of "Doll and Toy Makers" were it not for the fact that they also affected the postwar product development program of the Ideal Toy Company. In 1951, the company worked with a group of prominent black and white citizens led by Sara Lee Creech, a white intergroup relations activist inspired by the doll studies, to manufacture the first "anthropologically correct Negro doll." Named Sara Lee, the doll was introduced to the public with great fanfare, appearing with Eleanor Roosevelt and Ralph Bunche on the covers of both *Time* and *Newsweek*.[54] "Doll and Toy Makers" makes no mention of this activist history, even though Sara Lee was quite likely manufactured in the factory where its footage was shot. This was no doubt because the doll was discontinued in

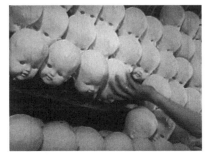

1953, crushed by the heavy political burden it was asked to bear; as historian Sabrina Lynnette Thomas notes, "not only was [it] assigned the role of healing racial wounds between white and black citizens [but it] also was expected to do the work of challenging the derogatory features of traditional Negro dolls and brokering racial acceptance from white citizens."[55] Still, despite its brief life span, Sara Lee's public debut as an "ambassador of peace" made skin color a central concern in subsequent understandings of the "lifelike" dimensions of dolls.[56] This concern finds expression in "Doll and Toy Makers" via the glaring whiteness of the doll parts that glide across the screen on the assembly line, their eerie, pale sameness contrasting sharply with the racial diversity of the workforce.

As the film unfolds, we see twelve people working on the dolls over the course of the episode: five white women; four dark-skinned, possibly Latino, men; two black women; and one white man.[57] This scrupulous attention to diversity was a reflection of AFL-CIO policy; according to Klein, the federation stipulated that *Americans at Work* should represent unions as successfully integrated organizations. Indeed, the only direct "orders" Meany gave the production team concerned the program's codes of racial representation: the films not only had to

include nonwhite workers but also should avoid showing "black people doing menial tasks."[58] "Doll and Toy Makers" scrupulously complied with this policy, but the effect was unnerving. At times the editing deliberately seems to contrast the blank whiteness of the dolls' faces with the human, racially coded specificity of the faces of the men and women who make them, creating a disjunctive sense of kinship and difference in the juxtaposition, for example, between the cat's-eye frames of a black woman's glasses and the eyebrows she is painting on a doll's decapitated head. The contrast is reiterated in a subsequent scene, where a dark-skinned man inspects row upon row of identical white heads. As we watch him sand their necks in preparation for attachment to the torso, the narrator comments on the importance of eliminating imperfections, the sameness of the dolls foregrounding the worker's human particularity.[59] Such instances of off-kilter language and stark black-and-white imagery suggest that Meany's policy for racial representation did not eradicate negative imagery altogether.

Directives for Negro representation were not the only AFL-CIO "teaching points" to make it into the film. The other—industrial cooperation—appears in a discussion of the dolls' flawless hand-painted faces ("their faces will be their fortunes, and the fortunes of worker

 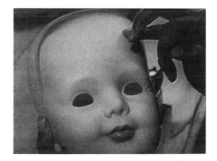

and manufacturer too") and over shots of skilled workers operating machines ("to produce enough dolls to keep up with the increasing human population, the modern craftsman must use man-made, man-run machines"). This phrasing portrays the dolls, the workers who make them, and the manufacturer as dependent upon the desires of the child, whose demands are more broadly symbolic of the economy as a whole. Such references to consumer demand (rather than the autocratic actions of employers) as the force to which labor was ultimately answerable were common to many episodes of *Americans at Work*, reflecting the quest for mainstream political participation that defined labor's postwar public relations efforts. It is as if the dolls are figures of the economic system as a whole: just as the workers endow the dolls with life, the demands of consumers animate the economic system. Like the doll, the economy is a kind of automaton; the energy that keeps it in perpetual motion is the managed equilibrium of supply and demand.

The possibility of this analogy is a reminder that in 1959, the very *idea* of the economy was a relatively recent invention. The postwar period saw the rise of economic planning as set of highly rational and unassailably objective processes, managed and rendered concrete in

policies, contracts, and statistics. As Timothy Mitchell notes, this vision of the economy as at once self-correcting and highly dependent upon technocratic expertise "did not emerge until the middle decade of the twentieth century [when] economists, sociologists, national statistical agencies, international and corporate organizations, and government programs formulated the concept ... as a self-contained, internally dynamic, and statistically measurable sphere of social analysis and political regulation."[60] Documentaries such as *Americans at Work* and *Industry on Parade* gave form to this new, concrete, manageable thing called the economy within the horizons of popular knowledge and belief, giving it life by depicting it as a phoenix forged in the factories of the war effort, reborn from the ashes of the Depression.

As much as it heralds union membership as a form of citizenship vital to the consumer economy, the anthropomorphic toy story of "Doll and Toy Makers" ultimately announces the ludicrousness of human labor in an era of automata. The replicants whose births we witness in the film are not just tools for the development of future consumer citizens made psychologically whole through play. As figures of the economy, they also anticipate a future in which simulation, rather than the concreteness of manufacturing, rules economic life—its di-

sastrous effects most trenchantly exemplified in the financial crises of 2008, precipitated in part by the false confidence induced by algorithmic, digitally modeled risk management.[61] This may seem like an overreading, but at least one observer from the period made the connection. In a 1963 article surveying current ideas about automation and computer simulation, institutional economist Robert A. Solo used Betsy Wetsy and other lifelike dolls to alert readers of the *Journal of Business* to the dangers of knowledge produced by the hypothetical manipulation of imagined scenarios based on symbolic representations: "How much shall we learn about the anatomy and psychology of the real thing by building and playing with baby dolls?"[62] We might turn the question around to ask it of television: how much would viewers learn about the lives and livelihoods of Americans at work by watching them on TV?

This, ultimately, is the issue that "Doll and Toy Makers" confronts us with. Its manifest goal is to demonstrate the primacy of an interracial union labor force in two intertwined processes of growth—the personal maturation of the consumer citizen and the economic development of the nation—but the insistent whimsy of Wolff's script, in combination with the anthropomorphic visual resonances of the dolls, ultimately subverts this intention. It also subverts the larger goal of *Americans at Work*, namely, to present viewers with the human face of commodity production, as opposed to the NAM's stentorian monologues about the majesty of industry.[63] Structured around the whimsical conceit that the dolls are alive, Wolff's narration ends up humanizing the *commodity* over the worker. As the dolls evolve into magical economic beings over the course of the episode they cannot help upstaging their makers. These questions about the agency, and will, of the rank-and-file worker raised by the film's gothic commodity fetishism will help conclude the story of governing by television told in this chapter, and this book.

## RIGHTS AND VOICES

Although "Doll and Toy Makers" was preoccupied with simulation, the larger goal of *Americans at Work* was representation, both in the sense of speaking for the rank and file and depicting them in visual language.[64] In this respect, television provided the corporatist labor leadership of the postwar period with an ideal form of governance. Showing the human face of labor was a way of signaling to the general public that the interests of labor were as legitimate as (if not identical with) those of business. But it was also a way of governing the rank and file themselves, providing the increasingly centralized and elite leadership of the trade union movement with a means of managing the constituency they represented. Putting the rank and file on TV allowed the bureaucrats of the AFL-CIO to signal their commitment to the people they spoke for at the bargaining table and in Washington without having to voice their concerns directly. Although it implied that the union members on-screen were themselves representatives of the organization and, as individuals, of the broader interest group constituted by labor, *Americans at Work* clearly circumscribed their place in the political process. The program was shot without sound, and its literal silencing of the voices of union members (to say nothing of the deafening din of the shop floor) was only the most obvious way that the public relations activity of labor leadership in the postwar period marginalized the rank and file. Representing them visually seemed close enough to representing them politically, an elision between image and polity that was fully consonant with emerging ideas of television's relationship to governance.

This conceptualization of televisual representation as an approximation of political advocacy was hardly unique to *Americans at Work*. Indeed, it is best glimpsed in network racial policies, such as NBC's "integration without identification," in which the commitment to the visual presence of black people on-screen occurred at the expense of, and indeed seemed intended to suppress, their political speech. This compensatory visibility also seems to structure the representation of nonwhite workers in *Americans at Work*; although Meany insisted on giving them presence on-screen, the program never commented on their presence in words. The ambivalence of this gesture was on a par with the ambivalence of AFL-CIO leadership when it came to the public support for civil rights. Although Meany was vocal in advocating civil rights and insistent on black representation in *Americans at Work*, he constantly resisted the efforts of A. Philip Randolph to initiate a more active antidiscrimination policy in member unions, investigating communist influence in local unions with far more zeal than when asked to pursue charges of segregation.[65] This situation makes Meany's efforts to ensure black representation in *Americans at Work* seem like a power play as well as an integrationist gesture. Documentary footage of black workers was a way for the AFL-CIO to tamp down black radicalism within the rank and file while asserting the legitimacy of its claims to represent workers of all colors.[66]

If such compensatory efforts to equate visual and political representation go unremarked, it is a testament to the degree to which televisual codes of representation seem equivalent to the mechanisms of government. Television's capacity to render the distant present and the invisible visible appears to map easily onto definitions of adequate political representation; the latter rest, as Hanna Fenichel Pitkin notes, on the idea that the will of the absent constituency is somehow made present through its representative. This constitutes a paradox insofar as the very concept of representation *requires* some kind of separation between representative and constituency, along with an agreed-upon system of codes that mediates (and thus translates) the relationship into a reasonable form of substitution. Struggles over political representation are often struggles over the terms of this mediation, Pitkin suggests, a claim borne out in the long history of positive image advocacy in U.S. media activism.[67]

As a means of representing the rank and file, *Americans at Work* was part of a wider struggle over the right to speak for workers in industrial relations, namely, the pitched battle over right-to-work legislation that took place at the end of the 1950s. The "paradox of representation" Pitkin analyzes would provide antiunion forces with a powerful rhetoric in this battle. Although labor leaders are elected to represent the rank and file in collective bargaining and in the political sphere, opponents of trade unionism historically have insisted that this process of representation is undemocratic, arguing instead that the right to work trumps the right to representation through a mediating—and thus intrinsically unrepresentative—agent, such as a union official. Right-to-work advocates seized on this pseudopopulist argument in the 1958 state elections, capitalizing on the negative image of labor generated by the McClellan hearings on racketeering with grassroots campaigns that claimed to articulate the feelings of a workforce supposedly disenfranchised by despotic union bosses. These campaigns did not simply show the rank and file; they also appeared to give them a voice, annexing the politics of visibility in which television representation registered as a form of advocacy.

The twenty-five-minute film *And Women Must Weep* (1958) is a particularly notorious example of the annexation of the rank-and-file voice in antiunion media campaigns, and its differences from AFL-CIO activism around right-to-work legislation are striking. Produced and distributed by the National Right to Work Committee, the film, like "Doll and Toy Makers," rested on the proxy subjectivity of the child, although the story it told was not a parable of economic citizenship but rather a mawkish melodrama that dramatized (with some license) conflicts leading up to the injury of a scab worker's baby during a 1957 strike in Indiana. In November 1958, the committee bought time to air the film in local television markets where right-to-work laws were on the ballot.[68] Using unknown (and presumably nonunion, possibly nonprofessional) actors to play union workers, the film ventriloquized rank-and-file discontents in dialogue scenes that showed union members coming to the growing realization that "Halley," a thuggish union boss, is infringing on their rights. "That plant don't open tomorrow," Halley jubilantly announces to a packed union hall on the eve of a strike. Privately, the membership questions his decision. "You know darned well we can't go on strike without an okay from International," says one. But the rank and file are powerless against their leader. "Halley's running the show. He must know what he's doing," another replies.

In case this dialogue seemed stilted and artificial, two sequences that framed the drama offered viewers a chance to hear from real people and learn their stories, adding verisimilitude to the film's claims to represent the point of view of the average worker. Both sequences use women to articulate the broader right-to-work message. In the first, a woman named Ann Stewart introduces the film, telling the camera that she was once a union official but left the labor movement after learning of the real-life events in the film. This conversion narrative is presumably intended as a template for the reaction of union members in the audience. "As a former union member and as a woman, this story terrifies me," she avows. Although her halting and incongruously emotionless speech betrays the fact that she is reading from cue cards, it also helps to confirm her status as a regular person, not an actor or a politician. In the second framing sequence, which concludes the film, the appearance of an "ordinary" person is a device for communicating the moral gravity and national importance of the events narrated on-screen. In it we meet the film's narrator, an actress who also plays the wife of an antiunion clergyman in the film's dramatic sequences. "It's been a real experience playing the role you've just seen. I've certainly learned a great deal," she tells the camera before introducing Winifred Greenfield, the woman on whom her character was based. Greenfield tells the audience that she supports right-to-work laws because "freedom is everybody's business"—a well-worn right-wing media catchphrase that lent a Cold War urgency to the repeal of New Deal policies.

The device of the actor who abandons a role is worth dwelling on, as such extravagant displays of sincerity and authenticity appear frequently in right-wing media activism in this period. (The device quite likely originated in Ronald Reagan's performance as host of *General Electric Theater*, a performance which inaugurated his media persona as a plain-spoken, charming representative of both the average man and the burgeoning right wing.) Another antiunion sponsor, the DuPont corporation, used an identical device in its ABC television series *DuPont Cavalcade Theater,* discussed in more detail in Chapter One. At the end of "Toward Tomorrow," a 1955 episode that told the story of the early hardships faced by black American diplomat Ralph Bunche, the actor who plays Bunche appears as himself and addresses the camera: "If you will forgive me for stepping out of character, it is a great privilege for an actor to portray a man such as Dr. Bunche." The device of the actor stepping out of character underscored the value of the ordinary person, a distilled signifier of sincerity, and direct address to the viewer helped position the foregoing drama within a broader governmental narrative. In testifying to the honor they felt at being chosen to play their roles, the scripted avowals of these out-of-character actors affirmed the national significance of the individuals, and the causes, their performances represented. This reverence for personal sovereignty, trumping class antagonisms and collective interests, seems calculated to prompt worship of the spirit of American individualism among viewers.

The mute images of workers in *Americans at Work* had little in common with such affirmative depictions of the individual. Instead they appear as ciphers of union membership, their humanity marshaled primarily in order to render the legitimacy of labor as an interest group. The contrast only highlights the ways that *And Women Must Weep*, with its extensive voicing of the feelings of the working individual and its willingness to break the frame of dramatic realism with direct address, succeeded in appropriating populist representational strategies associated in previous decades with the democratizing cultural governance of the Popular Front. Indeed, looking at the AFL-CIO's media campaign to defeat the 1958 right-to-work laws, it appears at first as if labor had wholly severed its relationship with this earlier mode of activist representation. AFL-CIO television broadcasts that aired in TV markets where the laws were on the ballot seem quite deliberate in their avoidance of both the image and the voice of the rank and file. They consisted of two types of material: a series of filmed political advertising spots featuring Democratic senator Herbert Lehman of New York and other governmental notables, and a star studded "television spectacular" that aired in California and Kansas (the latter was the only state in which voters would end up supporting the legislation).[69]

However, although these broadcasts seem to cede to antiunion forces the populist strategy of speaking in the voice of the worker, the "television spectacular" might be seen as the last gasp of Popular Front aesthetics in postwar labor media work. A filmed variety show, it featured George Jessel (long known as a union advocate), Eddie Cantor, and Sammy Davis Jr., as well as a speech by Eleanor Roosevelt.[70] This program's odd mixture of speechifying and showbiz contrasted sharply in style and tone with both *And Women Must Weep* and *Americans at Work*. It offered only a brief glimpse of an actual rank-and-file member, via a shot of a portly studio technician in overalls (almost a caricature) in a "backstage" sequence at the beginning of the program. Yet at the same time, the program's stars—all union members themselves—voiced frank denunciations of the right-to-work movement's populist strategy, particularly its language of fairness and equality for all workers.

One such speech, delivered by Sammy Davis Jr., is notable in that it exposed this language as a nefarious co-optation of the tenets of the civil rights movement. Davis no doubt hoped to counter the claims of right-to-work campaigners in Ohio and California, who were reportedly telling black workers that the legislation was a fair-employment-practices law.[71] Pausing between songs to warn the audience about "something being sold to you as the right to work," he goes on to suggest that "a law, like everything else, is known by the company it keeps." The monologue that follows condemns recent segregationist bombings in Clinton, Tennessee, and Atlanta, Georgia:

> Let's look at the states that have the right-to-work law. Arkansas has the right-to-work law. They also have a cat by the name of [Governor Orval] Faubus, too. There's also a state called Tennessee. You remember that state. You've read about it in the papers. That's where they bomb schools. And then there's a state called Georgia. That's where they bomb synagogues. I don't think we want the right to work in our state if minorities have no rights at all, and that's why I'm going to vote no, and why I ask [you], wherever you are, to vote against that phony right-to-work bill on your ballot.

Davis was not the first member of the Rat Pack to speak out against prejudice—recall Sinatra's Popular Front classic, the Academy Award–winning short *House I Live In*—but the candor with which he linked labor politics and civil rights was unusual for a celebrity in this period, particularly in the context of television entertainment. The direct indictment of Southern states is worth noting too. Such incendiary speech, delivered by a black man, would have been unthinkable in a network television broadcast at the time.

The program's use of a high-profile, outspoken, and multiracial celebrity cast contrasts sharply not only with the faux (and wholly white) populism of *And Women Must Weep* but also with the measured, cooperative tone of *Americans at Work*, intent on demonstrating labor's service to the public (as opposed to the more radical collective of "the people"). In *Americans at Work*, a residual Popular Front sensibility was visible only in glimpses, via the jarring collisions of word and image that ran through Wolff's scripts and provided a dark subtext to the Cold War economic nationalism of the AFL-CIO's teaching points. This unnamed variety show, on the other hand, merged star power, labor power, and black Americans' demands for empowerment in a manner more openly indebted to Popular Front–style media activism, even if it eschewed the language and imagery of the noble, toiling worker.[72] The program aired only a few weeks after *Americans at Work*'s debut, and their juxtaposition marks them as residual and emergent cultural practices, respectively. The variety program marked the end of this earlier era in cultural activism, whereas *Americans at Work* heralded the ascendancy of the modern labor movement's rationalist, interest-group-oriented governmental aspirations.

Taken together with the voiceless images of the black workers carefully included in *Americans at Work*, Davis' speech in this program communicates something of the paradoxical circumstances in which advocates of progressive politics found themselves when they turned to television as an instrument of governance, especially—as the chapters in this book have suggested—after the 1954 *Brown* decision. The abolition of segregation rewrote the governance of race and

irrevocably altered the structure of everyday life, making integration a matter of national moral leadership. Corporate sponsors such as DuPont appeared to take up this leadership position when they addressed the travails and triumphs of "the Negro," harnessing the cause of laissez faire capitalism to the narrative of American racial progress. But those who turned to television with the goal of actually realizing this narrative faced the limits of the medium's tenuous claim to legitimacy as a commercial institution working in the public service. Tensions between Southern stations and national networks duplicated and amplified the tensions between regional and federal authorities, the promise of their resolution pinned on the empty signifier of "balance." *Americans at Work* neatly conformed to industry conventions; it celebrated consumption while practicing "integration without identification" and balanced the industrial triumphalism of *Industry on Parade.* The program's conformity with broader ideas of liberal governance in this period is evident in the fact that it would become a cornerstone in Cold War cultural diplomacy. Like DuPont's biography of Bunche, *Americans at Work* enjoyed a long afterlife with the USIA, distributed overseas to show people oversees how American democracy empowers its workforce. Davis' impassioned speech, and that of the other stars who appeared on the variety program, might seem a more powerful demonstration of American democracy in action, but it spoke in a Popular Front idiom that was foreign to television and to the language of interest group politics.

From the perspective of the present, however, it is not celebrity activism that seems foreign. Far more alien to viewers today is the vision of the production-based economy propagated in *Americans at Work*, a vision anchored by optimistic stories about the power of U.S. manufacturing, the indispensability of union labor, and the intrinsic link between American workers and American consumers. It is impossible to imagine today that a film telling viewers about the people who make the products they consume would convincingly demonstrate the strength of the American economy—it would have to be shot in offshore factories, where inhuman working conditions and

correspondingly inhuman wages would induce not pride in American levels of production and consumption but rather shame at the rapacious and unsustainable search for profit among multinational corporations.

What's more, if someone were to attempt to make a film about the *domestic* sources of American economic power today, it would have to be shot in places other than the factory—in Wall Street boardrooms, inside the computer labs where risk is modeled and computed, and in the microscopic yet massive spaces of the electronic networks through which complex financial instruments, bundled to conceal rather than minimize risk, travel across the globe in the endless circuit of finance capital. These worlds are as mysterious to the present-day viewer as the factory of the 1950s. To be sure, finance in some form is all over television: in the financial news networks, in economic self-help programs that tell us how to maximize our personal worth through investments, and in the innumerable reality programs where entrepreneurs "flip" real estate purchases or compete for the backing of investors.[73] But such programs rarely claim to explain the total system of the economy as a whole and the place of the citizen within it. Still, as this book's epilogue will suggest, although contemporary entertainment programs and genres may seem to have nothing in common with the Establishment television of the 1950s, they offer a vision of civic life in the neoliberal present that it is worth exploring, as a way of tracing the links between older conceptions of TV as a machine for making citizens and the ones that are emerging in the media world of today.

# WESTERN U

## TELEGRAM

W. P. MARSHALL, PRESIDENT

The filing time shown in the date line on domestic telegrams is STANDARD TIME at point of origin. T

1957 FEB 21

NA139 PD ST LOUIS MO 21 254PMC

EDWARD REED FUNDS FOR THE REPUBLIC

60 EAST 42 ST

LOANED KSD A PRINT THE BUMS GAVE U

MARTIN QUIGLEY

Proj TV Quigley

120

(35)

1957 FEB 21 PM 4 45

MO 21 25 4PMC

OR THE REPUBLIC INC

RECEIVED

FEB 25 1957

THE FUND FOR THE REPUBLIC

THE BUMS GAVE US NOON SUNDAY

# EPILOGUE

FIFTIES TELEVISION is so closely identified with the period's hyperactive consumer culture that those sponsors who turned to TV with other things in mind besides selling products have largely been forgotten. To tell their stories is to establish their place in the historical record, but the foregoing account has been motivated by something more than a desire to set the record straight. I began this book with a certain curiosity about what men in power thought about television when their minds turned to the society emerging from the timeline of the New Deal and World War II. It was a society with a welfare state, albeit an uneven and imperfect one, and the implications of this were disquieting to many in the business world. Equally disquieting for business was the size and perceived power of the labor movement, even though management lobbies were distinctly more powerful. It was a society with a core ideological enemy, one with whom it was already waging proxy wars in distant lands. It was a society in which mass culture threatened high culture. And, perhaps most pressingly, it was a society with a major race problem on its hands.

Now, as I finish this work, our media system can no longer be described with words as simple as *broadcasting*. We have a collapsing economy. Unemployment is reaching Depression levels, and union membership is at an all-time low. Having forsaken manufacturing for finance, U.S. business is leveraged by an increasingly impecunious state that is more accountable to corporations than it is to its citizens. The United States is fighting a war discussed not in terms of fronts or parallels but rather in the language of torture and terror. And we have an African American president. If these situations seem disjunctive, they also speak to the specific alignments of culture, economy, and state that define this moment. What happened between then and now, and what did television have to do with it?

One set of stories about television's role in governance since the 1950s assigns a critical value to the image. It is commonplace to say that the sight of coffins and combat changed people's opinions about the Vietnam War, or, in the realm of entertainment television, that the representation of a particular group of people in, say, sitcoms, reflects their progress toward political and social equality.[1] Another, equally powerful (and arguably equally banal) set of narratives holds visual culture responsible for the progressive failure of government, arguing that the incessant "bombardment" of media images has reduced the citizenry's capacity to form reasoned opinion and induce ethical boundaries for their conduct. A third story about television's place in governance, and one I find more compelling than either of the foregoing ones, focuses on the source of that power, tracing how federal policy for media ownership and licensing has increasingly enabled the concentration of economic control in the hands of a few large companies. All three stories overlap: if I attribute more credence to the last, it is because the argument that economic power determines which, and how many, images people see seems to be the most fundamental, and thus the most fundamentally persuasive.

However, another way that these commonplace stories overlap has me troubled. Each has a tendency to describe the American people

and the TV audience in functionally equivalent terms, rarely stopping
to question the assumptions about the individuals, groups, interests,
and ideologies involved in such descriptions. The men who turned to
television as an instrument of rule in the 1950s didn't question them
either; indeed, the anxieties about the masses betrayed in these assumptions mark the course of liberal thought, in all of its conflicting,
contradictory forms, throughout the twentieth century and into the
twenty-first.[2] We cannot truly grasp the ways that media work with, or
against, the pragmatics of government at any particular moment in
U.S. history without knowing where these assumptions come from,
and what kinds of power relations they affirm. What the governing
classes thought about television in the fifties was inseparable from what
they thought about the people who watched it. In researching their
stories, I wanted to understand what lay beneath their beliefs about
viewers' race and racial attitudes, their class alignments, and their capacity for both reason and suggestibility. These elites often felt themselves to be superior to both the industry and its audience, but they
nevertheless turned to TV as a vehicle for persuading various imagined
viewers that thinking and acting a certain way was in their own interests. Scrutinizing the ways they went about this task revealed a great
deal about how postwar elites approached the period's political problems and the challenges to the power structure they foreshadowed,
particularly where matters of race were concerned.

But over the course of this research I always kept the present in
the back of my mind, wondering specifically about the expectations
that guide today's thinking about the ways that media might mold
people's conduct and steer their civic inclinations. And indeed, although
ideas about TV as a "laboratory for democracy" have changed radically
in the intervening years, in a number of senses the positions I encountered among the papers and TV programs left behind by the philanthropoids, the free enterprisers, the civic role players, and the labor
establishment of the 1950s were quite familiar.[3] Although there were
many reminders of the foreignness of the past, it seemed clear that
there was some kind of pathway leading from the postwar republic of
the airwaves to today's fantasies of a digitalized image culture that

proliferates democracy through users who are free at last to generate their own content and who access information and entertainment on demand.

Of course, today's media republic—a topsy-turvy world in which homeless people have Facebook accounts and reality TV provides lifestyle makeovers as a kind of social reform—would seem profoundly alien to the governing classes of the postwar decade.[4] Any explanation of the connection between their era and ours must address the technological proliferation of forms of media access and the so-called fragmentation of the audience that has occurred in the decades between, as well as the ways that the basic cast of characters involved in media governance has changed. The mainstream, functionalist argument that the progressive fragmentation of the media system corresponds to a progressively more fragmented—and by extension divided, alienated, and desensitized—society seems too simple, and too ready to assume the veracity of the marketing profession's insistence that demography is destiny. But how else can one compare conceptualizations of the mass audience in the three- (arguably four, if you include DuMont) network era of the fifties with the contemporary media environment?

First we must consider the collective nouns that describe media audiences as consumers and citizens in each moment. In 1961, when old ideas of governing by television were still active, Raymond Williams offered media scholars the indispensible insight that "there are in fact no masses, only ways of seeing people as masses."[5] But nowadays, the "disappearance" of the masses is the prevailing wisdom of branding and marketing. Williams' oft-cited dictum needs some revision, and indeed, its corollary seems more germane in today's media context: there are no individuals, only ways of seeing people as individuals. Or, more accurately, the predominant figure of the masses today is the individual. This is not the same as the abstract individual, talked about in terms of interest group membership, that dominated the Cold War language of political pluralism. Rather, contemporary citizen talk is dominated by singularizing personifications that stand for both political constituencies (moms, soccer and hockey; Joes, six-pack and plumber) and consumer segments (DINKs, buppies). And these individualizing images of populations cross and overlap each other as they circulate across media forms and platforms, from cable punditry to the casting circus of reality TV.

Second, we must grasp how this pervasive impulse toward demographic personification serves as a kind of civic discourse. Most obviously, it makes the concept of *lifestyle* central to practices of citizenship. Given that television is the preeminent purveyor of lifestyle in contemporary culture, it makes sense to investigate the ways that the industry's promiscuous exploitation of the concept speaks to today's civic investments and the power dynamics that drive them. This means focusing not on the "serious" programming forms that concern the chapters in this book—news reporting and analysis, cultural education, documentary, and so forth—but on the cheap, heavily branded, and commercialized landscape of basic cable channels, where reality programs about lifestyles (some good, some bad, some ugly) and demographic types (housewives, teenagers, entrepreneurs) dominate the broadcast day. And indeed, in a persuasive analysis of reality TV programming, Laurie Ouellette and James Hay propose that the format conforms closely to the dominant neoliberal logic of the Bush and Clinton governments, "in which privatization, personal responsibility, and consumer choice are promoted as the best way to govern liberal capitalist democracies." Lifestyle, they note, has become "one of the principal domains through which citizens are expected to look after themselves in the name of their own interests," making "rational choices in matters of health, consumption, family, and household." Under these circumstances, reality TV "shows us how to conduct and 'empower' ourselves as enterprising citizens."[6] But reality TV is also a profound symbol of neoliberal government's *failure* to protect its citizens: "It is a sign of the times that, in the absence of public welfare programs, hundreds of thousands of people now apply directly to reality TV programs for housing, affordable health care, and other forms of assistance."[7]

This grotesque situation not only demonstrates that TV remains central to mainstream conceptions of citizens' needs but also pinpoints how much the idea of governing by television has changed over the past five decades. No longer a top-down process guided by elite ideologues and reformers, television contributes to dominant conceptions of governance from the bottom up, disseminating the common sense of neoliberal political ideology throughout mainstream popular culture via the sociological spectacle of real people on reality TV. Although the civics lessons offered by contemporary reality TV may seem like "mere" entertainment, there is no clearer demonstration of the radical shifts in the conceptualization of the self, and its utility as a template for citizenship, that have taken place in the intervening years. As French sociologist Alain Ehrenberg pointed out in a 1998 article on the genre, "Long considered a window onto the world . . . television is more and more a window onto the self, onto the subject's internal conflicts and the difficulties they pose in life."[8] To grasp how this new conception of television as an apparatus for civic-therapeutic spectacle emerged, we have to look backward at the evolution of the medium since the end of the 1950s, when the TV programming initiatives described in the preceding chapters ceased. This epilogue will be, of necessity, a somewhat cursory account, but the point is not to provide an exhaustive summary of all changes in TV programming, policy, and politics in the past fifty years but rather to propose a kind of genealogy of the civic self that evolved and mutated out of the aspirations for television that drew the governing classes to the medium in its first decade.

The preliminary question to answer is why, exactly, the TV projects detailed in this book came to an end at the turn of the 1960s. A number of factors contributed to the situation. In 1960, the FCC for the first time officially acknowledged that commercial programming could be considered a public service, making nonprofit access to the for-profit airwaves that much harder.[9] Both the NAM and the AFL-CIO ceased production of their industrial documentary programs at this time, although the films continued to air on educational television stations. Compounding the problem of access, the networks themselves had developed a sudden interest in public service programming, expanding their news departments and putting together prestige documentary film teams in an effort to recuperate the cultural capital they lost in the quiz show scandals.[10] And the politically well-connected Ad Council, an organization of advertising agencies whose pro bono public service spots bought public relations credibility for the media industries, had by this point grown into a gatekeeping institution mediating access between charitable and social service organizations and TV.[11] Corporations continued to use TV to spread the pro–free enterprise message, but with the decline of anthology drama their outlets became limited—at least, that is, until the founding of the public television system at the end of the decade opened up new opportunities for institutional advertising.[12]

The establishment of PBS was not, however, a corporate initiative. Rather, it was the result of a concerted effort by philanthropic organizations, which early in the 1960s began to concentrate on nurturing the educational television network as an alternative to commercial programming. In 1967, the Public Broadcasting Act, incorporating the recommendations of the Carnegie Commission on Educational Television, made official the liberal philanthropic dream of an alternative to commercial TV. It granted state sanction to the idea that commercial TV had failed to serve the interests of the American people, and it enshrined in media infrastructure the idea that the most effective means for activating TV's promise as an instrument of self-governance was to offer viewers a prosocial, culturally diverse complement to the degraded fare offered by the networks. PBS thus seemed to solve the problems of uplift and education the fifties philanthropoids worried about when they tried reforming the system from within. It also, of course, cemented the terms for the 1970s culture wars, providing the Nixon administration with a convenient target in its weaponized form of authoritarian populism, even as Nixon aide Antonin Scalia was working to convince the president to treat PBS as a massive White House propaganda outlet.[13]

But another development had shifted the terms of governing by television at the turn of the 1960s as well. At around the same time that the projects detailed in this book ended, profound changes were under way in U.S. political culture. A new vocabulary of the civic self entered mainstream political discourse: the language of morality and individual sovereignty associated with the burgeoning conservative movement. This period is sometimes thought of as the high point of liberal hegemony—the bright future envisioned in Kennedy's talk of a New Frontier, the two-year window in which a Democratic majority in Congress passed the Great Society legislation—but from the perspective of the present, the fact that it also marks the rise of the modern conservative movement seems just as significant. Launched under the rallying cry of individual rights, the movement's rise was fueled by its adherents' zealous determination to wrest the moral position in governance away from racially liberal sectors of the establishment. It began as a grassroots movement based in local electoral politics, particularly when legislation concerning housing integration was on the ballot. Its infancy was ideologically nurtured by right-wing intellectuals and supported financially by a handful of superrich crusaders.[14] Television, including public service television, contributed to its development too. Ultraconservative Texas oil magnate H.L. Hunt saw local broadcasting as a way to awaken right-wing populism with rhetoric that was part racism, part anticommunist paranoia, and profoundly antielitist. For a time Hunt financed *The Dan Smoot Report*, a widely distributed conservative TV and radio program that aired in paid and public service time.[15] At around the same time future Republican senator Jesse Helms, then vice chairman of a regional North Carolina broadcasting chain, began airing nightly editorials on WRAL-TV, spreading vituperative rhetoric on the immorality of liberal foreign policy, homosexuality, desegregation, and other hot conservative talking points.[16]

The broadcasting industry's readiness to provide a forum for the insistent, racially coded rhetoric of crime and moral degeneracy that drove the conservative agenda made television a particularly useful tool. While the Fund for the Republic was wrapping up its project for distributing news film clips that countered sensational TV coverage of racial integration, first-term U.S. senator Barry Goldwater was persuading the NAM to fund and distribute free news coverage of the most contentious parts of the McClellan hearings on "improper activities in labor and management." The sessions in question concerned allegations of violence during a bitter strike at the Kohler plumbing fixtures plant in Milwaukee, and Goldwater, a member of the select committee that held the hearings, played a highly aggressive role within them. The hearings were, for the most part, a conservative morality play depicting organized labor as a force of criminal brutality, amoral power lust, and antidemocratic oppression. They culminated in the passage of the Landrum-Griffin Act in 1959, a corrosive piece of antilabor legislation that regulated the internal governance of unions, ostensibly in order to protect the sovereign individual rights of the rank and file.[17] The hearings were also important because they were Goldwater's first national exposure as a conservative figurehead, and indeed, although he is often remembered as a highly untelegenic man, his 1964 presidential campaign exploited the medium to the hilt. Shortly before the November elections, he delivered a Tuesday night speech in paid time on CBS that drew phenomenal ratings. In it, Goldwater proclaimed that "the moral fiber of the American people is beset by rot and decay." It was a milestone in that it definitively identified the newly, and tenuously, mainstreamed right as the moral conscience of the American people.[18]

In the meantime, while the right was starting to exploit television as a means for disseminating the new political morality, liberals increasingly made TV a moral target. Goldwater located the source of moral decay in crime, violence, and demands for racial reparation, but liberal moralists focused on the influence of the media. Senator Thomas J. Dodd spearheaded senate hearings focusing specifically on the effects of television violence and sexual representation on children. These hearings, notes William Boddy, helped legitimize the growing body of social scientific research on children and TV.[19] The idea that media images might endanger citizens, particularly young, gullible ones, became a matter of domestic policy in 1968, when the Johnson administration formed the National Commission on the Causes and Prevention of Violence. The commission's charge was to investigate seven social phenomena that might explain the rise in violence over the course of the decade. One of them was media; the other six were assassination, group violence, individual violence, law and law enforcement, firearms, and "American history and character."[20] In making TV a moral target on a par with guns and criminality,

liberal reformers in the 1960s effectively abandoned the idea of reha-
bilitating commercial television (and its audience) from within
through strategies such as sponsorship and program distribution.

By the 1970s, only vestiges of the 1950s models of governing by
television survived. PBS was publicly compared, however inaccurately,
to the experiments in cultural uplift the Ford Foundation carried out
with *Omnibus*, and echoes of the idealistic image of television as a
venue for local civic discussion could be heard in the FCC's 1972 policy statement requiring cable channels in large markets to carry programming produced by members of the local community (public access
channels, as they are now known).[21] But assumptions about how viewers use media to govern themselves had shifted. Most notably, the period saw the renewal of ideas about entertainment programming as a
sphere of political struggle. In one sense, this development was an
unintended by-product of new FCC guidelines designed to encourage
independent productions by limiting network ownership and syndication of programming. It brought new independent producers such as
MTM and Norman Lear to network TV, their "socially relevant" sitcoms retooling a shopworn genre for purposes of social critique. Advocacy groups got on the entertainment bandwagon too, collaborating
with producers to insert prosocial messages into prime-time programming. The most famous—and, on the right, notorious—of these collaborations was undoubtedly the two-part episode of *Maude* in which the
title character, played by Bea Arthur, decides to have an abortion, an
episode produced in consultation with the Washington, D.C.–based
Population Institute.[22]

In short, the beginning of the 1970s saw the bifurcation of ideas
about governing by television into two areas of programming and
policy. There was PBS, serving longhairs, children, community groups,
artists, and others who for various reasons were excluded from the demographic calculations guiding mainstream commercial programming. And then there were the networks, anxiously working to update
their staid images by seeking out controversial programming that spoke
directly, often didactically, about pressing social issues. This reinvention of network TV was a delicate process, as the abortion episode of

*Maude* makes clear. In a telling throwback to the constraining proto-
cols of balance active in the first decade of governing by television,
Lear met with the CBS standards and practices department to discuss ways of integrating "balance" into the episode. Their solution—
inserting a character who has also recently discovered she is pregnant
but who, unlike Maude, responds to the news with joy—reads as an
obvious appeasement gesture when viewed on-screen.[23] But it was still
not enough for the antiabortion activists who protested the episode;
the National Council of Catholic Bishops even went so far as to demand that CBS broadcast "a sequel in which Maude [a forty-nine-
year-old woman] gets pregnant a second time and has the baby."[24]

Despite—or perhaps because of—such controversies, the Lear years
saw the efflorescence of the popular idea that the positive representation of a particular social group or issue in entertainment TV is a sign
of political progress. It was supported by changes in the sitcom form
itself, which became less episodic and more serialized in its narrative
structure, a development that expanded the genre's emotional range.
Programs became more melodramatic, characters evolved over the
course of a series run, and the number of "messages" the genre sent
each season threatened to put Western Union out of business. With
these changes, sitcoms became a resource on which journalists, policy
makers, and the media industry itself drew when pointing to changes
in American culture and attitudes.[25] In 1973, evaluating the three
Lear programs then on the air, Lawrence Laurent of the *Washington
Post* praised them for containing "a measure of reality that was so com-
pletely missing for so many years in television comedy." He predicted
that "the huge audiences being attracted to the new—and controversial—
comedies" would benefit from the exposure: "caring, even objecting
to drama, is far better than no reaction and not caring at all."[26] Laurent's confusion of comedy and drama was symptomatic of the genre's
new seriousness. The sitcom was now a form of public service, raising
controversial issues, sparking debate, and bringing hidden assumptions out into the open.

There is plenty to quibble about in the political content of the
socially conscious sitcom of the 1970s—its racial politics favored white

liberal universalism over social and political change, recalling the anemic language of fellowship with which establishment integrationists appealed to their audiences in the *Brown* era, and the debates it sparked often seemed to dead-end on the question of whether Archie Bunker's illiberal attitudes lampooned bigotry or promoted it, a question whose either/or framing only shored up monolithic conceptions of the American public as a single, mass mind. But the promise of media representation as an arena for social struggle was a powerful and enduring one. It harked back to the days when labor and management competed, via documentary, to promote positive images of workers and industrialists respectively. And indeed, insofar as it reclaimed moralism from the forces intent on rolling back New Deal and Great Society social programs, the sitcom's cast of "exemplary"—if now sassy—Negroes (Florida Evans in *Maude* and *Good Times*, Benson in *Soap*), rational centrist mouthpieces (Edith Bunker, Maude's husband Walter Findlay), and stereotyped extremists (Archie Bunker, Fred Sanford) revived old conceptions of commercial TV as a vehicle in which the depiction of types is a way of talking to citizens about the underlying tenets of liberal capitalist democracy.

Although it still shapes the way we talk about the politics of genres such as the sitcom, the 1970s story of TV's renewed governing capacity through entertainment programming was never fully championed by the networks, as the meager PR credibility these shows brought was secondary to the unwelcome controversies that came with them. More crucially, because these shows were independent productions over which the networks exercised limited financial control, their success contributed little to the networks' coffers and, indeed, ran counter to their economic interests.[27] The networks therefore welcomed at first the deregulatory FCC agenda that took shape when Ronald Reagan came to power at the beginning of the 1980s, although they were unable to bring about the repeal of the finance and syndication rules that had fostered the socially conscious sitcoms of the 1970s (the rules would be amended in 1991 and finally revoked in 1995). Yet they also had reason to fear deregulation, as it quickly became clear that the FCC's master plan threatened their market dominance in TV. New communications policy opened the field for cable competition, and at the beginning of the 1990s, with the expansion of cable programming and the rise of Fox, cost cutting became a network imperative. Inevitably, the focus was on labor. Despite a series of industrywide strikes in the 1980s and early 1990s, nonunion sectors of the industry grew precipitously over the course of the decade. The cheap, nonunion production methods of reality TV emerged from this economic reorganization, as Chad Raphael notes in a deft analysis of the policy, financing, and production arrangements surrounding the genre's rise.[28]

A new vision of TV's capacity to provide a public service emerged with the rise of reality TV in the early 1990s, one in which, notes Raphael, "surveillance and voyeurism replace debate over public affairs ... and education is reduced to instructing viewers on how to avoid becoming a crime victim."[29] This prescient analysis indicates how much the ideology of civic governance we encounter in today's reality TV has its roots in Reagan-era communications policy. Although Raphael's assessment was focused on the spate of law-and-order reality programs popular in the early 1990s, such as *America's Most Wanted*, his diagnosis of the genre as the mouthpiece of privatizing governmental imperatives brings us back to the present day, in which reality TV is a symptom of a broader privatization of civic discourse and governance in U.S. political culture. Indeed, the genre's contemporary excesses—first born, as Raphael notes, from a perceived scarcity of production resources—speak to the excesses of privatized citizenship, a traumatic experience often expressed in the language of suffering and tears by those who are cast to play out the contemporary dramas of civic life on the reality TV screen.[30]

The Reagan FCC's impact on TV was thus not only economic; it also promoted a new picture of the citizen and the viewer. FCC chairman Mark Fowler succinctly stated the administration's viewpoint in a 1981 interview published in the conservative magazine *Reason*: "Why is it that we now single out one form—over-air television—and imbue it with specific social duties when we don't do the same for film for example? ... The television is just another appliance—it's a toaster with pictures."[31] In asking this question, Fowler entirely dismissed the basic tenet of broadcast reform since the rise of radio in the 1920s, namely, that the airwaves belong to the people and that broadcasters are required to provide programming that serves "public interest, convenience, and necessity." Instead, it implied that television programming was a commodity, its audience not citizens but consumers. The Reagan-era conceptualization of viewers as a market more than a polity was literalized in FCC cable TV policy, which stipulated that cable TV channels were not governed by public interest regulations. As John McMurria notes, the policy made official the Reagan-era idea that "viewers were paying individual customers not collective publics."[32]

The emergence of a privatized conception of TV viewership in the 1990s was only one of many shifts toward the neoliberal model of citizenship that gathered force under Reagan. The story is well known. However, as Lisa Duggan notes, its tellers do not always recognize "the continuities from Reagan through Bush I, Clinton to Bush II— the continuities of neoliberal policy promotion"—an oversight made possible by "the dominant political system and language [in which] conflicts between conservative Republicans and liberal Democrats have been shaped largely *within the terms* of neoliberalism."[33] But there are other continuities that go unrecognized too, ones that needled me forward as I researched and wrote this book about TV programs that are long forgotten, that were never popular, and which, in their anxiously didactic approach to U.S. race relations, seem far removed from media race talk in the present day. For one thing, the mockery of right wing ideologies we encounter in *The Daily Show* is not so far from the smug ridicule the Fund for the Republic had in mind when it sponsored commentators like Al Capp and Herblock. Moreover, although reality TV's voyeuristic promise of civic therapy is easy to dismiss as just so much gimmickry, there are nevertheless some uneasy overlaps between its visions of civic self-help and those of the social reformers who cast "ordinary people" to act out therapeutic race relations in the civic TV programs of the *Brown* era. Shows such as *The Real World, Big Brother,* or *Survivor,* for example, are amoral reworkings of these programs' invitation to observe and comment on

the parameters of civic conduct in groups. Even the trashiest programs—*The Hills*, say, or *The Real Housewives of New Jersey*—are
soapy showbiz throwbacks to the civic role play of the postwar period.
They too use ordinary people improvising particular character types
according to predetermined, if unwritten, scripts, and they share with
the earnest social science dramas of the 1950s not only an ostentatious
aesthetic of wooden acting but also, on the part of their cast members,
a grim determination to play to type. And finally, like the programs
sponsored by civic reformers in these years, lifestyle and makeover reality genres today rely heavily on the counsel of experts: psychologists,
style authorities, successful entrepreneurs, industry insiders, child
care professionals, and so forth.

When it comes to the messages of racial governance they strive to
send, these two moments in television's history of amateur social performance seem at first to be poles apart. If the integrationist media
projects of the intergroup relations movement saw television as a means
for ameliorating U.S. culture's racial conflicts, the writer-producers
of reality TV are more interested in heightening these conflicts for
dramatic effect. Still, when the genre does treat racial difference and
other forms of social inequality in therapeutic or reparative terms, it
often seems as if little has changed. When race takes center stage—
when Tyra Banks disciplines aspiring black models for playing the
race card, or when Judge Judy berates a Latina for having children
on welfare—it is clear that the experts appointed by reality TV, like
those of the *Brown* era, continue to advocate personal transformation
rather than political or economic critique as ways of handling racial
oppression.

A very diluted and adulterated form of social conscience thus remains active in the personal morality talk of reality TV's reparative
genres, and in fact, although I used the word *amoral* earlier, it is a
gross simplification to describe reality TV in such terms. Alongside
right-wing punditry, the genre is one of the preeminent outlets for
moralism in TV today. Shows such as *Judge Judy*, as Ouellette notes,
present themselves as "a moral and educational corrective to 'permis-
sive' entertainment, suggesting that the discourse of the 'public interest'

in broadcasting has not been squashed but reconfigured by neoliberal reforms."[34] In keeping with these reforms, the moral tales told by contemporary reality TV, which comprise its claims to serve the public, are all about personal responsibility and self-fulfillment, and they enjoin those who are depressed, grieving, or insecure not to conform to a particular system but to be *themselves*, to own their own stories and destinies.[35]

This personalizing vision of the civic self marks contemporary reality TV's debt not only to the racial morality that guided postwar liberal reformers in the 1950s but also to the conservative rallying around sovereign individualism that followed on their heels, and which appropriated their language of morality to serve the interests of white power. Because it is so personalized, this contemporary civic vision seems far removed from the moral promise of capitalism brokered by TVs pro–free enterprise sponsors in the postwar years, a promise explained in stentorian televised lectures on the American Economic System and the spurious idea of a labor-management truce. That is, of course, until one notices how much the talk of self-confidence and freedom of choice one encounters in reality TV's efforts to get people to work on themselves resembles the language of self-determination that business lobbies used in their TV campaigns for right-to-work laws in 1958.[36] The morality of reality TV is not the morality of conservative cultural politics—reality TV loves queers, freaks, psychos, cheaters, and militants—but as a language of self-governance predicated upon the capacity of television (and all post-TV media) to make everything personal, it evolves out of the changes in political culture, and in television's relation to governance, that began at the end of the 1950s and which have profoundly shaped the character of American conservatism in the years since.

This would be the place to bring up the Internet and the new capacities for self-governance—privatized and grassroots at one and the same time—that it promises the citizenry. But I leave that story for others to tell.[37] What concerns me, finally, is the fantasy of liberal democratic reform that television continues to nurture today. Viewers uninterested in, or horrified by, the tainted civic spectacle of reality

TV might feed these fantasies with Peabody Award–winning "quality" television programs—such as *House*, for example, a medical drama that tells stories about a wholly unrecognizable U.S. health care system, one in which renegade doctors with minuscule patient loads diagnose complicated cases seemingly free of oversight by medical insurers. It is a fantasy, to be sure, although the show's significance in contemporary visions of rehabilitated democracy is rendered very concretely in the fact that Kal Penn, one of the program's stars, quit the show to work in the Obama administration's public liaison office. The same might be said for Fox's hit FBI series, *24*. In January 2009, cast member Dennis Haysbert speculated that his role as a black president on the show made it easier for Americans to accept the idea of Obama's presidency; conversely, after a controversial episode in which the show's main character resorts to torture while interrogating a suspect, conservative pundit Laura Ingraham claimed on Fox News that because "the average American . . . loves the show *24*" it should be viewed as a "national referendum" (approving, of course) on torture—two odd moments that together convey not only commercial television's continued relevance in contemporary understandings of the citizenry and its (always seen as singular) political desires but also how easily such understandings can be appropriated to serve diverse political agendas.[38] Women and minorities play prominent roles in these and other quality TV programs about governance today; the fact that these supporting characters often serve as exemplary, truth-telling role models who help keep it real as the middle-class white antihero pursues his crusade is a further reminder of how little the terms of these fantasies have shifted.

If these quality dramas of governance cater to contemporary visions of justice, diversity, and reform, it is in part because of television's seemingly endless capacity to transform the workings of anonymous institutions into personal tales. But unlike the works of filmmakers such as Frederick Wiseman and Ken Loach, works that are often characterized in similar terms, the serial dramas of quality liberal television do not expose the inequities of the systems they depict. Rather, they translate commonsense ideas of social justice into narrative arcs that resolve, ultimately, in interpersonal dynamics, in the tenuous promise that people—and institutions—can change. A few programs using the serial form provide more substantial social critique (HBO's *The Wire* immediately springs to mind), although it's hard to deny that they are preaching to the progressive choir. To my mind, the point to take away from these moments when popular culture and political culture come together today is not so much the idea that television programs can help or hinder progressive visions of social reform by themselves, but rather that one of the challenges involved in changing today's political culture is acknowledging how much it rests on a persistent confusion between different ideas of representation: between narrative resolution and the resolution of inequality; between acting *out* fantasies of reform and acting *upon* them; between showing governance and sharing it; between the imagined citizens that constitute the audience and the actual people who watch TV.

# *Notes*

*Introduction:*

## TELEVISION AND POLITICAL CULTURE AFTER WORLD WAR II

1. Quoted in Frederic Bastiat, *The Law* (Irvington-on-Hudson, NY: Foundation for Economic Education, 1998), 48.

2. Michel Foucault, *Security, Territory, Population: Lectures at the Collège de France, 1977–78* (Basingstoke: Palgrave Macmillan, 2007), 49. See also Nikolas Rose's characterization in *Powers of Freedom: Reframing Political Thought* (New York: Cambridge University Press, 1999). "To dominate is to ignore or to attempt to crush the capacity for action of the dominated. But to govern is to recognize that capacity for action and to adjust oneself to it. . . . Hence, when it comes to governing human beings, to govern is to presuppose the freedom of the governed. To govern humans is not to crush their capacity to act, but to acknowlededge it and to utilize it for one's own objectives"(4).

3. With the exception of Michael Curtin's excellent study *Redeeming the Wasteland* (New Brunswick, N.J., 1995), the didactic television

culture of the 1950s has not received much sustained scholarly attention. No doubt this reflects the marginal status of these programs in relation to commercial programming. Largely unavailable in contemporary viewing formats, and in many cases neglected by collectors and preservation institutions, these programs are a lost archive in the history of U.S. politics and media. It is consequently difficult to estimate the total number of broadcast hours they filled. Still, taken together, the number of sponsored and unsponsored programs, from industrial films to cultural programs to public service announcements, that sought neither to entertain nor to sell but rather to mold viewers' attitudes and conduct surely constitutes a significant, if underrecognized, area of investment in early TV.

4. Ford Foundation, Report 012488, Ford Foundation Archives, New York, NY (hereafter Ford Foundation Archives).

5. This attitude is in many respects a reflection of enduring and contradictory perceptions of mass culture among elites and others who consider themselves outside the population that constitutes mass culture's intended audience. "Technologies of populism like television," Toby Miller notes, "are said to narcotize and repress but are, relentlessly, expected again and again to enliven and develop." Miller, *The Well-Tempered Self: Citizenship, Culture, and the Postmodern Subject* (Baltimore: Johns Hopkins University Press, 1993), xvi.

6. On Lippmann's TV set, see Robert Saudek Oral History Transcript, Ford Foundation Archives, and Robert Saudek letter to Walter Lippman, November 11, 1952, Series II, Box 6, Folder 305, *Omnibus* Collection, Wesleyan Cinema Archives, Wesleyan University, Middletown, CT (hereafter *Omnibus* Collection).

7. In the twentieth-century United States, such conceptualizations trace back at least to the Hoover administration's ruinous corporate liberal vision of an "associational state" run by businessmen, a vision modified but not abolished by the corporatist government of the New Deal. See Ellis Hawley, "The Discovery and Study of 'Corporate Liberalism,'" *Business History Review* 52 (1978).

8. The ascendancy of neoliberalism is an uneven and highly contested process, to be sure. Alternative visions have always persisted, both outside the apparatus of state government and within it, the latter most notably realized in Lyndon Johnson's Great Society programs of the 1960s. Still, "in a long perspective," as one Marxist sociologist

notes, such programs "appear as the last political alternative generated by capitalism before the tide of neoliberalism rose." (Bob
Connell, "Global Capitalism and the Australian Ruling Class," in
*Economics as a Social Science: Readings in Political Economy,* ed.
Frank Stillwell and George Argyrous [Sydney: Pluto Press, 2003],
49). On the other hand, the economic crisis that erupted in 2008
seems, at the time of writing, to have gone some way in discrediting
conceptualizations of the market as a moral, efficient, and self-
regulating system capable of modeling all forms of social life.
Whether this amounts to a discrediting of policies and programs
based on such conceptions remains to be seen.

9. See Peter Miller and Nikolas Rose, *Governing the Present: Adminis-
tering Economic, Social and Personal Life* (Boston: Polity, 2008), for a
detailed account of the neoliberal model of citizenship.

10. As Stuart Ewen notes, television was "a powerful social metaphor . . . a
communicative structure particularly suited to the molding and
maintenance of a *virtual public*" (*PR! A Social History of Spin* [New
York: Basic Books, 1996], 388). For an excellent account of the use of
industrial motivation films in this vein, see Heide Frances Solbrig,
"Film and Function: A History of Industrial Motivation Film," PhD
diss., University of San Diego, 2004.

11. Mortimer Jerome Adler, *How to Think About War and Peace* (New
York: Fordham University Press, 1995 [1944]), xlix.

12. Mary Smith to Sylvia Spence, February 28, 1957, Fund for the
Republic Records, Box 108, Folder 10, Seeley G. Mudd Manuscript
Library, Princeton University Library, Princeton University, used by
permission of the Princeton University Library (hereafter Fund for
the Republic Records).

13. "Report of the Public Policy Committee Annual Meeting, November
10, 1965," 13/2/209, Public Policy Committee Box, no folder number,
Advertising Council Archives, University Archives, University
of Illinois, Champaign-Urbana (hereafter Advertising Council
Archives).

14. Lisa Duggan, *The Twilight of Equality* (Boston: Beacon Press, 2003).

15. Miller and Rose, *Governing the Present,* 54–55.

16. Michel Foucault, *The Birth of Biopolitics: Lectures at the Collège de
France, 1978–79* (New York: Palgrave Macmillan, 2008), 186.

17. Pat O'Malley, Lorna Weir, and Clifford Shearing, "Governmentality, Criticism, Politics," *Economy and Society* 26, 4 (November 1997): 514.

18. I borrow this term from Roopali Mukherjee's *The Racial Order of Things: Cultural Imaginaries of the Post-Soul Era* (Minneapolis: University of Minnesota Press, 2006).

19. See Daniel T. Rodgers, *Contested Truths: Keywords in American Politics Since Independence* (Cambridge, MA: Harvard University Press, 1998), 213; John Fousek, *To Lead the Free World: American Nationalism and the Cultural Roots of the Civil War* (Chapel Hill: University of North Carolina Press, 2000), 42–62.

20. Miller and Rose, *Governing the Present,* 71.

21. For a full discussion of television's structural affinity with neoliberal models of governance, see James Hay and Laurie Ouellette, *Better Living Through Reality TV: Television and Post-Welfare Citizenship* (Malden, MA: Blackwell, 2008).

22. J.S. Mill: "We are eager for improvement in politics, education, even in morals, though in this last our idea of improvement chiefly consists in persuading or forcing other people to be as good as ourselves." *On Liberty* (Toronto: Courier Dover Publications, 2002), 79.

23. Ien Ang, *Living Room Wars: Rethinking Media Audiences for a Postmodern World* (London: Routledge, 1998), 5.

24. Radio and film had served for several decades as vehicles for cultural training and economic and political education, playing a key role in corporate public relations, state administration, voluntarist reform and, in the 1930s most notably, the radical and populist agendas that constituted the left's cultural front.

25. Barbara Cruickshank, *The Will to Empower: Democratic Citizens and Other Subjects* (Ithaca, NY: Cornell University Press, 1999), 123, 25.

26. Miller, *Well-Tempered Self,* xiv and passim. Citizenship is, in Toby Miller's words, "a polysemic category, open to contestation, an avatar for all parts of the spectrum . . . an open technology, a means of transformation ready for definition and disposal."

27. On the relationship between this emerging concept of global society and American nationalism see Fousek, *To Lead the Free World.*

28. Kate A. Baldwin, "Between Mother and History: Jean Strafford, Marguerite Oswald, and U.S. Cold War Women's Citizenship," *Differences* 13, 3 (2003): 83–120; Leerom Medovoi, *Rebels: Youth and the Cold War: Origins of Identity* (Durham, NC: Duke University Press, 2005); Penny von Eschen, *Satchmo Blows Up the World: Jazz Ambassadors Play the Cold War* (Cambridge, MA: Harvard University Press, 2004); Serge Guilbaut, *How New York Stole the Idea of Modern Art: Abstract Expressionism, Freedom, and the Cold War* (Chicago: University of Chicago Press, 1983). See also Donald E. Pease, "National Narratives, Postnational Narration," *MFS Modern Fiction Studies* 43, 1 (Spring 1997): 1–23.

29. The literature on the consumer citizen is extensive and too vast to be cited fully here. For two perspectives, see Toby Miller, *Technologies of Truth: Cultural Citizenship and the Popular Media* (Minneapolis: University of Minnesota Press, 1988); Lizbeth Cohen, *A Consumer's Republic: The Politics of Mass Consumption in Postwar America* (New York: Vintage, 2003).

30. Peter F. Drucker, "The Meaning of Mass Production," *Commonweal* 57, 22 (March 1953): 549.

31. Elizabeth Fones-Wolf, *Selling Free Enterprise: The Corporate Assault on Labor and Liberalism* (Urbana: University of Illinois Press, 1994), 112–13.

32. Henry C. Link, "How to Sell America to the Americans," *Business Screen* 9, 1 (1948): 20–21, emphasis in original.

33. "No Business Is an Island" (1954), filmstrip script, Series 12/2/207, Folder 786, Advertising Council Archives.

34. Robert Patterson, quoted in Mary L. Dudziak, *Cold War Civil Rights: Race and the Image of American Democracy* (Princeton, NJ: Princeton University Press, 2002), 111. Such opportunistic invocations of Cold War conflicts confirm Ellen Schrecker's suggestion that "many of the phenomena so casually ascribed to the Cold War are independent of it." To assume, for example, that the Cold War *produced* the U.S. promotion of global capitalism, she argues, is to ignore the many ways that "the ideological and institutional machinery for that venture developed in the years before and during World War II." Yet simultaneously, drawing on the same example, there is no doubt that the push to expand the relations of the market across globe drew its moral authority from the Cold War battle between the free world and

collectivism, and that the language of citizenship was one important rhetorical source for making such connections. Schrecker, "Introduction," in *Cold War Triumphalism: The Misuse of History After the Fall of Communism,* ed. Ellen Schrecker (New York: New Press, 2004), 7–8.

35. As one of the Fund's officers wrote, its goal was "to increase the capacity of citizens of our Republic to discuss, in a rational and orderly manner, the deep conflicts of liberty and justice that trouble us." Hallock Hoffman to Harry Ellwood, February 11, 1957, Box 111 Folder 3, Fund for the Republic Records.

36. Richard M. Fried, *The Russians Are Coming! The Russians Are Coming! Pageantry and Patriotism in Cold War America* (New York: Oxford University Press, 1998), 117.

37. This episode of *A Date with Liberty* is in the archives of the Peabody Awards at the University of Georgia.

38. Theodore Repplier to Thomas D'Arcy Brophy, March 31, 1952, Box 2, Folder 2. Thomas D'Arby Brophy Papers, State Historical Society of Wisconsin (hereafter SHSW).

39. On the rhetoric of maturity and manhood in this period, see Kyle A. Cuordileone, *Manhood and American Political Culture in the Cold War* (New York: Routledge, 1998).

40. Borstelmann, *The Cold War and the Color Line: American Race Relations in the Global Arena* (Cambridge, MA: Harvard University Press, 2001), 92.

41. Martin Luther King Jr., "A Letter from Birmingham Jail," *Ebony*, August 1963, 30.

42. Harry A. Millis and Emily Clark Brown, *From the Wagner Act to Taft-Hartley: A Study of National Labor Policy and Labor Relations* (Chicago: University of Chicago Press, 1950).

43. John Kenneth Galbraith, *American Capitalism: The Concept of Countervailing Power* (Boston: Houghton Mifflin, 1952).

44. Lionel Trilling, *The Liberal Imagination: Essays on Literature and Society* (Garden City, NJ: Doubleday Anchor, 1953); Geraldine Murphy, "Romancing the Center," *Poetics Today* 9, 4 (1988): 737–47.

45. C. Wright Mills, "The Structure of Power in American Society," in *Power, Politics and People: The Collected Essays of C. Wright Mills*, ed. Irving Louis Horowitz (New York: Ballantine, 1963), 31.

46. Cited in Mary Sperling MacAuliffe, *Crisis on the Left: Cold War Politics and American Liberals, 1947–1954* (Amherst: University of Massachusetts Press, 1978), 10. MacAuliffe's account offers a thorough and detailed overview of this shift in liberal alliances at the beginning of the Cold War.

47. Joseph Krutch, *Is the Common Man Too Common? An Informal Survey of Our Cultural Resources and What We Are Doing About Them* (Norman: University of Oklahoma Press, 1954).

48. Krutch, "Is the Common Man Too Common?" in *Is the Common Man Too Common?* 19.

49. In some ways, worrying about mass culture helped resolve the decades-long liberal concern with balancing the threat of propaganda against the need for expertise in information dissemination and the cultivation of reasoned opinion. See Brett Gary, *Nervous Liberals: Propaganda Anxieties from World War I to the Cold War* (New York: Columbia University Press, 1999).

50. Robert Saudek, quoted in "On with the Show," *Time*, January 5, 1957, 66. See also David R. Ebbitt, "Television," *New Republic*, January 2, 1956, 21.

51. On the term's nineteenth-century history, see Rodgers, *Contested Truths*, 80–111; on its use in New Deal social planning, see ibid., 206.

52. MacAuliffe, *Crisis on the Left*, 70. On populist responses to liberal elites in U.S. political culture, see David A. Horowitz, *Beyond Left and Right: Insurgency and the Establishment* (Urbana: University of Illinois Press, 1997).

53. Marya Mannes, "The People vs. McCarthy," *The Reporter*, April 27, 1954, 25–28.

54. Harold Lasswell, paraphrased in David M. Potter, "The America Round Table Discussions on People's Capitalism," *Digest Reports* (New York: Advertising Council, 1956), 55.

55. Art Preis, "The Myth of People's Capitalism," *International Socialist Review* 23, 1 (Winter 1962): 3–9.

56. Thomas A. Dalton letter, May 1, 1957, Box 13, Folder 31, Advertising Department Records, Accession 1803, E. I. du Pont de Nemours and Company, Inc., Collection, Hagley Business Museum and Library, Wilmington, Delaware (hereafter DuPont Advertising Department Collection).

57. For more on Up with People, see Rick Perlstein, *Nixonland: The Rise of a President and the Fracturing of America* (New York: Scribner, 2008), 179.

58. Quoted in "'We Talk Here. This Is a School for Talking': Participatory Democracy from the Classroom out into the Community: How Discussion Was Used in the Mississippi Freedom Schools," *Curriculum Inquiry* 28, 2 (Summer 1998): 182.

59. Rodgers, *Contested Truths*, 219.

60. NSC 68, reprinted in Thomas H. Etzold and John Lewis Gaddis, *Containment: Documents of American Policy and Strategy, 1945–1950* (New York: Columbia University Press, 1978), 386.

61. Daryl Michael Scott, "Postwar Pluralism," *Journal of American History* 91 (June 2004): 22. See also Alan Nadel, *Television in Black and White America: Race and National Identity* (Lawrence: University Press of Kansas, 2005), 115.

62. For a full explication of the rise of interest group politics, see Rodgers, *Contested Truths*, 176–226; for an incisive assessment, see Murphy, "Romancing the Center," 743. David Truman outlined the theory of interest groups in his 1951 classic *The Governmental Process*. For a critique, see Theodore Lowi, "Interest Group Liberalism," in *The End of Liberalism: The Second Republic of the United States* (New York: W.W. Norton, 1979). Lowi sees the 1960s and 1970s as the ascendancy of interest group politics, but the seeds are evident in conceptions of power sharing in the Eisenhower years—consider, for example, the manufactured professional, economic, and cultural diversity embodied in the memberships of the proliferating boards and committees that made up the infrastructure of Establishment networking.

63. Mills, "Structure of Power in American Society," 36–37.

64. See Medovoi, *Rebels*, for a full analysis of the ideological field in which "identity" became a political and developmental imperative.

65. Minutes, Advertising Council Board of Directors Meeting, September 16, 1954, Thomas D'Arcy Brophy Papers, Box 3, Folder 3, SHSW.

66. For good analyses of this developmental logic of liberal individualism, see Nicholas Sammond, *Babes in Tomorrowland: Walt Disney and the Making of the American Child* (Durham, NC: Duke University Press, 2005); Medovoi, *Rebels*.

67. Murphy, "Romancing the Center," 742.

68. See G. Edward White, *The Constitution and the New Deal* (Cambridge, MA: Harvard University Press, 2000).

69. For a good critique of the Cold War liberal assumption that "knowledge and expertise exist on an independent axis from politics and partisanship," see S.M. Amadae, *Rationalizing Capitalist Democracy: The Cold War Origins of Rational Choice Liberalism* (Chicago: University of Chicago Press, 2003), 36–37.

70. If the incorporation of a culture of experts in the establishment shored up the position of intellectuals in the governing classes, it also greatly limited their power therein. Under Roosevelt, argues Ira Katznelson, policy intellectuals could debate large-scale questions about the relationship between economy and society; by the beginning of the 1950s, policy debates were predicated upon the assumption that capitalist social relations were here to stay, and that what remained to be discussed was the technical matter of the correct administration of the growth-oriented economy and the pluralist polity. Katznelson, "Was the Great Society a Lost Opportunity?" in *The Rise and Fall of the New Deal Order*, ed. Steve Fraser and Gary Gerstle (Princeton, NJ: Princeton University Press, 1989), 189–90, 192.

71. For a critique of historical accounts extending the concept of consensus beyond the confines of the liberal establishment and into the population as a whole, see Gary Gerstle, "Race and the Myth of Liberal Consensus," *Journal of American History* 82 (1995): 579–86.

72. Mills, "Liberal Values in the Modern World," in *Power, Politics and People: The Collected Essays of C. Wright Mills* (Oxford: Oxford University Press, 1963).

73. Ibid., 191–92, 194.

74. Lucius Clay, December 6, 1953, Proceedings of the Meeting of the Board of Advisors of the TV-Radio Workshop, Series I, Box A, *Omnibus* Collection. This equation of state-run TV and propaganda was a corporate liberal bromide originating with Hoover himself. The privately run broadcast system, Hoover told the Department of Commerce's Radio Conference in 1925, produced "a greater variety of programs and excellence in service free of cost to the listener." If government-run broadcasting invited problems "of political, religious, and social conflicts in the use of speech over the radio which no

Government could solve," commercial broadcasting "preserved free speech to this medium." Herbert Hoover, Opening Address to the Fourth Radio Conference, 1925, in Senate Committee on Interstate Commerce, *Radio Control: Hearings Before the Committee on Interstate Commerce* (Washington, DC: 69th Congress, 1926), 50.

75. Legere to Martin, December 1956, Box 111, Folder 4, Fund for the Republic Records.

76. Peter Miller and Nikolas Rose, "Governing Economic Life," in *Foucault's New Domains,* ed. Mike Gane and Terry Johnson (New York: Routledge, 1993), 83.

77. Foucault, *Security, Territory, Population*, 47. For a full analysis of this role in relation to the public television system in the late 1960s, see Laurie Ouellette, *Viewers Like You? How Public TV Failed the People* (New York: Columbia University Press, 2002).

78. Thomas Streeter, *Selling the Air: A Critique of the Politics of Commercial Broadcasting in the United States* (Chicago: University of Chicago Press, 1993).

79. See Ellis Hawley, "Herbert Hoover, the Commerce Secretariat, and the Vision of an 'Associative State,' 1921–1928," *Journal of American History* (June 1974): 116–17.

80. James Weinstein, *The Corporate Ideal in the Liberal State, 1900–1918* (Boston: Beacon Press, 1968), xiii.

81. This language was first used in the Radio Act of 1927.

82. On the associations between sponsorship, patronage, and public service, see Roland Marchand, *Creating the Corporate Soul: The Rise of Public Relations and Corporate Imagery in American Big Business* (Berkeley: University of California Press, 1998): 192–93. See also Susan Smulyan, *Selling Radio: The Commercialization of American Broadcasting, 1920–1934* (Washington, DC: Smithsonian Institution Press, 1994), 70.

83. Robert McChesney, *Telecommunications, Mass Media, and Democracy: The Battle for the Control of U.S. Broadcasting* (New York: Oxford University Press, 1993), 92–93.

84. Weaver to James Webb Young, June 1, 1951, Box 6, Folder 315, *Omnibus* Collection.

85. James Webb Young, "Television-Radio Workshop," circa April 1950, Box 3, Folder 39, Rowan Gaither Papers, Ford Foundation Archives, 4.

For a useful discussion of the interconnection of showmanship and cultural programming in relationship to NBC programming strategies, see Pamela Wilson, "NBC Television's 'Operation Frontal Lobes': Cultural Hegemony and Fifties Program Planning," *Historical Journal of Film, Radio and Television* 15, 1 (1995).

86. On the rejection of the popular in the founding of American state-funded public service broadcasting systems, see Ouellette, *Viewers Like You*; see also Liz Jacka, "Democracy as Defeat: The Importance of Arguments for Public Service Broadcasting," *Television and New Media* 4, 2 (2003): 177–91.

87. See Ouellette, *Viewers Like You* for an excellent analysis of this process in the creation of the American Public Broadcasting System in the late 1960s.

*Chapter One:*
## SPONSORS AND CITIZENS

1. Philip Rieff, "Aesthetic Functions in Modern Politics," in *The Feeling Intellect* (Chicago: University of Chicago Press, 1990), 187–88.

2. Edward L. Bernays, "The Engineering of Consent," *Annals of the American Academy of Political and Social Science* 250, 1 (March 1947): 113–20.

3. J.A.R. Pimlott, *Public Relations and American Democracy* (Princeton, NJ: Princeton University Press, 1951), 240.

4. Review of *Nobody's Fool*, by Charles Yale Harrison, *Washington Post*, September 19, 1948, B5.

5. Roland Marchand, *Creating the Corporate Soul: The Rise of Public Relations and Corporate Imagery in American Big Business* (Berkeley: University of California Press, 2001), 164.

6. Ibid., 362.

7. Institutional advertisements served as vernacular complements to the evolving legislative and juridical processes that redefined corporations as citizens by extending to business organizations constitutional protections designed for individuals, from the highly contestable concept of "juristic personhood" to freedom of speech. See Toby Miller, *Cultural Citizenship: Cosmopolitanism, Consumerism, and Television in a Neoliberal Age* (Philadelphia: Temple University Press, 2007), 46. See also Barbara Johnson's discussion of the Dictionary Act in *Persons and Things* (Cambridge, MA: Harvard University Press,

2008), 12 and Thom Hartmann, *Unequal Protection: The Rise of Corporate Dominance and the Theft of Human Rights* (Emmaus, PA: Rodale Books, 2002). The anthropomorphic treatment of the corporation in government and in institutional advertising paralleled contemporaneous efforts to humanize the increasingly bureaucratic state through mass media, a process in which broadcasting would prove to be a key engine. The *locus classicus* of such efforts was Franklin Roosevelt's fireside chats (broadcast simultaneously on all networks), which relayed complex policy points in intimate, if involved, language. See Jason Loviglio, *Radio's Intimate Public: Network Broadcasting and Mass-Mediated Democracy* (Minneapolis: University of Minnesota Press, 2005), 9.

8. Peter F. Drucker, "The Meaning of Mass Production," *Commonweal* 57, 22 (March 6, 1953): 549.

9. On the difficulty of measuring the effects of institutional advertising, see Marchand, *Creating the Corporate Soul*, 198.

10. The most exhaustive account of the range and variety of media formats used in postwar corporate activism is Elizabeth A. Fones-Wolf, *Selling Free Enterprise: The Business Assault on Labor and Liberalism, 1945–60* (Champaign: University of Illinois Press, 1994).

11. Marchand, *Creating the Corporate Soul*, 233.

12. On proxy relations in market research, see Richard Maxwell, "Out of Kindness and into Difference: The Value of Global Market Research," *Media Culture and Society* 18, 1 (1996).

13. Michel Foucault calls this form of power *pastoral*, insofar as it is expressed as a form of care and service, and directed "at all and each in their paradoxical equivalence." *Security, Territory and Population* (New York: Palgrave Macmillan, 2007), 129. Visual media are often endowed with pastoral properties in efforts to use them to shape conduct and attitudes, particularly when these efforts are couched as a public service. As Ronald Greene notes in a very interesting study of the use of film at the YMCA in the twentieth century, "The norm of service had the potential of transforming class conflict into pastoral relationships of mutual care." Ronald Walter Greene, "Y Movies: Film and the Modernization of Pastoral Power," *Communication and Critical/Cultural Studies* 2, 1 (2005): 29. For a discussion of twenty-first-century manifestations of pastoral power in television, see Laurie Ouellette and James Hay, *Better Living Through Reality*

*TV: Television and Post-Welfare Citizenship* (Malden, MA: Blackwell Publishing, 2008), 11–12.

14. How to interpret the political valence of the statements that respondents made when they relayed their thoughts about DuPont programs and ads is a complicated question. It is commonplace in critical accounts of mass communications to see market research as an instrument of power; audience responses, in all of their complexity and diversity, might seem to hold evidence of resistance to such power. But such an interpretation, seeing the process in top-down, hegemonic-versus-subversive terms, would oversimplify the kinds of encounters that took place in the nexus of audience research surrounding institutional advertising. Although it certainly (and undesirably, from the DuPont perspective) provided an arena for criticizing social power and its mechanisms, participation in audience research hardly qualifies as "resistance."

15. See Donald F. Carpenter, "The Responsibility of Business Under the Current Administration," *Business Screen* 8, 13 (1952): 29–30.

16. For an example, see Chapter Four's account of the TV activities of the Fund for the Republic.

17. Gerard Colby Zilg, *DuPont: Behind the Nylon Curtain* (New York: Prentice Hall, 1974), 157.

18. House Report No. 998, 66th Congress, 2nd Session (Washington, DC: Government Printing Office, 1921), quoted in Zilg, *DuPont: Behind the Nylon Curtain*, 166.

19. DuPont publicity quoted in Marchand, *Creating the Corporate Soul*, 220.

20. BBDO pamphlet, "DuPont Company Advertising: A Glance Backward . . . a Look Forward," November 1952, Box 22, Folder 7, Advertising Department, Accession 1803, DuPont Advertising Department Collection.

21. William L. Bird Jr., *Better Living: Advertising, Media, and the New Vocabulary of Business Leadership, 1935–1955* (Chicago: Northwestern University Press, 1999), 188.

22. Memorandum from Wickliffe Crider to Brophy, Mills and Cox, January 6, 1956, Box 52, Folder 1, Thomas D'Arcy Brophy Papers, SHSW.

23. Bird, *Better Living*, 189.

24. Viewer mail excerpted in "Comment Report 'Cavalcade of America' Television October–November 1952," Box 10, Folder 22, DuPont Advertising Department Collection.

25. 1956 General Election Campaigns, Report of the Subcommittee on Privileges and Elections of the Committee on Rules and Administration, U.S. Senate, 84th Congress, 2nd Session (Washington, DC: Government Printing Office, 1957), 16, quoted in Henry A. Turner, "How Pressure Groups Operate," *Annals of the American Academy of Political and Social Science*, 319, 1 (September 1958): 63–72.

26. Robb De Graff to Wayne Tiss, August 22, 1955, Box 11, Folder 1, DuPont Advertising Department Collection.

27. For a chronological episode guide, see Martin Grams Jr., *The Official Guide to the History of Cavalcade of America* (Kearney, NE: Morris Publishing, 1998); commercials are listed as an appendix to the unauthored "Proposed Procedure: Development and Production of DSOM Commercials, 1958–1959 Season," n.d., Box 19, Folder 21, DuPont Advertising Department Collection.

28. "Report on Television Research" (response to June 15 request from the DuPont Executive Committee), September 29, 1955, Folder 9, Box 13, DuPont Advertising Department Collection.

29. Bird, *Better Living*, 243 n. 60.

30. "Report on Television Research," September 29, 1955, Folder 9, Box 13, DuPont Advertising Department Collection.

31. Photostat of carbon copy of letter from John Dollard to Harold Leo of BBDO, annotated by George P. Nielson to Robb M. De Graff, Box 10, Folder 13, DuPont Advertising Department Collection.

32. BBDO, "A Promotion, Publicity, and Merchandising Plan for 'Cavalcade of America,' 1954–1955," June 14, 1954, Box 5, Folder 22, DuPont Advertising Department Collection.

33. BBDO report, "Recommendations for du Pont's Continuing Use of Television," March 29, 1956, Box 6, Folder 7, DuPont Advertising Department Collection.

34. George P. Nielson, "Telling the Story of Chemistry to Television Viewers," speech to American Chemical Society, September 26, 1954, Box 12, Folder 18, DuPont Advertising Department Collection.

35. DuPont settled an antitrust suit with powder manufacturers in the teens; in the late 1940s it entered into protracted antitrust litigation over its long-standing interest in General Motors, eventually divesting itself of the stock in the early 1960s.

36. That season, *Cavalcade* ran on NBC on Wednesday evenings at 8:30 p.m.; it moved to Tuesdays at 7:30 p.m. on ABC after one year.

37. Harold Blackburn to F. Lyman Dewey, October 26, 1951, Box 4, Folder 21, DuPont Advertising Department Collection.

38. Mary Beth Haralovich, "Sitcoms and Suburbs: Positioning the 1950s Homemaker," *Quarterly Review of Film and Video* 11, 1 (May 1989).

39. Script ("as filmed"), "Mylar Polyester Film," December 2, 1953, Box 8, Folder 19, DuPont Advertising Department Collection. Audience research by John Dollard confirmed that women and men responded as indicated and that in general, women recalled "the personal rather than the mechanical and technical uses of 'Mylar.'" John Dollard, "Report No. 4," March 2, 1955, 80, Box 6, Folder 45, DuPont Advertising Department Collection.

40. "Speech by George P. Neilson—September 11, 1958," Box 19, Folder 19, DuPont Advertising Department Collection.

41. The paradigmatic instance of this language is the Advertising Council's "Miracle of America" campaign, which included a booklet in which "Uncle Sam" miraculously appears to explain the American economic system to a wide-eyed young boy. Series 13/2/279, AAAA Campaigns File, Folder 3, Advertising Council Archives, University of Illinois.

42. Script ("as filmed"), "Mylar Polyester Film," December 2, 1953, Box 8, Folder 19, DuPont Advertising Department Collection.

43. John Dollard, "Report No. 4," March 2, 1955, 79, Box 6, Folder 45, DuPont Advertising Department Collection.

44. Man, sixty-one, eighth-grade education, florist, quoted in ibid.

45. This idea that purchasing a product (or not) was a way of registering an opinion about the tone of a program or advertisement was an enduring theme in broadcast audiences' communication with sponsors, dating back to the days of radio. As Kathy M. Newman has pointed out in her study of audiences in the 1930s and 1940s, consumers often referred to their willingness to purchase a sponsor's product as a way of expressing their approval or disapproval of a particular program's narrative and style. Reclaiming some power for the "active" audience, Newman suggests that such responses may have led advertisers to fear "irritating" story lines and techniques more than any others. In the case of institutional advertising, however, the ideological equation of shopping and activism surely benefited sponsors more, as

it affirmed the figure of the consumer citizen perennially invoked in institutional advertising's claims for the equivalence of democracy and economy. Kathy M. Newman, *Radio Active: Advertising and Consumer Activism* (Berkeley: University of California Press, 2004), 191, 39. For an extended historical account of the equation of consumption and citizenship in the first half of the twentieth century, see Charles F. McGovern, *Sold American: Consumption and Citizenship, 1890–1945* (Chapel Hill: University of North Carolina Press, 2006); for a comparable account focused on the post–World War II period, see Lizabeth Cohen, *Consumer's Republic: The Politics of Mass Consumption in Postwar America* (New York: Vintage, 2003).

46. Charles Hackett, Memorandum to Chuck Crowley, December 24, 1957, Box 19, Folder 17, DuPont Advertising Department Collection.

47. Gallup and Robertson, "Report and Analysis of Commercial Performance, DuPont Show of the Month," September 12, 1958, Box 18, Folder 4, DuPont Advertising Department Collection; John Dollard, "Report No. 8," November 15, 1955, Box 6, Folder 49, DuPont Advertising Department Collection.

48. Advertest Report, "WAVE II," Box 4, Folder 6, DuPont Advertising Department Collection.

49. Male respondent quoted in Gallup and Robinson, "Television Impact Report on DuPont Show of the Month 'Crescendo,'" September 29, 1957, Box 18, Folder 1, DuPont Advertising Department Collection.

50. George P. Neilson, letter to Robb M. DeGraff, October 20, 1954, Box 8, Folder 22, DuPont Advertising Department Collection.

51. Bird, *Better Living*, 167.

52. For an excellent study of the use of film in these workplace programs, see Heide Frances Solbrig, "Film and Function: A History of Industrial Motivation Film," PhD diss., University of California, San Diego, 2004. See also Elizabeth A. Fones-Wolf, *Selling Free Enterprise: The Business Assault on Labor and Liberalism, 1945–60* (Champaign: University of Illinois Press, 1994).

53. Kim Phillips Fein, *Invisible Hands: The Making of the Conservative Movement from the New Deal to Reagan* (New York: W.W. Norton, 2009), 101; Fones-Wolf, *Selling Free Enterprise*, 83–84.

54. The Taft-Hartley Act's reform agenda was couched as the protection of both "management rights" and the interests of individual workers

who might be coerced into union membership. Stressing such liberal ideals as balance, fairness, and rights, it included among its key provisions an employer "free speech" clause designed to undermine the Wagner Act's concern with protecting workers from antiunion propaganda. In asserting management's rights of free expression, Taft-Hartley helped to advance the evolving matrix of legislative and ideological processes in which corporations acquire rights as citizens. Its protection of corporate speech did set standards for the form such speech should take, requiring that employers use a neutral tone when communicating their views to workers. It ruled that the dissemination of "any views, argument, or opinion . . . whether in written, printed, graphic, or visual form, shall not constitute or be evidence of an unfair labor practice under any of the provisions of this Act, if such expression contains no threat of reprisal or force or promise of benefit." However, as Bird notes, this feeble signal of a continuing federal commitment to protecting employees from management propaganda did not head off the resulting onslaught of dignified and fair-minded management communiqués lobbying against unions—on company time, in an avalanche of employee education films, and in print communications sent to workers' homes. Labor Management Relations (Taft-Hartley) Act, ch. 120, sec. 101, § 8(c), 61 Stat. 136 (1947); Bird, *Better Living*, 150, 167, 160. See also Fones-Wolf, *Selling Free Enterprise*, 43, 78. On the "individual worker" argument in Taft-Hartley, see George Lipsitz, *Rainbow at Midnight: Labor and Culture in the 1940s* (Champaign: University of Illinois Press, 1994), 171.

55. Ott Coelln, "Sponsored Films and Public Interest," *Business Screen* 9, 2 (1948): 4.

56. In October 1951, DuPont advertising department head William Hart mentioned the possibility of collaborating on HOBSO with Disney to Robert Saudek of the Ford Foundation's Television-Radio Workshop. Robert Saudek, letter to Walt Disney, October 18, 1951, Series II, Box 6, Folder 298, *Omnibus* Collection.

57. On NAM's adaptation of HOBSO, see Fones-Wolf, *Selling Free Enterprise*, 205.

58. S. Alexandra Rippa, "Dissemination of the Free Enterprise Creed to American Schools," *School Review* 67, 4 (Winter 1959): 413.

59. George Neilson, handwritten note to Robb DeGraff on letter from

Arnold Leo of BBDO, May 10, 1954, Box 9, Folder 6, DuPont Advertising Department Collection.

60. Michelle Kelley, "'Liberalism Stands for Freedom': The 'Fun and Facts About America' Film Series and the Postwar Ascendancy of Corporate Liberalism," seminar paper, Department of Cinema Studies, New York University, 2007.

61. Gallup and Robertson, "Report and Analysis of Commercial Performance, Du Pont Show of the Month," September 12, 1958, Box 18, Folder 4, DuPont Advertising Department Collection.

62. "Changing Times" commercial, airdate January 21, 1958.

63. Unsigned speech labeled "Information Networks Speech," April 10, 1958, Box 19, Folder 21, DuPont Advertising Department Collection.

64. Synopsis of "The Grand Design," p. 18 of "Proposed Procedure: Development and Production of DSOM Commercials, 1958–1959 Season," January 15, 1958, Box 19, Folder 21, DuPont Advertising Department Collection.

65. Charles M. Hackett, letter to C.E. Crowley, December 24, 1957, Box 19, Folder 17, DuPont Advertising Department Collection.

66. Ibid.

67. BBDO preliminary report, "Experimental Pilot Test #1—Du Pont Show of the Month Commercials," Box 16, Folder 4, DuPont Advertising Department Collection.

68. Ibid.

69. "Television Impact Report on Du Pont Show of the Month 'The Prince and the Pauper,'" October 28, 1957, Box 18, Folder 2, DuPont Advertising Department Collection.

70. "Television Impact Report on Du Pont Show of the Month 'Crescendo,'" September 29, 1957, Box 18, Folder 1, DuPont Advertising Department Collection.

71. Advertest Survey transcripts, Box 4, Folder 4, DuPont Advertising Department Collection. Livingston was the research director of DuPont's public relations department and the announcer in some of its early commercials, eventually replaced by the more telegenic Los Angeles actor Douglas Kennedy.

72. Chuck Crowley, annotations on letter from Leyton Carter of Gallup and Robinson to Robb M. DeGraff, August 21, 1957, Box 19, Folder 17, DuPont Advertising Department Collection.

73. "Television Impact Report on DuPont Show of the Month 'Crescendo,'" September 29, 1957, Box 18, Folder 1, DuPont Advertising Department Collection.

74. "'Cavalcade of America' Television Comment Report January, 1955," Box 10, Folder 27, DuPont Advertising Department Collection.

75. Advertest Report, "WAVE II," Box 4, Folder 6, DuPont Collection. Advertising men themselves seemed to agree with such assessments of the program. Bruce Barton, one of the founders of BBDO, wrote to the ad department after watching an episode of *Cavalcade* to say, "I thought the Cavalcade television show was dramatic, dignified, and a blessed event in contrast to so much of the cheap and tawdry stuff that now clutters up the programs." "Comment Report 'Cavalcade of America' Television October-November 1952," DuPont Advertising Department Collection.

76. Roland Marchand, *Advertising the American Dream: Making Way for Modernity, 1920–1940* (Berkeley: University of California Press, 1986), 89–94.

77. Viewer mail, n.d., Box 7, Folder 6, DuPont Advertising Department Collection.

78. "DuPont Cavalcade Theater Television Comment Report, September-October, 1955," Box 10, Folder 29, DuPont Advertising Department Collection. I did not tabulate the volume of viewer mail, but my sense is that most episodes garnered an average of two or three letters from viewers.

79. "Progress Report, July-Nov 1955," Box 13, Folder 4, DuPont Advertising Department Collection.

80. John Dollard, "Report No. 7," November 11, 1955, Box 6, Folder 48, DuPont Advertising Department Collection.

81. Ibid.

82. Ibid.

83. "DuPont Cavalcade Theater Television Comment Report, September-October, 1955," Box 10, Folder 29, DuPont Advertising Department Collection.

84. Ibid.

85. Ibid.

86. Ibid.

87. Ibid.

88. Ibid.

89. Melinda M. Schwenk, "'Negro Stars' and the USIA's Portrait of Democracy," *Race, Gender and Class* 8, 4 (October 2001): 116–39.

90. "DuPont Cavalcade Theater Television Comment Report, September-October, 1955," Box 10, Folder 29, DuPont Advertising Department Collection.

91. Ibid.

92. It seems significant that this man was the only respondent who worked in public relations, a field that might foster a certain amount of cynicism among insiders and might even exert a certain psychic toll on professionals outside of the white, mainstream establishment.

93. Unsigned speech labeled "Information Networks Speech, April 10, 1958," Box 19, Folder 21, DuPont Advertising Department Collection.

94. Charles Hackett, memorandum to Chuck Crowley, December 24, 1957, Box 19, Folder 17, DuPont Advertising Department Collection.

95. Taft-Hartley Act quoted in Eric N. Waltenburg, *Choosing Where to Fight: Organized Labor and the Modern Regulatory State, 1948–1987* (Albany: State University of New York Press, 2002), 20.

96. Donald F. Carpenter, "The Responsibility of Business Under the Current Administration," *Business Screen* 8, 13 (1952): 29–30.

97. Arnold Leo, letter to George Nielson, October 26, 1954, Box 8, Folder 22, DuPont Advertising Department Collection.

98. "Ideas for DuPont 'Show of the Month' Commercials," Appendix B, "Proposed Procedure: Development and Production of DSOM Commercials, 1948–1959 Season," n.d., Box 19, Folder 21, DuPont Advertising Department Collection.

99. Unsigned speech labeled "Information Networks Speech, April 10, 1958," Box 19, Folder 21, DuPont Advertising Department Collection.

100. Dollard's experience in television before DuPont hired him seems to have been limited to a brief stint as an audience researcher for *Omnibus* in 1953. Robert Saudek, letter to John Dollard, May 19, 1953, Series II, Box 5, Folder 231, *Omnibus* Collection.

101. Today, the project seems quite dated and even racist, especially when one encounters sentences like this one: "While Negroes, especially sweating Negroes and manual laborers, do have a strong odor, I

cannot detect a categorical difference between it and body odors of white people" (a statement Dollard made even more objectionable with a footnote confessing that his hay fever may have been the problem). John Dollard, *Caste and Class in a Southern Town* (Madison: University of Wisconsin Press, 1988 [1937]), 380.

102. John Dollard, "Report No. 7," November 11, 1955, Box 6, Folder 48, DuPont Advertising Department Collection.

103. Charles Hackett, memorandum to Chuck Crowley, December 24, 1957, Box 19, Folder 17, DuPont Advertising Department Collection.

104. John Nickel, "Disabling African American Men: Liberalism and Race Message Films," *Cinema Journal* 44, 1 (Autumn 2004), 33. For a good example of contemporaneous discussions of the "dignified Negro," see the discussion of the role played by Robert Earl Jones in this review of Elia Kazan's film *Wild River*: A.H. Weiler, "Kazan Film Is Drawn from Two Novels," *New York Times*, May 27, 1960, 22.

105. On the politics of respectability, see Evelyn Brooks Higginbotham, *Righteous Discontent: The Women's Movement in the Black Baptist Church, 1880–1920* (Cambridge, MA: Harvard University Press, 1993).

106. Ralph J. Bunche, "Nothing Is Impossible for the Negro," in *Ralph J. Bunche: Selected Speeches and Writings*, ed. Charles P. Henry (Ann Arbor: University of Michigan Press, 1995), 263.

107. "Bunche Receives City Hall Thanks," *New York Times*, May 18, 1949, 6; "Hoffman Honored by Carver Group," *New York Times*, January 6, 1954, 29; Paul Hofmann [*sic*], "Bunche Says '60 Is Year of Africa," *New York Times*, February 17, 1960, 15.

108. Numan V. Bartley, *The Rise of Massive Resistance: Race and Politics in the South During the 1950s* (Baton Rouge: Louisiana State University Press, 1969), 314.

109. Zilg, "Beyond the Nylon Curtain," 375.

110. Timothy J. Minchin, *What Do We Need a Union For? The TWUA in the South, 1945–1955* (Chapel Hill: University of North Carolina Press, 1997), 40. See also Timothy J. Minchin, *Hiring the Black Worker: The Racial Integration of the Southern Textile Industry, 1960–1980* (Chapel Hill: University of North Carolina Press, 1999), 236–37.

111. "Toward Tomorrow," BBDO report, n.d., Box 5 Folder 41, DuPont Advertising Department Collection; Louis Gallop of BBDO, letter to

Robert Marsh, October 13, 1955, Box 12, Folder 35, DuPont Advertising Department Collection.

112. Norman Johnson, letter to John Procope, October 13, 1955, Box 5, Folder 41, DuPont Advertising Department Collection.

113. Miller, *Cultural Citizenship: Cosmopolitanism, Consumerism, and Television in a Neoliberal Age* (Philadelphia: Temple University Press, 2007), 49.

114. Ben Keppel, in a study of Ralph Bunche's place in postwar political culture, accurately points out that although the show was "not entirely faithful to Bunche's biography," it remained "true to the symbolic and narrative conventions governing the representation of racial politics in popular culture." Ben Keppel, *The Work of Democracy: Ralph Bunche, Kenneth B. Clark, Lorraine Hansberry, and the Cultural Politics of Race* (Cambridge, MA: Harvard University Press, 1995), 75. The show's depiction of Bunche and Johnson certainly conformed to the requirements of postwar racial representation, most notably the schematically rendered figure of the "exemplary Negro," anatomized in the following chapter.

115. Mr. and Mrs. James Brown, Mrs. Robert Prindle, "DuPont Cavalcade Theater Television Comment Report, September-October, 1955," Box 10, Folder 29, DuPont Advertising Department Collection.

*Chapter Two:*
## THE POLITICS OF WOODEN ACTING

1. Martin Quigley, "Home-Grown TV in St. Louis," *Harper's*, July 1955, 39–44.

2. For a comparable understanding of film as a tool in democratic education, see Lea Jacobs, "Reformers and Spectators: The Film Education Movement in the Thirties," *Camera Obscura*, January 1990, 29–49.

3. Walter A. Jackson, *Gunnar Myrdal and America's Conscience: Social Engineering and Racial Liberalism, 1938–1987* (Chapel Hill: University of North Carolina Press, 1994), 280.

4. Stuart Svonkin, *Jews Against Prejudice: American Jews and the Fight for Civil Liberties* (New York: Columbia University Press, 1997), 1.

5. As a *New York Times* editorial noted, "a campaign of public education by community leaders" was crucial in ensuring that integration was "effected quietly and without incident." "St. Louis Sets an Example,"

*New York Times*, February 2, 1955, 26. See also Monroe Billington, "Public School Integration in Missouri, 1954–1964," *Journal of Negro Education* 35, 3 (Summer 1966): 253.

6. William Vickery, "Ten Years of Intergroup Education Workshops: Some Comparisons and Contrasts," *Journal of Educational Sociology* 26, 7 (March 1953): 293–302.

7. When two professors of communications surveyed a week of programming on all channels in New York City in 1951, they discovered that public issues program constituted 1 percent, or eight hours, of the broadcast week; of these, only half were categorized as "discussion and debate." Dallas Smythe, "The Consumer's Stake in Radio and Television," *Quarterly of Film Radio and Television* 6, 2 (Winter 1951): 123. The paucity of time devoted to public information programming is particularly notable given that the FCC licensing freeze at the time made it difficult to attract sponsors; one would expect stations to compensate by airing more "sustaining" or public service programs.

8. For one use of the term *ghetto* to describe Sunday afternoon, see Charles A. Siepmann, "Moral Aspects of Television," *Public Opinion Quarterly* 24, 1 (Spring 1960): 15.

9. Jack Gould, "Puzzling Phenomenon," *New York Times*, May 10, 1953, sec. XII. See also "Television in Review," *New York Times*, October 10, 1948, sec. XII; Leo M. Cherne, "Biggest Question on TV Debates," *New York Times Magazine*, March 2, 1952, 14.

10. Morris Novik testimony, FCC Docket No. 12782, Vol. 6, Record No. 173-90-50, Box 43, 1853 National Archives and Records Administration, Suitland, MD.

11. This is not to diminish the important role these programs played on a national level, as they were very conscious efforts to inform viewers about the agendas defining political culture. Indeed, it was not the storied 1954 *See It Now* broadcast that first exposed Senator Joseph McCarthy to public attack; a notable *American Forum* broadcast in December 1953 featured audience members posing polite, though pointed, questions to the sputtering and peevish senator. Thomas Doherty, *Cold War, Cool Medium: Television and McCarthyism and American Culture* (New York: Columbia University Press, 2003), 17.

12. Walter Lippmann, *Public Opinion* (New York: Free Press, 1997), 252.

13. Martin Quigley to W.H. "Ping" Ferry, January 30, 1957, Box 108, Folder 10. Fund for the Republic Records.

14. Leo Dratfield to Edward Reed, March 21, 1957, Box 108, Folder 10, Fund for the Republic Records.

15. Edward Reed, Memorandum to Officers of the Fund for the Republic, February 14, 1957, Box 108, Folder 10, Fund for the Republic Records.

16. Robert W. Wagner, "Films Without Endings," *AV Communication Review* 3, 2 (March 1955): 138; Harry Fleischman, "TV Film Spots," in *Television: Labor's New Challenge* (Proceedings of the First Annual Labor Television Workshop, New York City, September 7–8, 1954), Folder 17, Box 4, Morris Novik Papers, George Meany Memorial Archives, Silver Spring Maryland (hereafter George Meany Memorial Archives).

17. Fleischman, "TV Film Spots."

18. William E. Utterback, "Political Significance of Group Discussion," *Annals of the American Academy of Political and Social Science* 250 (March 1947): 39.

19. Paul Bergevin and Dwight Morris, *A Manual for Group Discussion Participants* (New York: Seabury Press, 1965), 9. The classic articulation of the problem of authoritarianism in U.S. political culture is T.W. Adorno, *The Authoritarian Personality* (New York: Harper and Brothers, 1950).

20. Kurt Lewin, "The Research Center for Group Dynamics at Massachusetts Institute of Technology," *Sociometry* 8, 2 (1945): 133. See also John L. Jackson Jr., *Social Scientists for Social Justice: Making the Case Against Segregation* (New York: NYU Press, 2001), 66.

21. Kenneth H. Recknagel, "Teamwork in Industry," *Journal of Educational Sociology* 26, 6 (1953): 259. The "two-step flow" model of opinion formation was first advanced in Paul Lazarsfeld et al., *The People's Choice: How the Voter Makes Up His Mind in a Presidential Campaign* (New York: Columbia University Press, 1948), and gained ascendancy in the field with the publication of Elihu Katz and Paul Lazarsfeld, *Personal Influence: The Part Played by People in the Flow of Mass Communications* (New York: Free Press, 1955). Katz and Lazarsfeld drew heavily on the literature on group discussion in formulating their model.

22. Sharon Beder, *Free Market Missionaries: The Corporate Manipulation of Community Values* (London: Earthscan Publications Ltd., 2006), 56. For an excellent analysis of the role of discussion in corporate

indoctrination Programs, see Chapter 3 of Heide Frances Solbrig, "Film and Function: A History of Industrial Motivation Film," PhD diss., University of California, San Diego, 2004.

23. *On Camera* is archived in the Peabody Awards Collection at the University of Georgia.

24. Conceived as a local experiment by John W. Studebaker, the town's assistant school superintendent, the project went national when Studebaker was appointed U.S. Commissioner of Education in 1938. See David Goodman, "Democracy and Public Discussion in the Progressive and New Deal Eras: From Civic Competence to the Expression of Opinion," *Studies in American Political Development* 18, 6 (Fall 2004) 90–91. See also William Keith, *Democracy as Discussion* (Lanham, MD: Lexington Books, 2007).

25. Kurt Lewin's "Action Research" paradigm in the study of group dynamics and the "two-step flow" model devised by Elihu Katz and Paul Lazarsfeld are two examples of this conception of individual-group relations. See Lewin, *Field Theory in Social Science* (New York: Harper, 1951); Katz and Lazarsfeld, *Personal Influence* (New York: Free Press, 1955). On the importance of group interaction in screening situations, see Giles, "The Present Status and Programs of Private Intergroup Relations Agencies," 415. The idea that the social environment was the basis for individual pathology was the framing for the *Brown* decision, which drew heavily on the findings of Kenneth Clark, Gunnar Myrdahl, E. Franklin Frazier, and other social and behavioral scientists when it asserted that living in a segregated world generated among Negro children "a feeling of inferiority as to their status in the community that may affect their hearts and minds in a way unlikely ever to be undone." *Brown v. Board of Education*, 347 U.S. 483 (1954), quoted in Ellen Herman, *The Romance of American Psychology: Political Culture in the Age of Experts* (Berkeley: University of California Press, 1996).

26. Giles, "The Present Status and Programs of Private Intergroup Relations Agencies," 418.

27. John P. Dean and Alex Rosen, *A Manual of Intergroup Relations* (Chicago: Phoenix Press, 1963), 12.

28. Ibid., 48.

29. For a critique of labor leadership's assimilation into interest group politics after the New Deal, see also Ira Katznelson, "Was the Great

Society a Lost Opportunity?" in *The Rise and Fall of the New Deal Order, 1930–1980*, ed. Steve Fraser and Gary Gerstle (Princeton, NJ: Princeton University Press, 1989), 185–211.

30. Claude C. Bowman, "Role-Playing and the Development of Insight," *Social Forces* 28, 2 (December 1949): 199.

31. J.L. Moreno, "The Concept of Sociodrama: A New Approach to the Problem of Inter-Cultural Relations," *Sociometry* 6, 4 (November 1943): 448, 446.

32. On the relationship between social roles and the technique of role play, see Moreno, "The Concept of Sociodrama," 438.

33. Such efforts to separate speech and conviction, argue Ronald Greene and Darrin Hicks in their history of debating teams in the Cold War United States, produced "a governing field between a person's first order convictions and his/her commitment to the process norms of debate, discussion, and persuasion." Because it seemed to model democratic virtue, competitive debate became "a game of freedom" that could be exported to other political systems, combating totalitarian repression by encouraging independent thought and active identification with ideas of the social as a field of rational action and choice. Ronald Walter Greene and Darren Hicks, "Lost Convictions: Debating Both Sides and the Ethical Self-fashioning of Liberal Citizens," *Cultural Studies* 19, 1 (January 2005): 121. On rational choice theory, see S.M. Amadae, *Rationalizing Capitalist Democracy: The Cold War Origins of Rational Choice Theory* (Chicago: University of Chicago Press, 2003).

34. On the role of play in military science and civil defense, see Sharon Ghamari-Tabrizi, *The Worlds of Herman Kahn: The Intuitive Science of Thermonuclear War* (Cambridge, MA: Harvard University Press, 2005); on the place of the prank in social science, see Anna McCarthy, "Allen Funt, Stanley Milgram, and Me: Postwar Social Science and the 'First Wave' of Reality TV," in *Reality TV: Remaking Television Culture*, ed. Susan Murray and Laurie Ouellette (New York: NYU Press, 2004). For a primary source on the place of play in corporate culture, see Charles H. Clark, *Brainstorming* (New York: Doubleday, 1958).

35. Vickery, "Ten Years of Intergroup Education Workshops," 298. Leerom Medovoi offers an exhaustive account of the rise of identity concepts in Cold War expressive culture and social thought in *Rebels:*

*Youth and the Cold War Origins of Identity* (Durham, NC: Duke University Press, 2005).

36. Moreno, "The Concept of Sociodrama," 449, 440.

37. The Urban League representative is introduced as "Mr. Bohannon." An oral history of Vivian Dreer mentions that Leo Bohannon was head of the local Urban League chapter in the 1950s. Vivian Dreer, interview by Doris Wesley, University of Missouri–St. Louis, 1995, in Western Historical Manuscript Collection, University of Missouri–St. Louis, www.umsl.edu/~whmc/guides/oral.htm. Reba Mosby's oral history records that Virgil Border, who runs the meeting in the film, was the head of the regional branch of the National Conference of Christians and Jews. Reba Mosby, interview by Dr. Richard Resh, St. Louis, Missouri, July 9, 1970, in Western Historical Manuscript Collection, University of Missouri–St. Louis, www.umsl.edu/~whmc/guides/bclp.htm.

38. Mrs. William T. Mason to Edward Reed, April 2, 1957, Fund for the Republic Records, Box 108, Folder 10.

39. William J. Sloan, "The Documentary Film and the Negro: The Evolution of the Integration Film," *Journal of the Society of Cinematologists* 4 (1964–65): 67.

40. Like many documentaries from this period, *A City Decides* was a dramatized essay that relied extensively on reenactment, hoping to set examples for other communities facing integration by showing how St. Louis citizens collectively addressed potential problems in the process. Its claim to documentary status is therefore very much a product of the period; *A City Decides* and other films using reenactment located the documentary idea not in the emergent cinema verité or direct cinema aesthetic but rather in the combination of a manifestly educational objective with the use of a nonprofessional cast playing either themselves or representative community members.

41. Cleo L. Harter, "But We Have No Problem!" *American Journal of Nursing* 58, 12 (December 1968): 1687–88.

42. J. Saunders Redding, *On Being Negro in America* (New York: Charter Books, 1951), 27, 9.

43. Ibid., 26.

44. Ross Posnock, *Color and Culture: Black Writers and the Making of the Modern Intellectual* (Cambridge, MA: Harvard University Press, 1998), 32.

45. J. Saunders Redding, *An American in India: A Personal Report on the Indian Dilemma and the Nature of Her Conflicts* (New York: Bobbs-Merrill, 1954).

46. George F. Kennan quoted in John Lewis Gaddis, *Strategies of Containment: A Critical Appraisal of American National Security Policy During the Cold War* (New York: Oxford University Press, 2005), 49. See also Anders Stephanson, *Kennan and the Art of Foreign Policy* (Cambridge, MA: Harvard University Press, 1989), 95.

47. Penny Von Eschen, *Race Against Empire: Black Americans and Anticolonialism, 1937–1957* (Ithaca, NY: Cornell University Press, 1997), 128. For an extended treatment of the role of black Americans in U.S. cultural diplomacy, see her *Satchmo Blows Up the World: Jazz Ambassadors Play the Cold War* (Cambridge, MA: Harvard University Press, 2004). See also Melinda M. Schwenk-Borrell, "Selling Democracy: The United States Information Agency's Portrayal of American Race Relations, 1953–1976," PhD diss., University of Pennsylvania, 2004.

48. K. Anthony Appiah, "No Bad Nigger: Blacks as the Ethical Principle in the Movies," in *Media Spectacles,* ed. Marjorie Garber, Rebecca Walkowitz, and Jann Matlock (New York: Routledge, 1993), 80. On the problematic exemplarity of Frederick Douglass in abolitionism, see Gustavus T. Stadler, *Troubling Minds: The Cultural Politics of Genius in the United States, 1840–1890* (Minneapolis: University of Minnesota Press, 2006).

49. See Christopher Castiglia, "Abolition's Racial Interiors and the Making of White Civic Depth," *American Literary History* 14, 1 (Spring 2002): 32–59 for a detailed account of this process in the nineteenth century. See John Nickel, "Disabling African American Men: Liberalism and Race Message Films," *Cinema Journal* 44, 1 (Autumn 2004): 27–28 for an account closer to the period under discussion here.

50. The biographies of the film's producers—Mark Kennedy, Nelam Hill, Ed Bland, and Eugene Titus—are fascinating, as is the production history and reception of *The Cry of Jazz*. It is too complex to go into here; for a full account see Anna McCarthy, "Screen Culture and Group Discussion in Postwar Race Relations" forthcoming in *Learning with the Lights Off: An Educational Film Reader,* edited by Devon Orgeron, Marsha Orgeron, and Dan Streible (Oxford: Oxford University Press, 2011).

51. Jazz critics, it should be noted also objected to the film's claims about the form's essential blackness, and its death. Bland to Hill, n.d. (circa 1960), Nelam L. Hill Papers, Box 1, Folder 8, Schomburg Center for Research in Black Culture, New York Public Library (Hereafter Nelam L. Hill Papers).

52. Robert Colby Nelson, "The Negro in the City," *Christian Science Monitor*, June 6, 1960, 27.

53. John O. Fritz to Nelam Hill, May 20, 1960, Box 3, Folder 8, Nelam L. Hill Papers.

54. Lennie to Barbara, April 15, 1959, Box 4, Folder 25, Nelam L. Hill Papers. See also Ernest Callenbach and Dominic Salvatore, review of *The Cry of Jazz*, *Film Quarterly* 13 (Winter, 1959), 60.

55. By my preliminary estimate, the extant materials from the KHTB office show a total of seventy-five requests or receipts for screenings. Thirty-three are from educational institutions. The next largest category is public library audio-visual departments, a total of twelve.

56. Edward Bland to Mark Kennedy, August 14, 1959, Box 3, Folder 14, Nelam L. Hill Papers.

57. Edward Bland to Nelam Hill, n.d. (circa 1960), Box 1, Folder 8, Nelam L. Hill Papers, See also Kenneth Tynan, "A Contrast in Black and White," *The Observer*, March 20, 1960 (clipping) Box 3, Folder 15. Nelam L. Hill Papers.

58. Mark Kennedy to Edward Bland, "March Equinoc '59," Box 3, Folder 14. Nelam L. Hill Papers.

59. Interview with Amiri Baraka, quoted in Lorenzo Thomas, "'Communicating by Horns': Jazz and Redemption in the Poetry of the Beats and the Black Arts Movement," *African American Review* 26, 2 (Summer 1992): 292.

60. Adler conceived of TV as something like a textbook; as he explained at the end of a program devoted to the question of how one might learn from television, "I often try to end one of my own programs with some questions unanswered, in order to evoke discussion which should begin as soon as the program is over." KGO-TV, "Learning from Television," circa 1953–54 (airdate unknown).

61. KGO-TV, "Learning from Discussion," ca. 1953–54 (airdate unknown).

62. When the Amarillo, Texas, library formed a group devoted to discussing the four-volume series *Great Ideas in Education* published by Adler's Great Books Foundation, Lillie Hostetler, the library's adult education director, reassured local newspaper readers that "*Great Ideas in Education* does not concern itself with political and social issues that recently have stirred Southern education." "Great Issues to Be Studied," *Amarillo Globe-Times*, January 1, 1957.

63. Michelle McCalope, "Blacks Furious over Exclusion from New Great Books of the Western World," *Jet*, November 19, 1990, 14.

64. Dana Polan, *Scenes of Instruction: The Beginnings of the U.S. Study of Film* (Berkeley: University of California Press, 2007), 363. See also Joan Shelley Rubin, *The Making of Middlebrow Culture* (Chapel Hill: University of North Carolina Press, 1992), 191.

65. Dwight Macdonald, "Three Hits, Five Errors," *Esquire*, June 1959, 63–66.

*Chapter Three:*
## THE ENDS OF THE MIDDLEBROW

1. Bernard Rosenberg, "Mass Culture in America," in Bernard Rosenberg and David Manning White, *Mass Culture: The Popular Arts in America* (Glencoe, IL: Free Press, 1957), 9. On American populism, see Michael Kazin, *The Populist Persuasion: An American History* (Ithaca: Cornell University Press, 1998) and David A. Horowitz, *Beyond Left and Right: Insurgency and the Establishment* (Champaign: University of Illinois Press, 1997).

2. Quoted in C. Scott Fletcher, "For the Board of the Adult Education Fund," Box 2, Folder 24, Rowan Gaither Papers, Ford Foundation Archives.

3. H. Rowan Gaither Jr. et al., *Report of the Study for the Ford Foundation on Policy and Program* (Detroit: Ford Foundation, 1949), table of contents.

4. The term *philanthropoid* was originally coined by Frederick P. Keppel, president of the Carnegie Foundation. Dwight Macdonald, *The Ford Foundation: The Men and the Millions* (New York: Reynal Press, 1956), 96.

5. Robert Maynard Hutchins to Jack Skirball, October 4, 1955, Box 108, Folder 2. Fund for the Republic Records. See James Sloan Allen, *The Romance of Commerce and Culture: Capitalism, Modernism, and the*

*Chicago-Aspen Crusade for Cultural Reform* (Chicago: University of Chicago Press, 1983), 103, and Dwight Macdonald, *Against the American Grain* (New York: Random House, 1952), 257, for very similarly worded quotes from Hutchins on liberal education.

6. Unlike the activist alliance for nonprofit broadcasting in the 1930s, educational broadcasting advocates in the 1950s did not push their arguments to the point of asserting that regulatory acquiescence to corporate influence was the cause of the problem. Glenda R. Balas, "Domestic Values and National Security: Framing the Battle for Educational Frequencies in 1950–51," *Journal of Communication Inquiry* 25, 4 (2001): 414–37.

7. Robert Saudek, "Report on *Omnibus* 1953–1954 season," n.d., Series I, Box A, *Omnibus* Collection.

8. Letter to Hoffman, Davis, and Katz from Robert Hutchins, Nov. 14, 1951, Reel 1145, "General Correspondence: TV," Ford Foundation Archives.

9. Laurie Ouellette, *Viewers Like You? How Public TV Failed the People* (New York: Columbia University Press, 2002), 45–47.

10. Jack Gould, "Sweeping and Imaginative in Conception, *Omnibus* Makes Video Debut," review originally published in the *New York Times*, November 10, 1952, reprinted in *Watching Television Come of Age: The New York Times Reviews by Jack Gould*, edited by Lewis L. Gould (Austin: University of Texas Press, 2002), 121; Jack O'Brien review quoted in William C. Hughes, *James Agee*, Omnibus, *and Mr Lincoln: The Culture of Liberalism and the Challenge of Television, 1952–1953* (Lanham, MD: Scarecrow Press, 2004), 55.

11. Ford Foundation press release, August 14, 1952, Series 1, Box A, *Omnibus* Collection.

12. Robert Saudek oral history transcript, 56, Ford Foundation Archives.

13. Dwight Macdonald, *The Ford Foundation: The Men and the Millions* (New Brunswick, NJ: Transaction Publishers, 1989), 95.

14. Telegram to Ford Foundation from Hoffman, January 19, 1951, James Webb Young General Correspondence, R1146, Ford Foundation Archives.

15. Letter to Ping Ferry from Earl Newsom, with attached speech by James Webb Young, "Some Advertising Responsibilities in a Dynamic Society," May 1, 1951; James Webb Young, "Address to Advertising

Council of Rochester, Inc.," January 15, 1951, Reel 1146, General Correspondence, Ford Foundation Archives.

16. Letter to William Benton from James Webb Young, April 2, 1951, Reel 11, General Correspondence, "TV," Ford Foundation Archives; James Webb Young Oral History, Ford Foundation Archives, 11.

17. See Robert Griffith, "The Selling of America: The Advertising Council and American Politics, 1942–1960," *Business History Review* (Autumn 1983): 388–412.

18. James Webb Young, "Television-Radio Workshop," Series 1, Box A, *Omnibus* Collection.

19. Promotional pamphlet for *Omnibus*'s fourth season, Series 1, Box A, *Omnibus* Collection.

20. *Omnibus: Television's Golden Age* (VHS, New River Media, 1994), dir. Michael Ritchie.

21. Transcript of January 29, 1954, radio broadcast, Series I, Box C, *Omnibus* Collection.

22. Henry Hohman to George Benson, December 10, 1953, Series IV, Box 17 Folder 739, *Omnibus* Collection. See also James Webb Young, Oral History Transcript, Ford Foundation Archives, 12.

23. Dwight Macdonald, "Masscult and Midcult," in *Against the American Grain*.

24. See publicity materials, Series I, *Omnibus* Collection, as well as Morton M. Hunt, "Report on the Television-Radio Workshop," 1955, Unpublished Report 010610, Ford Foundation Archives.

25. Marianne Conroy, "Acting Out: Method Acting, the National Culture, and the Middlebrow Disposition in Cold War America," *Criticism* 35, 2 (Spring 1993): 241.

26. Macdonald, *The Ford Foundation*, 90.

27. Ouellette, *Viewers Like You,* 189.

28. On *Omnibus*'s relationship to PBS, see ibid., 43–44.

29. Ibid., 55.

30. Ibid., 55, 188, 146.

31. For an engaging account of these collaborations, see Francis Stonor Saunders, *The Cultural Cold War: The CIA and the World of Arts and Letters* (New York: The New Press, 1999).

32. Another example would be Mortimer Adler's postwar popular education programs, or the Great Books Foundation of the Encyclopaedia Britannica.

33. Dyke Brown, quoted in Francis X. Sutton, "The Ford Foundation: The Early Years," *Daedalus* 116 (Winter 1987): 59.

34. On the role of the middlebrow in domestic projects of containment, see Andrew Ross, *No Respect: Intellectuals and Popular Culture* (New York: Routledge, 1989), 47. For a thorough and truly excellent account of *Omnibus'* place in the Ford Foundation's cultural Cold War, see Hughes, *James Agee,* Omnibus, *and Mr. Lincoln,* 41–65.

35. See Toby Miller and Justin Lewis, "Introduction to Part V," in *Critical Cultural Policy Studies,* ed. Miller and Lewis (Oxford: Blackwell Publishing, 2002), for a good discussion of the role of the museum in such programs of cultural governance.

36. B. Stratton, Minutes of Program Meeting, June 23, 1953, Series III, Box 5, Folder 267, *Omnibus* Collection.

37. George Perkovich, *India's Nuclear Bomb: The Impact on Global Proliferation* (Berkeley: University of California Press, 1999), 24; Robert J. McMahon, *The Cold War on the Periphery* (New York: Columbia University Press, 1994), 180.

38. Howard B. Schaffer, *Chester Bowles: New Dealer in the Cold War* (Washington, DC: Institute for the Study of Diplomacy, 1993), 54; Chester Bowles, *The New Dimensions of Peace* (Santa Barbara, CA: Greenwood Press, 1974), 18.

39. Willard S. Hertz, *Roots of Change: The Ford Foundation in India* (New York: Ford Foundation, 1961), 6.

40. Nicole Sackley, "Passage to Modernity: American Social Scientists, India, and the Pursuit of Development, 1945–1961," PhD diss., Princeton University, 2004, 176.

41. Saudek to Ahern, August 20, 1953, Series III, Box 5, Folder 271, *Omnibus* Collection.

42. Rickey to Bowles, July 14, 1953, Series III, Box 5, Folder 225, *Omnibus* Collection; Ahern to Rickey, July 31, 1953, Series III, Box 5, Folder 271, *Omnibus* Collection.

43. The broadcast is archived on 16 mm kinescope in four places: the Paley Center for Media, Syracuse University, Wesleyan University, and the Library of Congress, where I watched it.

44. With the exception of George Cukor's *Bhowani Junction* (1956), which is set in 1947, the year of Indian independence, these conventions are remarkably uniform across the minor subgenre that might be called "Hollywood Raj." See, for example, *The Rains of Ranchipur* (1955), the two Victor Mature vehicles *Zarak* (1956) and *The Bandit of Zhobe* (1958), and *Northwest Frontier* (1959).

45. The conflict over the plows was reported by Cornell anthropologist Morris Opler. Sackley, "Passage to Modernity," 195–96.

46. The most well-documented instance of this is Howard K. Smith's assertion that CBS chairman William Paley told him that it was against network rules to take sides on controversial issues after viewing Smith's 1961 documentary "Who Speaks for Birmingham." Stephen Vaughn, *Encyclopedia of American Journalism* (New York: Routledge, 2008), 482. See also Jeff Alan and James M. Lane, *Anchoring America: The Changing Face of Network News* (Chicago: Bonus Books, 2003), 172; Sasha Torres, *Black, White and in Color: Television and Black Civil Rights* (Princeton, NJ: Princeton University Press, 2003), 17–19.

47. Gardner Murphy, *In the Minds of Men* (New York: Basic Books, 1953). The title of the book, *In the Minds of Men,* was taken from the preamble of the UNESCO constitution: "Since wars begin in the minds of men, it is in the minds of men that the defenses of peace must be constructed." The phrase is interesting in the way it links UNESCO to Paul Hoffman's rhetoric of "waging peace."

48. Sackley, "Passage to Modernity," 211–83.

49. Vijay Prashad, *The Darker Nations: A People's History of the Third World* (New York: The New Press, 2008), 200.

50. "A Man on Foot," *Time*, May 11, 1953, 32–37.

51. On Federal Theater and "neglected publics," see Part Two of Paul Sporn, *Against Itself: The Federal Theater and Writers' Projects in the Midwest* (Detroit: Wayne State University Press, 1995).

52. Carol Anderson, "From Hope to Disillusion: African Americans, the United Nations, and the Struggle for Human Rights, 1944–1947," *Diplomatic History* 20, 4 (1996): 549–51.

53. "The U.S. Negro: 1953," *Time*, May 11, 1953, 58.

54. Richard Wright, *The Color Curtain: A Report on the Bandung Conference* (Jackson, MS: Banner Books, 1995).

55. Elizabeth Forsling, untitled review, Series III, Box 5, Folder 264, *Omnibus* Collection.

56. Forsling, untitled review, Series IV, Box 18, Folder 795, *Omnibus* Collection. Forsling would become the original publisher of *Ms.* magazine but quit after the first issue, suing Gloria Steinem for misrepresenting the magazine's politics. Nick Ravo, "Elizabeth F. Harris, 77, the First Publisher of *Ms.*" *New York Times*, August 7, 1999, C16.

57. James Baldwin, "Everybody's Protest Novel," in *Notes of a Native Son* (Boston: Beacon Press, 1984), 14, 18.

58. Linda Williams, *Playing the Race Card: Melodramas of Black and White from Uncle Tom to O.J. Simpson* (Princeton, NJ: Princeton University Press, 2001), 63.

59. Reading the musical as a classic text of Cold War orientalism, Christina Klein argues that "Small House of Uncle Thomas" linked abolitionism and anti-imperialism to reveal "the debt that postwar discourses of modernization and expansion owed to nineteenth century sentimentalism." For Klein, "representations of Cold War internationalism carried the residual traces of older discourses that imagined transcending the boundaries of difference at home," and the moral at the end of the story, which sees the new king, Chulalongkorn, liberalizing the culture of his court, is that "Siam has learned the lessons of *Uncle Tom's Cabin*." Interestingly, two productions were staged in Moscow in 1951. Harrison E. Salisbury, "What They Read and See in Moscow," *New York Times*, February 18, 1951, 27. In 1958, a New York company called Colorama Features issued a rerelease of the 1926 Universal version, with narration and an introduction by actor Raymond Massey, known for his portrayal of Abraham Lincoln in the 1940 film adaptation of the Robert Sherwood play *Abe Lincoln in Illinois*. A.H. Weiler, "View from a Local Vantage Point," *New York Times*, October 5, 1958, X7. See also Williams, *Playing the Race Card*, 135.

60. Klein, *Cold War Orientalism*, 207, 213.

61. Although she had originally included the whipping scene, Violett was relieved to remove it when Saudek's staff told her that the play needed to be shortened to accommodate another segment appearing on the broadcast. Ellen M. Violett, interview by author, New York, November 13, 2008.

62. Michele Wallace, "Uncle Tom's Cabin: Before and After the Jim Crow Era," *TDR* 44, 1 (Spring 2000): 153.

63. Ellen M. Violett, interview; Ellen M. Violett to Paul Feigay, personal papers of Ellen M. Violett.

64. Violett, "Overall Note," personal papers of Ellen M. Violett. Emphasis in original.

65. Ellen M. Violett, interview.

66. Lionel Trilling, *The Liberal Imagination* (New York: Doubleday, 1950). See also Trilling's 1962 summary of Baldwin's argument: "Only a mode of art which was subtle and complex and untrammeled by social theory could truly propose the idea of freedom by exhibiting the true nature of man." Lionel Trilling, "James Baldwin," in *A Company of Readers: Uncollected Writings of W.H Auden, Jacques Barzun, and Lionel Trilling from the Reader's Subscription and Mid-Century Book Clubs*, ed. Arthur Krystal (New York: Free Press, 2001), 154.

67. Lionel Trilling, "*Uncle Tom's Cabin* by Harriet Beecher Stowe," in *American Panorama: Essays by Fifteen American Critics on 350 Books Past and Present*, ed. Eric Larrabee (New York: NYU Press, 1957), 318; George F. Whicher, "Literature and Conflict," in *The Literary History of the United States*, 3rd ed., ed. Robert E. Spiller et al. (New York: Macmillan, 1963), 583. Stowe, Trilling declared in his short essay, was "no genius, but she had a very competent talent and she could tell a good straightforward story . . . She was an intelligent woman and there is intelligence in her novel." Like Violett, Trilling associated the novel's reputation for melodramatic excess (a quality he deplored) with its history on the popular stage, although his own essay confused the two when it included Eliza's escape from the bloodhounds in a list of the book's contributions to "American lore" (the bloodhounds are an embellishment from the theatrical adaptations). Despite this generous, if backhanded, evaluation, Trilling is associated with the midcentury dismissal of *Uncle Tom's Cabin* by a number of critics and literary historians. See Jane Tompkins, "Sentimental Power: *Uncle Tom's Cabin* and the Politics of Literary History," in *Ideology and Classic American Literature*, ed. Sacvan Bercovitch and Myra Jehlen (New York: Cambridge University Press, 1987), 267–70; see also Donald Pease, "New Americanists. Revisionist Interventions into the Canon," in *Revisionary Interventions into the Americanist Canon*, ed. Donald E. Pease (Durham, NC: Duke University Press, 1994), 9. Trilling's conflation with this position may stem from the degree to which he championed *Huckleberry Finn*, a novel frequently

held up to Stowe's for comparison. See Jonathan Arac, "*Uncle Tom's Cabin* vs. *Huckleberry Finn*: The Historians and the Critics," *Boundary 2* 24, 2 (Summer 1997).

68. Baldwin, "Everybody's Protest Novel," 19, 23.

69. Stowe herself stressed the moral weakness of the wastrel St. Clare, and, by contrasting his affectionate treatment of Topsy with abolitionist Ophelia's distaste for the child, used him as a figure for the ambiguous position of the "good master" within the horrors of the plantation system.

70. Lani Guinier, "From Racial Liberalism to Racial Literacy: *Brown v. Board of Education* and the Interest-Divergence Dilemma," *Journal of American History* 91, 1 (June 2004): 100.

71. Ellen M. Violett to Paul Feigay, personal papers of Ellen M. Violett.

72. Edwin J. Lukas to Max Wylie, November 26, 1954; Wylie to Lukas, December 2, 1954, Series IV, Box 15, Folder 610, *Omnibus* Collection.

73. Martin Quigley relayed Saudek's thoughts about covering integration in *Omnibus* in an undated letter to Robert Hutchins on May 25, 1955. Box 109, Folder 1, Fund for the Republic Records.

74. Alice O' Connor, *Social Science for What? Philanthropy and the Social Question in a World Turned Rightside Up* (New York: Russell Sage Foundation, 2007): 92.

75. According to Macdonald, both the Reece Commission's investigation and that of the Cox Commission two years earlier reflected factional animus among Republicans, specifically opposition among isolationist Taft Republicans to Eisenhower and the internationalist wing of the party with which the Ford and Rockefeller families stood. Neither investigation would end up damaging the foundation. The Cox Commission had found no evidence of communist infiltration or the subversion of free enterprise in American philanthropy in its final report, issued in early 1953. The Reece Commission, formed at the peak moment of McCarthyism under a new Republican congressional majority, would conclude at the end of 1954 that tax-exempt organizations *were* supporters of subversion, but by then the backlash against McCarthy was in full swing and the committee report was widely criticized in congress and in the press. Macdonald, *The Ford Foundation*, 27–34. See also Francis X. Sutton, "The Ford Foundation: The Early Years," *Daedelus* 116 (Winter 1987): 83.

76. Ellen M. Violett, interview.

77. Rosetta LeNoire to Ellen M. Violett, n.d., personal papers of Ellen M. Violett.

78. Robert Saudek Oral History Transcript, 45, Ford Foundation Archives; Forsling, untitled review, Series IV, Box 18, Folder 795, *Omnibus* Collection.

79. Dennis to Ford, April 5, 1955, Series IV, Box 14, Folder 581, *Omnibus* Collection.

80. Faucette to Saudek, April 7, 1955, Series IV, Box 14, Folder 581, *Omnibus* Collection.

81. Saudek to Dennis, n.d., Series IV, Box 14, Folder 581, *Omnibus* Collection.

82. Saudek to Dennis, n.d. Series IV, Box 14, Folder 581, *Omnibus* Collection; Saudek to Faucette, n.d., Series IV, Box 14, Folder 581, *Omnibus* Collection.

83. Robert Saudek Oral History Transcript, 56, Ford Foundation Archives.

84. Edwin J. Lukas to Max Wylie, November 26, 1954; Wylie to Lukas, December 2, 1954, Series IV, Box 15, Folder 610, *Omnibus* Collection.

85. Wylie to Saudek, February 24, 1955, Series IV, Box 14, Folder 581, *Omnibus* Collection.

86. It was not until the 1970s, when an episode of the sitcom *Maude* showed the main character deciding to have an abortion, that the FCC would consider complaints applying the Fairness Doctrine to nonfactual programming. See Kathryn C. Montgomery, *Target Prime Time: Advocacy Groups and the Struggle over Entertainment Television* (New York: Oxford University Press, 1990), 42.

87. Ellen M. Violett, personal communication with the author, March 26, 2008.

88. George Cotkin, "Middle-Ground Pragmatists: The Popularization of Philosophy in American Culture," *Journal of the History of Ideas* 55, 2 (April 1994): 284; Rubin, *The Making of Middlebrow Culture*, 85; Marianne Conroy, "Acting Out: Method Acting, the National Culture, and the Middlebrow Disposition in Cold War America," *Criticism* 35, 2 (Spring 1993): 239–64.

89. On the segregationist invocation of balance see William G. Thomas III, "Television News and the Civil Rights Struggle: The Views in Virginia and Mississippi," *Southern Spaces*, November 3, 2004, www. southernspaces.org/contents/2004/thomas/4a.htm.

90. Stephen F. Lawson, *Black Ballots: Voting Rights in the South, 1944–1969* (Lanham, MD: Lexington Books, 1999), 213–14. This "both sides" rhetoric was common among politicians interested in appeasing southern voters after *Brown*. Kennedy used it several times, as in a 1963 television statement on Martin Luther King Jr.'s plan to lead a march in Birmingham, Alabama, denouncing "extremists on either side." Quoted in Rick Perlstein, *Before the Storm: Barry Goldwater and the Unmaking of the American Consensus* (New York: Nation Books, 2001), 204.

91. Thurgood Marshall to Dwight D. Eisenhower, September 6, 1956, quoted in Karen Anderson, "The Little Rock School Desegregation Crisis: Moderation and Social Conflict," *Journal of Southern History* 70, 3 (August 2004): 611. See also Garth E. Pauley, *Modern Presidency and Civil Rights: Rhetoric on Race from Roosevelt to Nixon* (College Station: Texas A&M University Press, 2001), 72–73.

92. Everett Wheeler, "The Unofficial Government of Cities," *Atlantic Monthly*, March 1900.

93. Macdonald, *The Ford Foundation*, 101–2.

94. "My interpretation of the 12th floor lunchroom as a community enterprise is that the individual's rights who make up the community should be respected by all fellow members. Otherwise it's all shot." Memo from Cynthia Colby to workshop staff, December 23, 1954, Series III, Box 5, Folder 274, *Omnibus* Collection; Macdonald, *The Ford Foundation*, 95.

95. Robert Saudek to Mary Ahern, August 20, 1953, Series II, Box 5, Folder 271, *Omnibus* Collection.

96. Paul Feigay memo to Robert Saudek, March 25, 1953, Series III, Box 5, Folder 271, *Omnibus* Collection. According to Saunders, this film was funded by the CIA (295).

97. Sutton, "The Ford Foundation: The Early Years," 55; Milton Katz to Program Committee, January 8, 1954, Ford Foundation Archives.

98. Rowan Gaither to Program Committee, October 29, 1953, Box 3, Folder 39, Rowan Gaither Papers, Ford Foundation Archives.

99. Katz to Gaither, January 22, 1954, Box 3, Folder 39, Rowan Gaither Papers, Ford Foundation Archives. Saudek's reaction is documented in a January 28 letter to Nathan Pusey, Series I, Box A, folder "Advisory Board," *Omnibus* Collection.

100. Fred Cole to William McPeak, January 21 [1955], Series II, Box 8, Folder 229, William McPeak Papers, Ford Foundation Archives.

101. William McPeak, "TV Roundup" (handwritten notes), n.d., Series II, Box 8, Folder 229, William McPeak Papers, Ford Foundation Archives. Saudek never quite managed to escape the taint of television in the eyes of the foundation officers. When I told Violett about McPeak's note, she commented, "The entire 'golden age' ain't that good and never was. [There was] censorship on every level. Never giving a character a Jewish name, for instance, was an unwritten law." Ellen M. Violett, personal communication with the author, March 26, 2008.

102. Alex McNeil, *Total Television* (New York: Penguin, 1996), 616.

103. J. Saunders Redding, *On Being Negro in America* (Indianapolis: Bobbs-Merrill, 1951); James Ralph, *Northern Protest: Martin Luther King, Jr., Chicago, and the Civil Rights Movement* (Cambridge, MA: Harvard University Press, 1993), 59.

104. John Fousek, *To Lead the Free World: American Nationalism and the Cultural Roots of the Civil War* (Chapel Hill: University of North Carolina Press, 2000), 89.

*Chapter Four:*
## LIBERAL MEDIA

1. Robert Maynard Hutchins, quoted in *Los Angeles Times*, "His Concern: Morals, Not Course Credits," May 29, 1977, H5.

2. On the paralysis of liberal intellectuals, see Mary Sperling MacAuliffe, *Crisis on the Left: Cold War Politics and American Liberals, 1947–1954* (Amherst: University of Massachusetts Press, 1978), 85–86.

3. Thomas C. Reeves, *Freedom and the Foundation: The Fund for the Republic in the Era of McCarthyism* (New York: Alfred A. Knopf, 1969), 276. It is difficult to determine with precision the exact amount the Fund spent on television. My estimate of around $700,000 is based on figures given in the Fund's papers for the following programs (amounts in thousands of dollars): *Al Capp Show* (20); *Herblock's Week* (200); Newsfilm Project (200); *A City Decides* (35); *Survival*

*and Freedom* (50); *Barrier* (35); *Dateline: Freedom* 60; script contest (75). The Fund backed additional TV ventures, but I have not been able to locate figures for these.

4. Frank K. Kelly, *Court of Reason: Robert M. Hutchins and the Fund for the Republic* (New York: Free Press, 1981), 39.

5. "Recommendations for Board Action" quoted in Reeves, *Freedom and the Foundation*, 84.

6. Hutchins, "A Sickness Afflicting Our Country," speech upon receiving Sidney Hillman Foundation award, January 28, 1959, Box 143, Folder 1, Fund for the Republic Records.

7. Unfortunately, most of the broadcasts produced or subsidized by the Fund appear to be lost. Three pilot episodes of the 1956 historical biography series *A Date with Liberty* are housed in the Peabody Archives of the University of Georgia (the series appears never to have actually aired); the documentary *A City Decides* is available on DVD from its producers, Charles Guggenheim Associates; selected Fund-sponsored episodes of *The Mike Wallace Interview* are available for viewing on the website of the Ransom Center in Texas, the archive where Wallace's papers are housed; and the stock footage house MacDonald and Associates owns some newsfilm clips and a WGBH series apparently sponsored by the Fund right before it moved to Santa Barbara. I have been unable to locate any other examples of the Fund's television projects. However, the paper trail surrounding their sponsorship, production, and distribution is preserved in the Fund for the Republic Records, housed at Princeton University's Seeley G. Mudd library. The scripts, correspondence, and memoranda that compose this substantial archive provide a deep sense of what liberal media advocacy entailed in the mid-1950s, and of the forces—both external and internal—against which it struggled.

8. Dwight Macdonald, *The Ford Foundation: The Men and the Millions* (New York: Reynal, 1956), 79.

9. Civil rights legislation, many segregationists reasoned, was an excess of government that illegitimately applied "force and coercion in areas of personal and social relations" and encouraged "uniformity and collectivism." David A. Horowitz, *Beyond Left and Right: Insurgency and the Establishment* (Chicago: University of Illinois Press, 1996), 278, 279.

10. Hallock Hoffman to Edward Reed, August 12, 1955, Box 111, Folder 5, Fund for the Republic Records. Emphasis added.

11. Nancy Bernhard, *U.S, Television News and Cold War Propaganda, 1947–1961* (Cambridge: Cambridge University Press, 2003), 57–59, 103–9, 184–87; Sasha Torres, *Black, White and in Color: Television and Black Civil Rights* (Princeton, NJ: Princeton University Press, 2003), 21.

12. Marcia Legere to George Martin, December 1956, Box 111, Folder 4, Fund for the Republic Records.

13. Thomas W. Chrystie quoted in Reeves, *Freedom and the Foundation*, 87.

14. Pegler, quoted in Reeves, *Freedom and the Foundation*, 54.

15. Fulton Lewis Jr., quoted in Reeves, *Freedom and the Foundation*, 58.

16. The actual Civil Rights Congress had been listed as a subversive organization by the attorney general's office in the 1940s. "Tax-Exempt Foundations: Hearings Before the Special Committee to Investigate Tax-Exempt Foundations and Comparable Organizations," House of Representatives, 83rd Congress, 2nd session (Washington, DC: Government Printing Office, 1954), 25–26 [hereafter Reece Commission Report).

17. Reece Commission Report, 38–40.

18. "Red Hiring Is Defended by Hutchins," *Washington Post*, November 8, 1955, 34. Hutchins' remarks were a reprise of comments he made at the National Press Club that January, an occasion on which he excoriated Reece, calling the commission's report "wild and squalid" and accusing it of exploiting public fears in the service of political ambition and revenge. See Reeves, *Freedom and the Foundation*, 103–4.

19. Hallock Hoffman to Edward Howden, October, 21, 1954, Box 110, Folder 1, Fund for the Republic Records.

20. Gloria Biggs, "Young Hoffmans Work for Understanding in Family, Community, and World," *Christian Science Monitor*, May 11, 1953, 12.

21. W.H. Ferry Oral History, Ford Foundation Archives, 112.

22. Howard Chernoff to Hutchins and W.H. Ferry, December 8, 1954, Box 110, Folder 5, Fund for the Republic Records.

23. Jack Skirball to Howard Chernoff, December 6, 1954, Box 110, Folder 5, Fund for the Republic Records.

24. W.H. Ferry to Howard Chernoff, December 13, 1954, Box 108, Folder 5, Fund for the Republic Records. From their description, the Capp

pilots seem to be a variant of the *Al Capp Show*, which aired on NBC in 1952. In that version, Capp provided humorous commentary on sketches meant to illustrate the foibles and blind spots of the average American. A copy of the show is in the Peabody Archives. It is not particularly funny.

25. W.H. Ferry to David Freeman and Edward Reed, January 21, 1955, Fund for the Republic Records, Box 108, Folder 5.

26. Edward Reed, memorandum to Ping Ferry, February 9, 1954, Box 108, Folder 5, Fund for the Republic Records.

27. See the following for different accounts of the cultural work of NBC's "integration without identification" policy: Kathryn C. Montgomery, *Target: Prime Time* (Oxford: Oxford University Press, 1990), 15–16; Dianne Brooks, "'They Dig Her Message': Opera, Television, and the Black Diva," in *Hop on Pop: The Politics and Pleasures of Popular Culture*, ed. Henry Jenkins, Tara McPherson, and Jane Shattuc (Durham, NC: Duke University Press, 2002), 309; Thomas Doherty, *Cold War, Cool Medium: Television, McCarthyism and American Culture* (New York: Columbia University Press, 2003), 75.

28. In fact, self-censorship was an explicit part of the policy. As Vice President Edward D. Madden explained, "Scenes containing racial minority stereotypes are cut out from old film features 'by the hundreds every month.'" In censoring these images, NBC was no doubt influenced by increasing pressure from the NAACP, which led a long campaign to get CBS to cancel the television version of *Amos 'n Andy*. "NBC's Talent Has No Color," *Variety*, March 18, 1953, 34.

29. Montgomery, *Target: Prime Time*; Michele Hilmes, *Radio Voices: American Broadcasting, 1922–1952* (Minneapolis: University of Minnesota Press, 1997), 270.

30. *Christian Science Monitor*, "Devoted to the Documentary," May 23, 1955, 6 (clipping) Box 108, Folder 8, Fund for the Republic Records.

31. Reggie Schuebel, memorandum, March 28, 1955, Box 108, Folder 8, Fund for the Republic Records. Despite the name, Reggie Schuebel was a woman.

32. The file for this project includes letters of inquiry from interested organizations. These consisted for the most part of labor groups and liberal churches (Unitarians and Quakers). The churches were

bulwarks of grassroots liberalism in the midcentury United States and among the Fund's core constituency. Box 108, Folder 8, Fund for the Republic Records.

33. Press release, Box 110, Folder 7, Fund for the Republic Records.

34. Stephen E. Fitzgerald to Frank Kelly, October 4, 1956; Fleischman-Hillard to Fund for the Republic, October 12, 1956, Box 109, Folder 1, Fund for the Republic Records.

35. *London News-Chronicle*, untitled review, August 20, 1958, quoted in Peggy Miller to Charles Guggenheim, August 21 1958, Box 108, Folder 10, Fund for the Republic Records.

36. George S. Mitchell, "Memorandum," February 15, 1957, Box 108, Folder 10, Fund for the Republic Records.

37. Reed to PF, DFF, FKK, JL, HH, February 14, 1957, Box 108, Folder 10, Fund for the Republic Records.

38. The episodes that have achieved some notice focused on homosexuality, often via prurient and homophobic angles such as "homosexuals who stalk and molest children." One notable episode featured the young secretary of the Mattachine Society. Although his face was obscured in the broadcast, his employer watched the show and recognized his voice. He was fired the next day. Stephen Tropiano, *The Prime Time Closet: A History of Gays and Lesbians on TV* (New York: Hal Leonard, 2002), 3–4. See also Edward Alwood, *Straight News: Gays, Lesbians, and the News Media* (New York: Columbia University Press, 1998), 31–32.

39. Hal Hoffman to Ping Ferry, n.d., Box 109, Folder 4, Fund for the Republic Records.

40. Elizabeth Huling, undated critique Box 109, Folder 4, Fund for the Republic Records.

41. Hallock Hoffman to Paul Coates, December 8, 1955, Box 109, Folder 4, Fund for the Republic Records.

42. Hoffman to Files, November 9, 1955, Box 109, Folder 4, Fund for the Republic Records.

43. In 1956, another media worker tried to explain to Fund officers why appealing to viewers' emotions was important, proposing a TV series in which "some sympathetic personality [such] as James Stewart would portray the man with the answers in conversations on specific aspects of civil rights." This approach, he suggested,

would "avoid sterility and preaching and . . . permit viewers to identify themselves with the man asking the questions." Fund officers do not appear to have been enthusiastic. George Martin to Edward Reed, March 20, 1956, Box 11, Folder 4, Fund for the Republic Records.

44. "Civic Groups Will Hear Bias Head," *San Mateo Times*, September 15, 1958, B2; "Willie Will Get House After All," *San Mateo Times*, November 14, 1957, 1.

45. Memo of agreement between Edward Howden of Council and station KRON-TV, January 20, 1956, Box 109, Folder 10, Fund for the Republic Records.

46. Edward Howden, "Notes on General Approach and Evaluation of Impact," n.d., Box 110, Folder 2, Fund for the Republic Records.

47. David Freeman to Edward Howden, September 29, 1955; Edward Reed to Hallock Hoffman, May 10, 1955, Box 110, Folder 1, Fund for the Republic Records.

48. Newsfilm Project Proposal, September 28, 1954, Box 111, Folder 6, Fund for the Republic Records.

49. In early 2005, print media widely reported that since taking office, the Bush administration made extensive use of VNRs to promote positive attitudes toward its military actions in Afghanistan and Iraq and to seek acceptance of its domestic policy initiatives. See David Barstow and Robin Stein, "Under Bush a New Era of Prepackaged News," *New York Times*, March 13, 2005, 1. As John Caldwell points out, the practice made viral marketing "a sanctioned form of publicly funded communication." In insisting that the question of whether to identify the source of planted material was a matter properly left up to individual stations, Bush effectively engaged in a form of ad hoc policy making that legitimized the proliferation of VNRs and other viral news forms. John Thornton Caldwell, *Production Culture: Industrial Reflexivity and Critical Practice in Film and Television* (Durham, NC: Duke University Press, 2008), 313–14. On early uses of newsfilm for PR purposes, see Eric Barnouw, *A History of Broadcasting in the United States,* vol. 3: *The Image Empire* (New York: Oxford University Press, 1970), 43–44.

50. Docket item attached to Hallock Hoffman memorandum to Edward Reed, August 12, 1944, Box 111, Folder 5, Fund for the Republic Records.

51. Hallock Hoffman to Edward Reed, August 12, 1955, Box 111, Folder 5, Fund for the Republic Records.

52. For most of its lifespan the Newsfilm Project relied on both stringers and camera crews from the Movietone syndicate for footage. It contracted INS-Telenews to shoot its stories in August 1956, seven months before the fund declined to renew the project. George Martin to Nick Archer, August 15, 1956, Box 111, Folder 4, Fund for the Republic Records.

53. George Martin to Robert Hutchins, April 12, 1957, Box 110, Folder 9, Fund for the Republic Records.

54. Martin gives the total number of clips as seventy-four in a letter to Margaret Herrmann, January 30, 1957, Fund for the Republic Records, Box 111, Folder 3; an undated 1957 clipping from *Variety* announcing the closure of the project estimates that a total of 115 clips were produced. *Variety*, "Fund for Republic Newsfilmery Axed" clipping, Box 112, Folder 3, Fund for the Republic Records.

55. The number of local or network news programs using the clips each week varied greatly; the Louisville story, for example, was shown on four stations and on NBC's *John Cameron Swayze and the News* and reached around twelve and a half million viewers, while the Florida doctor story aired on one station and reached an estimated six hundred thousand. George Martin, "Newsfilm Project Progress Report as of October 29, 1956," Box 111, Folder 4, Fund for the Republic Records.

56. George Martin to Roger Sprague, August 15, 1956, Box 111, Folder 4; handwritten notes, undated, Box 111; Folder 9, Fund for the Republic Records.

57. Marcia Legere to George Martin, August 6, 1955, Box 111, Folder 5, Fund for the Republic Records.

58. George Martin to Frank L. Kelly, May 31, 1956, Box 111, Folder 4; Bill Meadows to Newsfilm Project, November 27, 1956, Box 110, Folder 9, Fund for the Republic Records.

59. Questionnaire responses, n.d., Box 112, Folder 2, Fund for the Republic Records.

60. WLBT-TV questionnaire responses, n.d., Box 112, Folder 2, Fund for the Republic Records.

61. This assessment of Sanders comes from 1967 FCC testimony by WLBT general manager Fred Beard, quoted in Kay Mills, *Changing Channels: The Civil Rights Case That Transformed Television* (Jackson: University Press of Mississippi, 2004), 103; Dick Sanders quoted in Allison Graham, *Framing the South: Hollywood, Television, and Race During the Civil Rights Struggle* (Baltimore: John Hopkins University Press, 2001), 10. For a detailed account of responses to WLBT among Jackson's black citizens, including those who testified against the station in FCC hearings, see Steven D. Classen, *Watching Jim Crow: The Struggles over Mississippi TV, 1955–1969* (Durham, NC: Duke University Press, 2004).

62. Steven D. Classen, personal communication with the author, November 10, 2008.

63. KWTX questionnaire responses, n.d.; KTSM-TV questionnaire responses, n.d., Box 112, Folder 2, Fund for the Republic Records. KTSM-TV had invoked its regional autonomy earlier that year when it refused a story about a southern California real estate agent whose license was revoked for selling a home in a white neighborhood to a Mexican American family. Someone, presumably Bryson, returned the accompanying comment card to the fund with a note: "Here in El Paso, relations with Mexican-origin citizens is excellent. We see no purpose in pointing out that a Latin American was discriminated against elsewhere." "Production Record," April 9, 1956, Fund for the Republic Records.

64. George Martin, "Progress Report," May 23, 1956, Box 111, Folder 4, Fund for the Republic Records.

65. Minutes of lunch meeting, August 5, 1954; "Notes on George Martin's visits to California stations," n.d., Box 111, Folder 6, Fund for the Republic Records.

66. "Production Record," June 28, 1956, Box 111, Folder 9, Fund for the Republic Records.

67. "Production Record," March 18, 1956, Box 111, Folder 9, Fund for the Republic Records.

68. "Suggested Film Script" appended to press release for March 18, 1956, Box 111, Folder 4, Fund for the Republic Records. A pencil annotation on the cover suggests that West Coast stations, including KVEC-TV, received the footage as a preedited, fully realized news story.

69. See Garth E. Pauley, *Modern Presidency and Civil Rights: Rhetoric on Race from Roosevelt to Nixon* (College Station: Texas A&M University Press, 2001), 72–73. Eisenhower had actually used the phrase "extremists on both sides" in private already, in a March 30 letter to Billy Graham. Gary Scott Smith, *Faith and the Presidency: From George Washington to George W. Bush* (New York: Oxford University Press, 2006), 251. By 1960, he had expanded its purview within his political philosophy to encompass "almost every economic, political, and international problem that arises." Letter to Lucy Eisenhower, May 6, 1960, quoted in Allan J. Lichtman, *White Protestant Nation: The Rise of the American Conservative Movement* (New York: Atlantic Monthly Press, 2008), 185.

70. Hoffman to Howden, September 20, 1954, Box 110, Folder 1, Fund for the Republic Records.

71. "Cameraman's Dope Sheet," n.d., Box 111, Folder 4, Fund for the Republic Records. On the statute, see Dean Sinclair, "Equal in All Places: The Civil Rights Struggle in Baton Rouge, 1953–1963," *Louisiana History* 39, 3 (Summer 1998): 357.

72. Harrison Harkins to Hallock Hoffman, October 28, 1955, Box 111, Folder 5, Fund for the Republic Records.

73. Described by producer George Martin as "an extreme right wing group," this was likely not the same as the Congress of Cultural Freedom detailed by Frances Stonor Saunders in *The Cultural Cold War: The CIA and the World of Arts and Letters* New York: (New Press, 2001). George Martin to Frank L. Kelly, September 14, 1956, Box 110, Folder 9, Fund for the Republic Records.

74. Transcript of phone conversation between Bethuel Webster and George Martin, August 1, 1956, Box 111, Folder 4, Fund for the Republic Records.

75. In May, for example, eleven of the thirteen stories in preparation concerned civil rights. Knopf to George Martin, May 9, 1956, Box 111, Folder 8, Fund for the Republic Records.

76. George Martin to Roger Sprague, n.d. [CWCA August 15], Box 111, Folder 4, Fund for the Republic Records. See also August 14, 1956, letters to television news directors in Box 111, Folder 9, Fund for the Republic Records.

77. Knopf to George Martin, August 28, 1956; Legere to George Martin, November 30, 1956, Box 111, Folder 8, Fund for the Republic Records.

78. Frank Kelly to George Martin, September 28, 1956, Box 111, Folder 4, Fund for the Republic Records.

79. Loescher to George Martin, September 17, 1956, Box 111, Folder 4, Fund for the Republic Records. Loescher may have been inspired by an article by liberal journalist I.F. Stone condemning Eisenhower's "extremists on both sides" approach, which appeared on the same day as his communication with Martin. See "Eisenhower Goes Neutralist—on Civil Rights," in I.F. Stone, *The Best of I.F. Stone* (New York: Public Affairs Books, 2007), 171–73.

80. Paul Jacobs to Robert Hutchins, May 23, 1957, Box 112, Folder 3, Fund for the Republic Records.

81. Peck quoted in Yasuhiro Katagiri, *The Mississippi State Sovereignty Commission: Civil Rights and States Rights* (Jackson: University Press of Mississippi, 2001), 13.

82. Ibid., 14; George Martin to Robert Hutchins, May 21 1957, Box 12, Folder 3, Fund for the Republic Records.

83. Katagiri, *The Mississippi State Sovereignty Commission*, 14.

84. Station lists, June 6 and June 4, Box 112, Folder 3, Fund for the Republic Records.

85. George Martin to Robert Hutchins, May 21, 1957, Box 112, Folder 3, Fund for the Republic Records.

86. Torres, *Black, White, and in Color*, 41.

87. George Martin to Frank Kelly, September 14, 1956, Box 111, Folder 4, Fund for the Republic Records.

88. Shanley nevertheless called the documentary "admirably balanced," suggesting (Treasury Department notwithstanding) that the *fact* of showing "both sides," and not the manner in which each was treated, was all that was needed to meet the requirements of balance. Jack Shanley, "TV: Documentary on Bias," *New York Times*, June 17, 1957, 47.

89. Robert Hutchins, quoted in Frank Kelly, *Court of Reason: Robert Hutchins and the Fund for the Republic Records* (New York: Free Press, 1981), 116–18.

90. Robert Hutchins, memorandum to the board, quoted in Reeves, *Freedom and the Foundation: The Fund for the Republic Records in the Era of McCarthyism* (New York: Knopf, 1969), 242, 243, 244.

91. Memorandum by Adam Yarmolinsky and Dave Freeman, quoted in Kelly, *Court of Reason*, 128. Emphasis in original.

92. Ibid., 261.

93. W.H. "Ping" Ferry Oral History, Ford Foundation Archives, 108.

94. Carol Bernstein Ferry, quoted in James Arthur Ward, *Ferrytale: The Career of W.H. "Ping" Ferry* (Palo Alto, CA: Stanford University Press, 2001), 157.

95. For an in-depth discussion of Hoffman's argument, see Matthew Lasar, "Right out in Public: Pacifica Radio, the Cold War, and the Political Origins of Alternative Media," *Pacific Historical Review* 67, 4 (November 1998): 520–28.

96. The Fund's last venture in TV appears to have been the discussion program *The Press and the People*, which aired on Boston educational station WGBH in 1960. I am grateful to J. Fred MacDonald for alerting me to this program.

97. Hutchins and his staff initially considered publicizing the Basic Issues program with a seven-hour telethon, but they were dissuaded by the incredulity and horror with which media professionals responded to it, among them Eric Sevareid and Edward R. Murrow. Letter to Frank Kelly from Eric Sevareid, November 10, 1958, Box 143, Folder 18, Fund for the Republic Records.

98. Wallace built this reputation at the DuMont network, where he hosted a show called *Nightbeat*. Although his ABC program continued to be called *The Mike Wallace Interview* after the Fund took over as sponsor, fund officers referred to the show as *Survival and Freedom*, and I will adopt their usage.

99. C.H. Percy, president, Bell and Howell Company, to Robert Hutchins, June 17, 1958, Box 144, Folder 1, Fund for the Republic Records.

100. The classic text of postwar sociology's anatomy of opinion as a two-step flow in which elites play a crucial role is Elihu Katz and Paul Lazarsfeld, *Personal Influence: The Part Played by People in the Flow of Mass Communications* (New York: Transaction Publishers, 1955).

101. Wallace first posed the question to William O. Douglas on May 11, 1958, asking it again in an interview with Aldous Huxley on May 18, 1958. The first episode of *Survival and Freedom*, broadcast April 27, 1958, featured theologian Reinhold Niebuhr. It, and sixteen

others, may be viewed on the website of the Harry Ransom Center in Austin, Texas, along with forty-eight preceding episodes of *The Mike Wallace Interview.*

102. On the publicity surrounding the show, see Kelly, *Court of Reason*, 144–55.

103. Mark Kennedy to Nelam Hill, May 12, 1960 Box 3, Folder 15, Nelam L. Hill Papers.

104. Ted Yates to Don Coe, June 23, 1958, Box 144, Folder 1, Fund for the Republic Records.

105. Mimeographed statement June 15, 1958, by Robert Hutchins on ABC's refusal to broadcast the Henry Cabot Lodge interview after it had been edited. Box 144, Folder 1, Fund for the Republic Records. The argument was publicized by Jack Gould, the *New York Times* TV columnist, whom Hutchins castigated in a passionate, if unconvincing, letter subsequently printed in Gould's column. Jack Gould, "TV: Sound Journalism," *New York Times*, June 17, 1959, 59; "TV: Reply by Hutchins," *New York Times*, June 28, 1958, 67.

106. John Daly to Robert Hutchins, June 24, 1958, Box 144, Folder 1, Fund for the Republic Records.

107. Malin and Carskadon to Robert Hutchins, June 20, 1958, Box 144, Folder 1, Fund for the Republic Records. Wallace obliquely referred to the incident in the interview with Harry Ashmore on June 29, 1958, shortly after the cancelled Lodge broadcast, asking Ashmore, a Fund board member, about a hypothetical situation in which a politician being interviewed for a newspaper might demand the right to review his remarks before they were printed: "Do you think that a reporter can make that kind of an agreement and retain his integrity?" Ashmore's lengthy and equivocal reply stressed the difference between television and print media, and proposed, singling out Wallace, that TV journalists had "taken some of the worst faults of my trade and translated it into the new medium." Harry Ashmore, *The Mike Wallace Interview*, June 29, 1958. Digitized kinescope available online at www.hrc.utexas.edu/collections/film/holdings/wallace.

108. Dwight Macdonald, *Against the American Grain: Essays on the Effects of Mass Culture* (New York: Random House, 1962), 251.

*Chapter Five:*
## LABOR GOES PUBLIC

1. George Meany to Frank Stanton, September 14, 1953, Morris Novik Papers, Folder 8, Box 1, George Meany Memorial Archives.

2. Frank Stanton to George Meany, September 15, 1953, Morris Novik Papers, Folder 8, Box 1, George Meany Memorial Archives.

3. Ira Katznelson, "Was the Great Society a Lost Opportunity?" in *The Rise and Fall of the New Deal Order, 1930–1980*, ed. Steve Fraser and Gary Gerstle (Princeton, NJ: Princeton University Press, 1990) 191.

4. As James Gray Pope notes, labor's capitulation to the U.S. political system is tellingly conveyed in the fact that the only Taft-Hartley provision to which labor leaders advocated direct opposition was the ban on union political expenditures. Pope, "The Thirteenth Amendment Versus the Commerce Clause: Labor and the Shaping of American Constitutional Law, 1921–1957," *Columbia Law Review* 102, 1 (January 2002): 110.

5. William Green, "Labor Day Message," *American Federationist*, September 1947, 4.

6. Daniel T. Rodgers, *Contested Truths: Keywords in American Politics Since Independence* (Cambridge, MA: Harvard University Press, 1998), 211.

7. Green, "Labor Day Message," 4.

8. G.W. Johnstone to K.R. Miller, March 31, 1955, Series 1, Box 155, Folder 1955, National Association of Manufacturers Collection, Hagley Museum and Library, Wilmington, Delaware (hereafter National Association of Manufacturers Collection).

9. During the 1930s, the NAM produced and sponsored a syndicated radio drama, *American Family Robinson*. Despite its populist rhetoric and folksy images, the show was saturated with dialogue attacking labor and the New Deal. According to William L. Bird, Networks refused to run the program as an unsponsored, or "sustaining," broadcast (*Better Living*, 58–59). However, Elizabeth Fones-Wolf suggests that the program had some success finding local station managers who would agree to air the program as a public service. Elizabeth Fones-Wolf, "Creating a Favorable Business Climate: Corporations and Radio Broadcasting, 1934 to 1954," *Business History Review* 73, 2 (1999): 234. As she notes, the program was not well

received in the trade press: *Variety* judged it "likely to cause resentment," and dismissed it as "unadulterated propaganda" (253).

10. *Industry on Parade* fact sheet, April 1955, Box 157, Folder 1955, National Association of Manufacturers Collection; NAM advertisement quoted in Bird, *Better Living*, 162.

11. "AFL-CIO's New Film Series Available," *AFL-CIO News*, December 27, 1958, 7.

12. Gerald Pomper, "The Public Relations of Organized Labor," *Public Opinion Quarterly* 23, 4 (Winter 1959–60): 487; Roscoe Born, "AFL-CIO Slates TV Campaign to Improve Public View of Unions," *Wall Street Journal*, July 29, 1958, 15. Study copies of *Americans at Work* can be purchased from the George Meany Memorial Archives.

13. Roscoe Born, "AFL-CIO Slates TV Campaign to Improve Public View of Unions," *Wall Street Journal*, July 29, 1958, 15; "100 TV Stations Showing 'Americans at Work,'" *AFL-CIO News*, July 11, 1959, 7.

14. Undated Norwood Studios brochure, Rogers C.B. Morton Collection, Wendell H. Ford Research Center and Public Policy Archives, University of Kentucky Library, Lexington, Kentucky.

15. S. Paul Klein, telephone interview with the author, December 23, 2008.

16. Wolff's poem "No More Rhetorical Questions, Please, Mr. Congressman" appeared in the Federal Writers Project magazine *Direction* (vol. 6, no. 2) in 1943, in an issue devoted to winning entries in the publication's Summer Fiction Contest.

17. "As Read Narration for Cement Makers," January 15, 1960, *Americans at Work* viewbook, vol. 4, Education Department Papers, George Meany Memorial Archives; "As Read Narration for Cereal Makers," April 29, 1960, Education Department Papers, George Meany Memorial Archives.

18. *Americans at Work* viewbook, vol. 4, Education Department Papers, George Meany Memorial Archives.

19. S. Paul Klein, telephone interview with the author, December 23, 2008.

20. "Operation Entertainment" script, n.d., Morris Novik Papers, Folder 12, Box 1, George Meany Memorial Archives.

21. William Alexander, *Film on the Left* (Princeton, NJ: Princeton University Press, 1981); Michael Denning, *The Cultural Front* (New York: Verso, 1996), 268.

22. "Papermen's Paper," *Industry on Parade*; "Narration for Meat Cutters Film," airdate unknown, *Americans at Work* viewbook, vol. 3, Education Department Papers, George Meany Memorial Library.

23. One difference between the two was that *Industry on Parade* tended to focus on more than one factory, tracing the production of related commodities. One episode, for example, moves from a story about the editor of an in-house plant newspaper to a story about the production of ink ("Paperman's Paper," airdate unknown, available online at (www.archive.org/details/papermans_paper); *Americans at Work*, on the other hand, was more likely to stay within a single factory, although at times—as in the documentary about sugar discussed later in this chapter—it moved across locations, following a commodity from the moment of extraction of raw materials to its final packaging. Writer S. Paul Klein explained this approach as a conscious attempt to appear more educational than *Industry on Parade*. S. Paul Klein, telephone interview with the author, December 23, 2009.

24. Elizabeth Fones-Wolf, *Waves of Opposition: Labor and the Struggle for Democratic Radio* (Urbana: University of Illinois Press, 2006), 244.

25. Guy Nunn, a local Detroit TV and radio news commentator sponsored by the UAW, was a prominent voice in local labor media in the postwar period.

26. Pomper, "The Public Relations of Organized Labor," 491, 494.

27. In this light, the small differences between the two programs are as telling as their similarities. Most notable is *Industry on Parade*'s pointed avoidance of organized labor: unions were rarely mentioned in its fables of prosperity. In contrast, almost every other episode of *Americans at Work* seemed to stress labor's collaboration with management. "Unions and industry cooperate," proclaimed one episode about workers building intercontinental ballistic missile silos, ending on the question of whether the missile bases "will stand forever silent or erupt in sudden fury at the next moment." Although uncharacteristically ominous, the reference to national security was typical of the language of industrial partnership in *Americans at Work*, which often stressed labor's commitment to the technological promise of a bright future for the nation. "In cooperation with engineering and management," the narrator announced in an episode on industrial rubber workers, "theirs is a never-ending story that sometimes reads

like a science thriller." With such characterizations, *Americans at Work* suggested parallels between the patriotic contributions of labor during World War II and its cooperation with business in the Cold War growth economy. "Narration for Building Trade Workers Film" episode script, n.d., *Americans at Work* viewbook, vol. 2, Education Department Papers, George Meany Memorial Archives; "Narration for Industrial Rubber Workers Film," January 22, 1960, *Americans at Work* viewbook, vol. 1, Education Department Papers, George Meany Memorial Archives.

28. Morris Novik, "Labor and Politics on TV," Address to the First Annual Labor Television Workshop, September 7–8, 1954, 6a, Morris Novik Papers, Folder 17, Box 4, George Meany Memorial Archives.

29. Middle commercial, script for *Both Sides*, broadcast on ABC on May 17, 1953, Morris Novik Papers, Folder 7, Box 1, George Meany Memorial Archives.

30. Radio networks had long required that labor organizations tone down any suggestion of radicalism in order to gain access to public service time, and the AFL had a history of cooperation, even complacency, when it came to the restraints imposed by network policy. Fones-Wolf, *Waves of Opposition: Labor and the Struggle for Democratic Radio*, 72–74, 103–5.

31. J.K. Galbraith, *American Capitalism: The Concept of Countervailing Power* (Boston: Houghton Mifflin, 1952).

32. Robert Griffith, "Dwight D. Eisenhower and the Corporate Commonwealth," *American Historical Review* 87, 1 (February 1982): 109; Stanley Aronowitz, "Cracks in the Bloc: American Labor's Historic Compromise and the Present Crisis," *Social Text* 5 (1982): 41.

33. Nelson Lichtenstein, *State of the Union: A Century of American Labor* (Princeton, NJ: Princeton University Press, 2003), 99, 232–33. See also Aronowitz, "Cracks in the Bloc," 40, and George Lipsitz, *Rainbow at Midnight: Labor and Culture in the 1940s* (Chicago: University of Illinois Press, 1994), 176–78.

34. Aronowitz, "Cracks in the Bloc," 40; Al Campbell, "The Birth of Neoliberalism in the United States: A Reorganization of Capital," in *Neoliberalism: A Critical Reader*, ed. Alfredo Saad-Filho and Deborah Johnston (London: Pluto Press, 2006), 196.

35. Michel Foucault, *The Birth of Biopolitics: Lectures at the Collège de France* (New York: Palgrave Macmillan, 2008), 226.

36. Campbell, "The Birth of Neoliberalism in the United States," 196; United States Bureau of Labor Statistics, "Union Members in 2007," press release, January 25, 2008.

37. Michele I. Naples, "The Unraveling of the Union-Capital Truce and the U.S. Industrial Productivity Crisis," *Review of Radical Political Economics* 18, 1–2 (1986): 110–18. See also Campbell, "The Birth of Neoliberalism in the United States." For an analysis of how labor-management struggles over productivity played out in the sphere of consumption, see Meg Jacobs, *Pocketbook Politics: Economic Citizenship in Twentieth-Century America* (Princeton, NJ: Princeton University Press, 2007), 220–61.

38. "Narration for Papermakers Film," airdate unknown, *Americans at Work* viewbook, vol. 1, Education Department Papers, George Meany Memorial Archives; "As Read Narration for Sugar Workers," February 28, 1960, Education Department Papers, George Meany Memorial Archives.

39. Karl Marx, *Capital*, vol. III: *The Process of Capitalist Production as a Whole* (New York: International Publishers, 1967 [1894]), 830.

40. For a good case study of industry's southward journey, see Jefferson Cowie, *Capital Moves: RCA's 70-Year Quest for Cheap Labor* (Ithaca, NY: Cornell University Press, 1999).

41. "Outgoing Cargo!" *Industry on Parade*, airdate unknown, online at Prelinger Archives, www.archive.org/details/IndustryOnPa.

42. Karl Marx, *Capital*, vol. 1, trans. Ben Fowkes (New York: Penguin Classics, 1976), 163; "As Read Narration for Upholstery Workers," *Americans at Work* viewbook, vol. 2, AFL-CIO Education Department Papers.

43. "Narration for Meat Cutters Film," *Americans at Work* viewbook, vol. 3, Education Department Papers, George Meany Memorial Archives.

44. Denning, *The Cultural Front*, 123.

45. Sharon Ghamari Tabrizi, *The Worlds of Herman Kahn: The Intuitive Science of Thermonuclear War* (Cambridge, MA: Harvard University Press, 2005), 240.

46. Ibid., 238.

47. As T.J. Jackson Lears has observed, the grotesque is an idiom central to the discourse of consumption and its excesses. The development of the hypervisual world of twentieth-century consumer culture advanced

via efforts within the corporate realm to discipline advertising's carnivalesque animism with scientific, rational functionalism. *Fables of Abundance: A Cultural History of Advertising in America* (New York: Basic Books, 1995), 251.

48. Edward Dimendberg, "These Are Not Exercises in Style: *Le Chant du Styrene*," *October* 112 (Spring 2005): 65.

49. "As Read Narration for Doll and Toy Makers Film," *Americans at Work* viewbook, vol. 3, Education Department Papers, George Meany Memorial Archives.

50. My identification of the doll as Betsy Wetsy is based on close scrutiny of photographs on a number of websites devoted to doll collecting, among them dollinfo.com and dollreference.com. The untitled Ideal promotional film appears on a DVD entitled *Classic Doll Commercials from the Fifties and Sixties*, available for order from the website www.tvdays.com.

51. On the postwar relationship between media, toys, and child development, see Nicholas Sammond, *Babes in Tomorrowland: Walt Disney and the Making of the American Child, 1930–1960* (Durham, NC: Duke University Press, 2005); Sean Griffin, "Kings of the Wild Backyard: Davy Crockett and Children's Space," in *Kids' Media Culture*, ed. Marsha Kinder (Durham, NC: Duke University Press, 1999), 102–21. On the history of the toy industry's place in American child rearing see, among others, Gary Cross, *Kid's Stuff: Toys and the Changing World of American Childhood* (Cambridge, MA: Harvard University Press, 1997).

52. Kenneth B. Clark and Mamie P. Clark, "Racial Identification and Preference in Negro Children," in *Readings in Social Psychology*, ed. Theodore M. Newcomb and Eugene L. Hartley (New York: Henry Holt, 1947), 602.

53. Ben Keppel, *The Work of Democracy: Ralph Bunche, Kenneth B. Clark, Lorraine Hansberry, and the Cultural Politics of Race* (Cambridge, MA: Harvard University Press, 1995), 21.

54. Eleanor Roosevelt championed the idea of Sara Lee and helped shepherd the prototype through the design process. The doll's features, modeled on more than a thousand photographs of black children's faces, were subtly asymmetrical in order to achieve greater realism, and the thorny question of skin tone ("soft medium brown") was resolved by a "color jury" comprising Zora Neale Hurston, Ralph Bunche, Walter F. White, and other prominent black public figures.

Sabrina Lynette Thomas, "Sara Lee: The Rise and Fall of the Ulti-mate Negro Doll," *Transforming Anthropology* 15, 1 (2007): 40, 42, 43.

55. Ibid., 47.

56. Ibid., 48 n. 4.

57. The multiracial makeup of this workforce makes sense, given that the Ideal Toy Company had factories in Hollis, a largely black neighbor-hood in the New York borough of Queens, and in the ethnically diverse city of Newark, New Jersey. Given the large Galician Spanish immigrant population in Newark's Ironbound district, where the Ideal factory was located, it is possible that some of the workers shown in the film are of Iberian descent.

58. S. Paul Klein, telephone interview with the author, December 23, 2009. According to Klein, the importance of showing interracial unions meant that very few episodes of *Americans at Work* were shot in the South.

59. This was not the only episode to hint at a strange contrast between the commodity's white perfection and the racialized humanness of the nonwhite worker. Wolff's script for the documentary about sugar featured narration explaining that "the undesired color of residual molasses is whipped off the crystals to take them nearer to the desired whiteness" over a shot of a black worker staffing a centrifuge that separates molasses from sugar crystals.

60. Timothy Mitchell, *Rule of Experts: Egypt, Techno-Politics, Modernity* (Berkeley: University of California Press, 2002), 4.

61. On the rise of risk as an integral part of economic citizenship, see Randy Martin, *The Financialization of Daily Life* (Philadelphia: Temple University Press, 2002).

62. Robert A. Solo, "Automation: Technique, Mystique, Critique," *Journal of Business* 36, 2 (April 1963): 178.

63. S. Paul Klein, telephone interview with the author, December 23, 2009.

64. On the distinction between representation and simulation, see Jean Baudrillard, *Simulations*, ed. Sylvère Lotringer, trans. Paul Foss, Paul Patton, and Philip Beitchman (New York: Semiotext(e), 1983), 11.

65. Gilbert Jonas, *Freedom's Sword: The NAACP and the Struggle Against Racism in America, 1909–1969* (New York: Routledge, 2005),

283–84; Robert H. Zieger, *American Workers, American Unions: The Twentieth Century* (Baltimore: John Hopkins University Press, 2002), 221–22.

66. The equation of visibility on-screen with political representation is a long-standing fallacy central to liberal humanist approaches to the study, and practice, of media institutions. "If representational visibility equals power," one feminist critic observes, "then almost-naked young white women should be running Western culture." Another makes the same observation in obverse terms: "There are probably more African-American women judges in one week of prime time television than in the entire American judiciary—a simulacrum of racial equality absent the demand to actually achieve it." Peggy Phelan, *Unmarked: The Politics of Performance* (New York: Routledge, 1993), 10; Laura Kipnis, *Ecstasy Unlimited: On Sex, Capital, Gender, and Aesthetics* (Minneapolis: University of Minnesota Press, 1993), 6. For a critique of this representational logic in the context of the situation comedy, see Anna McCarthy, "*Ellen*: Making Queer Television History," *GLQ* 7, 4 (2001): 593–620.

67. Hanna Fenichel Pitkin, "Commentary: The Paradox of Representation," in *Representation*, ed. Roland Fenichel and John W. Chapman (New York: Transaction, 1968), 41–42.

68. Advertisement, *Oakland Tribune*, October 16, 1958, E25; advertisement, *Idaho State Journal*, October 29, 1959, 16; advertisement, *Post Register* (Idaho Falls), October 29, 1958, 12; TV listing, *Salinas Journal* (Kansas), October 31, 1958, n.p.; TV listing, *Los Angeles Times*, November 3, 1958, 31. It should be noted that *And Women Shall Weep* experienced a long afterlife in antiunion activism; it was a staple of employer activism against unions in the workplace. See Joseph A. Pichler and H. Gordon Fitch, "And Women Must Weep: The NLRB as Film Critic," *Industrial and Labor Relations Review* 28, 3 (April 1975): 395–410. The legislation was on the ballot in six states: California, Colorado, Idaho, Kansas, Ohio, and Washington. Voters in only one state, Kansas, approved the legislation.

69. Morris Novick to F.E. Black, October 23, 1958, Box 2, Folder 12, Morris Novick Papers, George Meany Memorial Archives.

70. The program's title is unknown; an incomplete version is archived at the Library of Congress.

71. "Phony Civil Rights Pitch Used to Push 'Work' Law," *AFL-CIO News*, May 24, 1958, 6.

72. As Michael Denning notes, the 1930s and 1940s witnessed "a remarkable and contradictory politics of mass culture, producing the phenomena of left-wing 'stars' and 'socially conscious' nightclubs, radio broadcasts, and picture magazines." Denning, *The Cultural Front*, 83.

73. Randy Martin, *The Financialization of Daily Life* (Philadelphia: Temple University Press, 2002).

*Epilogue*

1. Chester Pach and Todd Gitlin offer persuasive revisions of the popular, and largely media-generated, account of the relationship between television and opinions for or against U.S. involvement in Vietnam. See Chester Pach, "The War on Television: TV News, the Johnson Administration, and Vietnam," in *A Companion to the Vietnam War*, ed. Marilyn Blatt Young and Robert Buzzanco (Oxford: Blackwell, 2002); Todd Gitlin, *The Whole World Is Watching: Mass Media in the Making and Unmaking of the New Left* (Berkeley: University of California Press, 2003). For a critique of the idea that sitcoms are an expression of the progressive liberalization of American society, see Anna McCarthy, "*Ellen:* Making Queer Television History" *GLQ* 7, 4 (2001): 593–620.

2. Brett Gary, *The Nervous Liberals: Propaganda Anxieties from World War I to the Cold War* (New York: Columbia University Press, 1999).

3. Laurie Ouellette and James Hay, *Better Living Through Reality TV* (Malden, MA: Blackwell, 2008), 220.

4. Phred Dvorak, "On the Street and on Facebook the Homeless Stay Wired," *Wall Street Journal*, May 30, 2009, 1; Ouellette and Hay, *Better Living*, 7 John McMurria, "Desperate Citizens and Good Samaritans: Neoliberalism and Makeover Reality TV," in *Television and New Media* 9, 9: 305–332.

5. Raymond Williams, *Culture and Society 1780–1950* (New York: Columbia University Press, 1983), 300.

6. Ouellette and Hay, *Better Living*, 2, 86.

7. Ibid., 4–5. For an account of a reality program that literally promised philanthropic assistance to the underclass, see Anna McCarthy, "Reality Television: A Neoliberal Theater of Suffering," *Social Text* 93 (Fall 2007): 17–41.

8. Alain Ehrenberg, "La Vie en Direct ou les Shows de l'Authenticité," *Revue Esprit*, January 1993, 31 (my translation).

9. The FCC's Report and Statement of Policy Re: Commission en Banc Programming Inquiry *(25 Fed. Reg. 7291*, July 29, 1960), known as the Programming Policy Statement made this allowance in the broader context of new "ascertainment" procedures requiring that stations conduct research in the community to determine the kinds of programs local citizens thought would best serve their interests.

10. See Michael Curtin, *Redeeming the Wasteland: Television Documentary and Cold War Politics* (New Brunswick, NJ: Rutgers University Press, 1995).

11. See David L. Paletz, Roberta E. Pearson, and Donald L. Willis, *Politics in Public Service Advertising on Television* (New York: Praeger, 1977).

12. Bird, *Better Living: Advertising, Media, and the New Vocabulary of Business Leadership, 1935–1955* (Evanston, IL: Northwestern University Press, 1999), 244.

13. Laurie Ouellette's *People Like You? How Public Television Failed the People* (New York: Columbia University Press, 2002) is the definitive account of this process. On the Scalia memo, see Rick Perlstein, *Nixonland: The Rise of a President and the Fracturing of America* (New York: Scribner 2008), 596.

14. For a good overview, see Rick Perlstein, *Before the Storm: Barry Goldwater and the Unmaking of the American Consensus* (New York: Hill and Wang, 2002).

15. Heather Hendershot, "Cold War Right-Wing Broadcasting: H.L. Hunt, Dan Smoot, and the Unraveling of Consensus Culture," paper presented at the annual meeting of the American Studies Association, October 12, 2006; William O'Neill, *Coming Apart: An Informal History of America in the 1960s* (Chicago: Quadrangle Books, 1971). The program's host, Dan Smoot, was a former FBI agent best known today for his influential right-wing screed *The Invisible Government*, a book that accused a strange collection of Establishment bedfellows— the Council on Foreign Relations, the Committee on Economic Development, and the vestigial and impotent Public Policy Committee of the Advertising Council, among others—of conspiring to create a global socialist state. Perlstein, *Before the Storm*, 152.

16. Lisa Duggan, "Jesse Helms: American Bigot," obituary, *The Nation*, July 6, 2008, online edition.

17. Perlstein, *Before the Storm*, 38–39; "Kohler Hearing Film Costs Paid by NAM," *AFL-CIO News* April 12, 1958, 1, 2; "NAM's Kohler Films Being Probed by FCC," *AFL-CIO News*, April 19, 1958, 2; "TV Stations Rebuked on Use of NAM Films," *AFL-CIO News*, August 8, 1958, 8; Reuel Schiller, "From Group Rights to Individual Liberties: Post-War Labor Law Liberalism, and the Waning of Union Strength," *Berkeley Journal of Employment and Labor Law* 20, 1 (1999).

18. Robert E. Baker, "Goldwater Says Decay 'Starts at the Top,'" *Washington Post and Times-Herald*, October 21, 1964, A5. See also Perlstein, *Before the Storm*, 484.

19. William Boddy, "Senator Dodd Goes to Washington: Investigating Video Violence," in Lynn Spigel and Michael Curtin, eds., *The Revolution Wasn't Televised: Sixties Television and Social Conflict* (New York: Routledge, 1997).

20. *Progress Report of the National Commission on the Causes and Prevention of Violence to President Lyndon B. Johnson* (Washington, DC: Government Printing Office, 1969).

21. FCC Third Report and Order, 46 FCC 2d.143, 184 (1972).

22. For a detailed account of the negotiations involved in this episode, and public responses, see Kathryn Montgomery, *Target Prime Time: Advocacy Groups and the Struggle over Entertainment Television* (New York: Oxford University Press, 1989), 29–50.

23. Ibid., 32.

24. Quoted in ibid., 36.

25. See Todd Gitlin, *Inside Prime Time* (New York: Pantheon Books, 1983), Chapter 3, especially 212–14.

26. Lawrence Laurent, "Controversial Comedies Win High Ratings," *Washington Post and Times-Herald*, February 4, 1973, TVC9.

27. It should be noted that the socially conscious sitcom producers were by no means the primary beneficiaries of the finance and syndication rules. Although the laws were originally intended to support small producers, Hollywood benefited most. See Mara Einstein, *Media Diversity: Economics, Ownership, and the FCC* (Mahwah, NJ: Lawrence Erlbaum Associates, 2003), 45.

28. Chad Raphael, "The Political-Economic Origins of Reali-TV," *Reality TV: Remaking Television Culture*, ed. Laurie Ouellette and Susan Murray (New York: NYU Press, 2004).

29. Ibid., 129.

30. For an elaboration on this argument see McCarthy, "Reality Television."

31. Mark S. Fowler, quoted in *Television Digest* Oct. 19, 1987: 4.

32. John McMurria, "Regulation and the Law: A Critical Cultural Citizenship Approach," in *Media Industries: History, Theory, and Methods*, ed. Jennifer Holt and Alisa Perren (Malden, MA: Blackwell, 2009), 176.

33. Lisa Duggan, *Twilight of Equality: Neoliberalism, Cultural Politics, and the Attack on Democracy* (Boston: Beacon Press, 2004), xv, emphasis added.

34. Laurie Ouellette, "Take Responsibility for Yourself: *Judge Judy* and the Neoliberal Citizen," in *Reality TV: Remaking Television Culture*, ed. Susan Murray and Laurie Ouellette (New York: NYU Press, 2004), 227.

35. On the evolution of depression as a disease of responsibility, see Alain Ehrenberg, *La Fatigue d'Etre Soi: Depression et Société* (Paris: Odile Jacob, 1998).

36. On the connection between labor discourse and self-help, see Micki McGee, *Self-Help, Inc.: Makeover Culture in American Life* (New York: Oxford University Press, 2005).

37. Two good places to start would be Thomas Streeter, "'That Deep Romantic Chasm': Neoliberalism and the Computer Culture," in *Communication, Citizenship, and Social Policy: Rethinking the Limits of the Welfare State*, ed. Andrew Calabrese and Jean-Claude Burgelman, (New York: Rowman and Littlefield, 1999), 49–64, and Fred Turner, *From Counterculture to Cyberculture: Stewart Brand, the Whole Earth Network, and the Rise of Digital Utopianism* (Chicago: University of Chicago Press, 2006).

38. Mike Parker, "I Opened Door to Obama Win," *Sunday Star*, January 11, 2009, 28. I am grateful for Christopher Finlay of the University of Pennsylvania for telling me about Laura Ingraham's statement, which aired on Fox News' *The O'Reilly Factor* on September 13, 2006. This is not to say that progressives should not continue to appropriate the collective politics of mass culture for their own ends. However, as Stephen Duncombe argues in a persuasive critique of these illusory correlations, progressives must abandon the belief that reform can happen if people renounce the pleasures that popular culture affords and train themselves to ignore the desires it activates. Instead, he

suggests, we must consider the possibility that the popularity of such "degraded" forms as reality TV (or, I might add, of quality drama's complementary reassurances of progress) is a recognition of real structural inequalities and a way of voicing commitments to their resolution. Stephen Duncombe, *Dream: Re-imagining Progressive Politics in an Age of Fantasy* (New York: The New Press, 2007), 108.

# Index